Train Tracks

Train Tracks

Work, Play and Politics on the Railways

Gayle Letherby and Gillian Reynolds

Oxford • New York

First published in 2005 by
Berg
Editorial offices:
1st Floor, Angel Court, 81 St Clements Street, Oxford, OX4 1AW, UK
175 Fifth Avenue, New York, NY 10010, USA

Berg is the imprint of Oxford International Publishers Ltd.

Library of Congress Cataloguing-in-Publication Data
Letherby, Gayle.
   Train tracks : work, play and politics on the railways/Gayle Letherby
and Gillian Reynolds.
      p. cm.
   Includes bibliographical references and index.
   ISBN 1-84520-083-7 (pbk.)—ISBN 1-84520-082-9 (cloth)
   1.   Railroads--Social aspects. 2.   Railroad travel—Social aspects.
I. Reynolds, Gillian. II. Title.

HE1031.L48 2005
306.3—dc22   2005005532

British Library Cataloguing-in-Publication Data
A catalogue record for this book is available from the British Library.

ISBN-13 978 1 84520 082 4 (Cloth)
ISBN-10 1 84520 082 9 (Cloth)
ISBN-13 978 184520 083 1 (Paper)
ISBN-10 1 84520 083 7 (Paper)

Typeset by Avocet Typeset, Chilton, Aylesbury, Bucks
Printed in the United Kingdom by Biddles Ltd, King's Lynn

www.bergpublishers.com

Contents

Illustrations

Acknowledgements

As a joint endeavour this book has been a joy to write. We have been able to indulge our interest in trains and train travel and our friendship. However, as with all research and writing projects, there is a need to acknowledge the help and contributions of others. We are grateful, of course, to the many people who took part in our research as respondents: as well as providing us with essential data they – and others – encouraged us with their ongoing enthusiasm for our project. The finished product is our own responsibility.

We would like to thank Paul Bywaters and other members of the Centre for Social Justice, Coventry University, and Tim Strangleman (London Metropolitan University) for support, encouragement and critical insight; David Bill (Billy) for the cover picture and line drawings; Dave McAlone, John Hunt, Robert Hart, Mike Jager and Henry Lewis for permission to use artwork; 'Jon', whom Gillian met at York station, for permission to take a photograph for use in this book; and the anonymous traveller who kindly agreed to photograph us at work on the train. We are also grateful to Clive Reynolds for valuable technical support, and to Kathryn Earle and Hannah Shakespeare for using carrots rather than sticks during the production of our manuscript.

Introduction
The Train Now Standing ...

Initial Thoughts

> Oh, you're writing a book about trains and train travel, how great. And if you are late finishing it you can write in the introduction – 'We are sorry for the delay and for any inconvenience to your reading' [laughter].
>
> Janet – UK

In this book we consider work, play and politics on the train and as such explore social and cultural aspects of the train and train travel. As two sociologists, our aim in this book is to begin to make visible an area of everyday life largely ignored by social scientists. Although transport is an area that has been explored, this has more often been in the process of examining exclusion, poverty, inner city life or urban planning. As Edward de Boer (1986) notes, '(t)here is hardly a tradition of studying the social aspect of transport'. This is a serious omission as the train and train travel hold an important place in many people's lives. As a cultural icon and/or a focus of leisure pursuits, as a formal or constructed place of work and in terms of personal and public politics, the train holds significance.

Drawing on social and cultural theory, secondary analysis of cultural artefacts (including 'on-board' magazines, TV programmes, literature and films, and historical documents) and the analysis of primary data (collected via single and focus group interviews and email) from worldwide train travellers, workers and enthusiasts, we consider in this book the practical and political significance of the train both historically and to date. As two British scholars with easier access to the politics and experience of the British railways, we are largely concerned here with an exploration of the experience of trains and train travel in Britain. At times, however, we make comparisons with trains and train travel in other cultures, not least because some of our respondents comment on their worldwide relationship with trains.

We are not suggesting that our analysis is completely unique. Stephen Page (1999) briefly explores aspects of British train travel in the context of tourism and Chris Rojek and John Urry (1997) also address the part which travelling plays in tourism. In both these publications, however, the social phenomenon of what actually goes on during a journey and also the fascination in which trains are held as a cultural icon and social symbol are generally overlooked. Some writers have examined the place of trains in cultural nostalgia whilst others explore the railway industry from economic and historical perspectives (e.g. White 1995; Divall 2003; Marchant 2003; Strangleman 2004). While all these writers address briefly some areas of interest to us, none have brought together, as we do, the combined consideration of:

● travellers' experiences of being on a train (as distinct from experiences of service provision);
● railway workers' experiences of working on the train and for the railway industry;
● perceptions of trains and train travel among rail enthusiasts;

which we believe enables the concept of the train to be analysed as a cultural and social phenomenon in its own right.

In the introduction to his book *Parallel Lines, or Journeys on the Railway of dreams*, Ian Marchant (2003: 13) notes that: 'The first chapter, or introduction, of any self-respecting railway book is always called something along the lines of "Departures" or "The Train now Standing" ... The last chapter is always, always always called "All Change" and is invariably about Beeching. Fans of the genre will find this aspect of my book ... reassuringly familiar.' Although we have not completely conformed to stereotype, you will see that we too have attempted humorous titles for our chapters:

Introduction The Train Now Standing
Chapter 1 Points and Branch Lines
Chapter 2 Leaves on the Line
Chapter 3 Signs and Signals
Chapter 4 All Aboard the 'Play Station'
Chapter 5 Working on the Line
Chapter 6 Standing Room Only
Reflections Light at the End of the Tunnel?

Our personal interest and affection for trains and train travel are shared by many of the authors that we cite throughout this book and by the majority of our respondents (as highlighted by the quote with which we began). However, this affection is not merely the preserve of those represented here – as authors and/or respondents – because the train holds a place in many people's hearts. But, as Janet's account suggests, this affection is often tinged with frustration, and humour is just one of the ways in which this frustration is manifested. This tension between affection and frustration is present throughout this book.

Our own affection for and frustration with trains and train travel have intensified through data collection and writing. It has even begun to structure the gifts we buy each other: for example, a London and North Eastern Railway (LNER) mouse mat; a birthday book complete with copies of railway posters; an Australian train tea towel; and a book, the inside sleeve of which highlights once more the affection/frustration dichotomy:

<blockquote>
PAINS ON TRAINS
A COMMUTERS GUIDE TO THE 50 MOST IRRITATING TRAVEL
COMPANIONS
You have seen them, heard them, smelt them, been touched by them and had
your commuting life made miserable by them. Welcome to the world of
Pains on Trains.
Pains on Trains come in a variety of shapes and sizes, but all are destined
to add woe to the life of the modern commuter. This book gives you the
opportunity to lighten your journey by indulging in the craze that's set to
sweep the nation's travelling fraternity – 'pain-spotting'. From *The Broadsheet*
to *The Mobile Phoner*, and from *The Nose Picker* to *The Over Your Shoulder*,
you'll be able to have hours of fun with the person sat next to or opposite you,
without them even knowing.
START PAIN-SPOTTING TODAY AND PUT THE FUN BACK INTO
COMMUTING! (Holmes and Reeves 2003: unpaginated)
</blockquote>

Ideologies and Discourses

A Tale of Two Trains

The affection and frustration that people feel for trains and train travel are closely linked to issues of nostalgia and consumerism. As Jack Simmons (1991a: 10) notes: 'For all the discomfort, and sometimes the strong hostility, that railways might arouse in Britain, the general affection for them lasted, and is apparent still. It derives ultimately from a certain pride in the fact – clear beyond argument – that Britain pioneered the mechanically-worked railway.' Furthermore, as Marchant (2003: 306–7) points out, there are two railway 'systems': a real railway and a railway of our imaginations: 'One railway, the railway that you sit on every morning to another ... pointless day in a drab office ... is the fruit of political corruption, institutional indifference and short-term profiteering. No one loves it, because it is unlovable. The other railway, the romantic railway, the railway of memory and dreams ... is deeply lovable because it isn't entirely real.'

We can find both the 'nostalgic railway of our dreams' (from steam engines to the pleasure we feel sitting in an old-fashioned carriage with exit doors and windows that open between the seats) and the 'railway of consumerism and quality' (late trains and league tables, smart uniforms and customer charters) in contemporary discourse. Thus, the nostalgic railway of our dreams:

Santa & Steam – A Victorian Christmas
The Churnet Valley Railway invites you to join them for their traditional Victorian Christmas.
Sit back and enjoy our seasonal favourite, the Churnet Valley Railway's Santa & Steam Specials.
Travel with us on an 8 mile round journey through the hidden valley whilst Santa strolls through the train handing out wonderful presents to each girl and boy and sherry and mince pies to mums and dads. Garland filled coaches, clowns and magicians add to the festive atmosphere.
Begin your journey from our splendid Victorian station where time has stood still, with period attractions, music and merriment, souvenirs and curios and a visit to Santa's workshop (Churnet Valley Railway 2003)

and the railway of consumerism and quality:

Tilting Trains make us feel sick
Travellers say that £11 million Italian-built Pendolino trains are so smooth they have suffered a 'subtle vibration' which has 'turned their stomachs'.
The trains are not allowed to tilt round bends until next September and top speed is 110 mph until the London to Glasgow line is upgraded. It is feared that once tilting starts and speeds rise to 140 mph passengers will feel worse ... Virgin customer services assistant Ken Pointer said: 'If a passenger feels ill, we report it to the train manager and offer a glass of water.'
A Virgin Trains spokesman said: 'There has been a minority of cases where customers have suffered a form of motion sickness. But many people have told us the trains are smooth.' (Leake 2003: 42)

At times these two discourses meet, even clash. At several points in this book, for example, we refer to the journey from Exeter to Plymouth along the South Devon coast, a journey that for many epitomizes the romantic, nostalgic train (see Fig. 1). But as Marchant (2003: 300) notes:

Figure 1 Dawlish station, Devon. Previously published on the front cover of Ransom (2001). Copyright: Dave McAlone. By permission.

In places, this remaining line goes along the sea wall. Waves break over the line. Virgin have just invested a vast amount of money in new trains to run their cross-country services from Penzance to Plymouth to Bristol and beyond. These trains keep breaking down every time they go over the sea wall. Salt gets into their delicate parts, far more delicate than on any of the steam engines which used to navigate the line.

As we write this book it is fair to say that there is a crisis in public transport in Britain:

> What really did for Railtrack was not government double-dealing but the underlying structural weakness of the company and the wider railway industry, coupled with arrogant and incompetent mismanagement on a gigantic scale. The three crashes at Southall in 1997, Ladbroke Grove in 1999 and finally at Hatfield at the end of 2000, and the gradual exposure of the potential liabilities that the company faced, caused its share price to plummet to under £4. (Strangleman 2002b: 2.4)

> You have to get the Treasury to make a realistic commitment to the 10–year transport plan. Railways need double the £33.5 billion the government has earmarked. With £60 billion in the kitty you might then be able to get an additional £20 billion from the private sector. It's a lot of money but it is needed

to catch up a backlog of 30 to 40 years of underinvestment by Labour and Tory governments. (Steven Norris, former Conservative transport minister and transport consultant, cited by Carr-Brown 2002: 13)

With this in mind it is possible to argue, as Andrew Murray (2002: xii) does, that discussions about the railways are a 'microcosm of the wider debate about the role of the public and private sectors, the proper scope of market forces and, more generally, what values and whose interests should drive public policy'. Despite this, the train and train travel still remain for many an important part of our history and our future. Thus, the discourses of trains and train travel are complex and varied.

Discourses of Trains and Train Travel

Michel Foucault (1980, 1984) suggests that discourses are historically variable ways of specifying knowledge and truth and it is through discourses that we are encouraged to see what is and is not 'the truth'. For Foucault then, '[d]iscourses are not merely linguistic phenomena, but are always shot through with power and are institutionalised as practices' (Foucault cited by Ransom 1993: 134).

Foucault (1984: 100) argues that it is necessary to recognize that there is not a simple divide between accepted and excluded discourse, or between a dominant and dominated discourse. He suggests that we must recognize 'a multiplicity of discursive elements that can come into play in various strategies' that can transmit, produce and reinforce power, but also expose power, which makes it possible to thwart it. Another way to describe these dominant discourses is as 'authoritative'. Authoritative discourses are, clearly, discourses that are seen to have most value (by some people at least, and always by those with the power to define). One of the problematic features of any notion of discourse is that it is difficult to assess where a discourse begins and ends, not least because these become part of the fabric of understandings in our daily lives. A dominant discourse can be defined as one which is imposed on people, and an authoritative discourse as one accepted by people; and such discourses frequently have institutional power but may be appropriated into individuals' lives and as useful ways to explain events and experiences.

A Foucauldian analysis of discourse, then, can allow us to see more of the relationships of power between different interest groups at any specific historical period. 'Knowledge' is a 'matter of the social, historical and political conditions under which, for example, statements come to count as true or false' (McHoul and Grace 1995: 29). Power, however, does not merely emanate from the top downwards; it can emerge from anywhere.

As noted above, we are concerned with both the discourse of romance and that of consumerism and quality in this book. But that is not all. In engaging with these two very different images of the train and train travel we also consider the significance of the other ways in which the 'truth' and the 'knowledge' of the railway are understood. As a whole, this book represents a challenge to current dominant discourses surrounding, for example, the use to which train space is put and the characteristics and experience of train-spotters. In the first half of the book – Chapters 1, 2 and 3 – we concentrate more on public and policy discourses, drawing on the experience and views of our respondents to help us critique these. In Chapters 4, 5 and 6 our respondents' accounts are to the fore and as such, in the second half of the book, we focus on lay discourses and offer this as a challenge to previous work in this and related areas.

Locating Our Work

Themes and Issues

In respect of trains and train travel, the issues of time and space are considered in detail by Wolfgang Schivelbusch (1986). In his book on the development of the railway (particularly in Europe) he refers to the railway as the nineteenth-century symbol of modernity. He argues that the railway was seen as a key agent in the annihilation of space and time in that it denaturalized transport by speeding it up, and changed our perception of the landscape from detailed to panoramic: 'Transport technology is the material base of potentiality, and equally the material base of the traveler's space–time perception … If an essential element of the given socio-cultural space–time continuum undergoes changes, this will affect the entire structure; our perception of space–time will also lose its accustomed orientation' (Schivelbusch 1986: 36).

Further, for Schivelbusch, with the development of the railway the journey itself ceased to be an active part of the journey, with only departure and arrival as the real events. This, of course, does not sufficiently acknowledge the train as a place in and of itself. Thus, unlike Schivelbusch and Kerry Hamilton and Stephen Potter (1985), we argue that 'the train' has never been merely a series of boxes on wheels to move people from one place to another, but the journey itself is frequently a work time or a leisure time and of interest in itself. Our aim, therefore, is to extend, in an empirical way, understandings and meanings of trains and train travel by exploring activities surrounding and within the train.

The concepts of time, space and place have been problematized as much by those from other disciplines – cultural theorists and social geographers – as by sociologists. A number of varying definitions of the concepts have emerged, sometimes in contradiction to each other (Massey 1993). Drawing on our own and other disciplines – including geography, history, cultural studies – our main aim in this book is to 'unwrap' the train and train travel as social phenomena which can be analysed in their own right. We explore a number of theoretical themes:

Space and Place. The train is an identifiable space in which certain activities take place for a specified length of time. It is also a place in at least two senses: (i) a site with material boundaries and parameters within which people can move around in the space thus created; and (ii) a symbolic 'place' which is constructed purely in people's heads when they identify and articulate their specific activities. Additionally, the train/place travels through other 'spaces' which impact upon the activities of those using the train space and those who observe the train on its journey.

Time. Although often perceived as fixed, natural and unchanging, time is constructed in a number of different ways during train travel. There is 'clock' time, including times of departure and arrival; 'historical' time, which denotes the constructional historical period of railways, the geographical areas through which trains run, and also the historical time in which research in undertaken; and 'work' time and 'leisure' time which mark out the times for beginning and ending those activities and which are not always synonymous with 'clock' time.

Power and Identity. Gender, age, class, ethnicity and disability all have a bearing on the train experiences, as passengers, as railway enthusiasts and as railway workers. At times, consumer 'power' is significant; at others, rail travellers feel powerless in the face of confused and confusing services. Issues of identity and difference are also relevant to the relationships between and amongst train users and watchers and railway workers. Furthermore, the experience and pleasure of rail enthusiasts and railway workers are affected by, amongst other things, historical shifts in the control of the railways and therefore of rail enthusiasts.

Public and Private. Trains are normally supremely public spaces, not just in the number of people who may be standing or seated, but also open to those who walk through and 'explore' the train in its full length. Yet the activities that people undertake in that space are largely of a private or personal nature. The train space, therefore, is the site of conflict and negotiation in social interactions that are themselves often culturally specific, or even unarticulated in terms of cultural etiquette. Etiquette is also part of the public activity of train watching, an activity which takes place in public but which is often a private and personal endeavour.

Risk. Historically, and to date, references to safety and danger are a part of any discussion of trains and train travel. In addition, and with reference to the themes and issues mentioned above, there are times when those who occupy the space within and around the train put their 'public' and 'private' identities at risk. Also significant in terms of social theory is the view that we are living in a progressively risk-structured society.

Some of these themes we consider in all chapters, some in just a few.

Outlining Our Book

Having detailed the themes and issues pertinent to our analysis we now outline the structure of the book.

In Chapter 1, Points and Branch Lines: Locating the Train in Time, Place and Space, we consider the relevance of social theory in developing a historical and contemporary analysis of the train and train travel. We draw on a range of disciplines and consider further the theoretical themes underpinning our analysis. In Chapter 2, Leaves on the Line: Current Discourses of the Train, we extend the social and political discussion begun in Chapter 1 through attention to the place of the train in historical and contemporary discourse.

In Chapter 3, Signs and Signals: Finding the Train in Western Culture, we consider how the train is embedded in Western and patriarchal culture. Trains and train travel form the backdrop of films, children's television programmes, books and songs and symbolize progress, power and sex. This cultural analysis is extended in Chapter 4, All Aboard the 'Play Station': Leisure and the Train, in which we argue that the train is not just used to travel to and from leisure activities but is a space and place of leisure and a source of spectacle in its own right.

In Chapter 5, Working on the Line: Working Patterns and the Train, we consider the experiences of people who work on and for trains (as railway employees), people who use the train to and from their occupation and passengers who use the train as a space in which to work. Our point here is once again that trains are not merely boxes on wheels that move people from A to B but spaces in which a different work time is constructed. Yet the space and place of the train are structured by issues of personal politics and we consider this in relation to the experience of railway personnel and train users and fans in Chapter 6, Standing Room Only: Personal Politics and the Train.

Finally, in Final Reflections: Light at the End of the Tunnel? we pose some questions for both the future of trains and the future directions of our research.

The 'Place' of the Railway Station

Any discussion of trains and train travel must of course include, in passing at least, reference to the railway station. Just as there are whole books about trains and train travel, there are, of course, also whole books about railway stations. The romantic nostalgia that many feel for the train is also felt in relation to the place where the passengers board and disembark, the historical home of the 'stationmaster', the contemporary home of the 'Buffet QuickStop'. For example, Jeffrey Richards and John MacKenzie (1986: vii–viii) describe the railway station as a living, breathing space that is 'instantly recognized when depicted in the theatre, the cinema, painting, photographs, poetry, novels and travel works'. Similarly, Nicholas Whittaker (1995: 125–6) argues that: 'However indifferent people have become to trains, anyone with a smidgin of poetry in their soul can't fail to be fascinated by the comings and goings of a railway station.' In addition, the symbolic meanings of the Gothic, Classical or Renaissance style stations need to be contrasted with the modern, functional – and some would suggest soulless – station and the abandoned stations in various states of preservation or decay that remain as a reminder to Beeching's closure of routes, and thus stations, in Britain in the 1960s (Huntley 1993: 2). With stations as with trains, therefore, we need to consider both romanticism and issues of consumerism and quality.

The railway station was and is the focus of train activity, a place where people meet and part; buy books, newspapers, socks and ties and greetings cards, and any type of food and drink that one can imagine. It is also the destination of material goods needed for town and city life. Our romantic view, though, as always, needs to be tempered with a historical and contemporary sprinkling of reality:

> the familiar landmarks of [our] lives have been bulldozed, leaving them bewildered and uncertain. The big city station from which they saw off their loved ones to war, from where they left for their honeymoons and holidays, where they kept their romantic trysts under the station clock, has been obliterated or at the very least altered out of all recognition. (Richards and MacKenzie 1986: 6)
> ... a centre of news, gossip and advice, the home of bookstall and telegraph office. Its disappearance has been followed in many cases by that of the

village shop, the village post office, even the village pub – the slow, inexorable process of urban decay ... The station was ... a gateway through which people passed in endless profusion on a variety of missions ... There are countless individual stories encapsulated in the photographs of migrant workers arriving in Continental stations or commuters pouring into the London termini, of the Jews being herded on to trains headed for death-camps, or of armies departing for half a dozen different wars. (Richards and MacKenzie 1986: 7)

Figure 2 Departure board at sunny Manchester Piccadilly station. Copyright: Gillian Reynolds. By permission.

Thus, discourses of affection and frustration are relevant here too and, although not central to our analysis, the railway station has a place in our book and we make reference to it throughout (see Fig. 2).

Motivation and Method

Background and Beginnings

Our work here brings together areas of our individual expertise in a new way. We have each undertaken research and writing, focusing on aspects of difference and diversity (with reference to gender, disability, sexuality and so on) in relation to private and public identities, and have previously addressed the themes and issues that we consider here. More specifically we have also each undertaken research on areas of work and workplace. In addition, we share a history of observing and using the train. Our interest in this area, then, is stimulated by our own experiences and further supported by our ongoing relationship with trains and train travel. We are, of course, not the only ones:

> It was one of those rare days. Work had been enjoyable and I was in a good mood ... I got to the station in plenty of time, expecting to unwind on the commute home.
>
> Not long into the journey, it started. The guy opposite on his mobile, addressing the entire carriage. 'I can't believe it! The Evening Standard have just published my article! It's fantastic, I'm so pleased!' ... No sooner was one call finished than the next began, repeating the same words over and over again (had he been rehearsing in the toilet all day?) ... His voice was so loud ... Everyone in the carriage had to endure his attempts to impress – surely there was no other reason for so much noise over such a trivial event.
>
> But every cloud has a silver lining. It struck me that commuting life is made more miserable by some of the characters who travel on the trains. On studying my fellow commuters more closely, I noticed that there were many different types of annoying people, some more common than others, some certainly more irritating and some even amusing. Virtually everyone tolerates them and only rarely does anyone make a stand. Then revenge came to me, like a bolt out of the blue. Pains on Trains, that's it! – fighting back on behalf of the embattled commuter who can derive some entertainment value at the expense of those who make a bad journey still worse. I would, of course, like to thank the clot who made this particular journey especially bad. Without his help I would still be gritting teeth and rolling my eyes. If only I could be bothered to find out his name. (Holmes and Reeves (2003) – Preface by Andrew Holmes, pp. 6–7)

Auto/biographical Underpinnings

It is already clear, then, that our interest in this area is located in the auto/biographical. As such our work is part of an established sociological tradition. For example: 'You must learn to use your life experiences in your intellectual work: continually to examine it and interpret it. In this sense craftsmanship [*sic*] is the centre of yourself and you are personally involved in every intellectual product upon which you work' (Mills 1970: 216).

A critical and reflexive form of autobiography ... has the sociological potential for considering the extent to which our subjectivity is not something that
gets in the way of our social analysis but is itself social ... I would suggest
that the key point is that 'society' can be seen to be, not 'out there', but
precisely located '*inside our heads*', that is, in our socially located and structured understandings of 'my-self', 'my-life', 'me-as-a-person', and so forth.
(Ribbens 1993: 88, original emphasis)

Despite this, there are some who suggest that auto/biographical work
is both unacademic and self-indulgent. But, like Judith Okely and Helen
Callaway (1992: 2), we believe that there is a fine line between 'situating
oneself' and 'egotistical self-absorption' and, like Okely (1992), we also
believe that 'self-adoration' is quite different from self-awareness and a
critical scrutiny of the self. Indeed, those who protect the self from
scrutiny could well be labelled self-satisfied and arrogant in presuming
their presence and relations with others to be unproblematic.

Given all of this, and before we go any further, we aim to introduce the
reader to some of our own connections to trains and train travel. Thus:

Gillian

Trains were an integral part of my entire childhood. The line from London to
Penzance ran a couple of miles from our home village. The local level crossing – or the bridge on which we could become mystically enveloped by the
smoke from the engines – were favourite destinations for cycle rides.

At least three times a year my two siblings and I were deposited on a train
at Exeter, to be met at Salisbury by our grandparents. So regular was this trip
that we were given three matching suitcases as Christmas gifts. Our grandparents lived beside the London to Bournemouth line and – joy of joys – there
was a signal at the end of their garden. I have been told that by the time I was
one year old, I would sit in the high chair and copy the movement of the signal:
while it signalled 'up', all eating, drinking, and other activities of life came to
a standstill. As 'railway children' we cultivated friendliness with drivers and
firemen of the steam era by throwing windfall apples to them when they were
waiting at the signal. As I grew older and more reflective, I would study the
passengers, wondering who they were, where they were going and why; and
whether they were wondering who I was and what my life was like.

As I reached my teenage years and fell in love with a young man who
wanted to see life and so went to the 'smoke' (London) to find it, I spent (too)
many hours waiting on station platforms, anticipating the ecstasy of reunion
or the despair of impending parting. Meanwhile, trains would come and go,
and station announcers would reel off long lists of romantic-sounding place
names.

Thus the train became an icon of adventure and exploration for me which
stays with me even as I approach my sixties. Despite a series of rail disasters,

overcrowded or cancelled trains, and dirty stinking carriages, trains remain my preferred mode of transport. I still enjoy sitting on a station platform – even the bleak, draughty subterranean platforms at Birmingham New Street – watching humanity coming and going; watching the amazing technology that is the train, moving relentlessly along parallel strips of metal; watching the rhythmic dipping of those strips under the weight of the rolling stock. Railways and formation dancing have much in common!

I continue to use trains for both work and leisure – I have been known to go to a station and purchase a ticket for the next departing train without even knowing beforehand where that train will be going. I have met many others who enjoy similar pastimes – rail fans, for example, who travel not with each other but with lists of engine and rolling-stock numbers, national rail timetables, video cameras, tape recorders, two-way radios (and, increasingly, laptop computers). Researching for this book was an opportunity to explore not only the train *per se*, but also my own love affair with it.

Gayle

As a non-car-driver, whose parents also never owned a car, the train has always been important in my life. As a child I remember travelling with my parents in trains with discrete carriages with their own doors to the platform and trains with small carriages off a large corridor (just the type of carriage that I imagine Harry and Ron sitting in when I read Harry Potter novels now). When on a long journey, and for a treat, we might have our lunch in the restaurant carriage – served on white linen and eaten passing through the countryside. We left Liverpool, the city of all our births, when I was seven and in the next few years lived in various places across the UK, finally settling in Cornwall, so trips to visit family often involved long journeys.

My first experience of travelling alone was when I was sixteen and my parents waved me off for a two-week holiday in Liverpool with my grandmother, aunt and uncle. This was the first of many thousands of hours alone on the train. Since then the train has been the vehicle that has transported me to and from boyfriends, to and from college and to and from work. Although most of these journeys are spent alone I also travel with others both for journeys to work and for leisure. At present I live in the Midlands area of England and my current job involves my travelling about sixty miles to and from work at least once a week (I stay close to work in the meantime) and I seem to be travelling to another part of the country for a meeting or a conference at least once a fortnight. My mother still lives in Cornwall and I visit her and other friends and family regularly. I am friendly with all of the staff at my local railway station and they spend a considerable amount of time working out best routes and prices for me.

The train is an important place for me – a space where I work and play. 'I'm on the train' is a phrase that I could use more than anyone I know. Sometimes I reflect on the number of days of my life that I've spent on the track. But it's not time that's been wasted, it's been productive and enjoyable, not least because it's led to and informed my part in the production of this book.

As we write this book we realize that our historical relationship with the train and train travel – Gillian largely as watcher, Gayle largely as traveller – has structured our debate throughout. Reflecting back on our accounts, we suggest that Gayle's experience of 'being on' and Gillian's of 'looking at' are both significant to our analysis. In addition, we can both identify with the discourse of affection, of the 'nostalgic railway of our dreams':

> When we go to Cornwall particularly, there are rituals about different parts of the journey. I know it so well, I could fall asleep really and wake up and know where we were almost. But like there's one bit – Dawlish and Teignmouth – it's like a ritual. Whatever I'm doing I have to stop and look at the sea while we're going through Teignmouth and Dawlish. It's such a wonderful part of the journey, especially when it's rough and the sea is coming over the train. It's kind of like 'we're there now, we're there' – but there's still another two and a half hours to go! (Gayle)

> there's a part of the journey that goes through the Fens, and my heart aches because I love it so much. It's so flat and you can see for miles and miles. And because you can see for miles, then after a while you get to know each individual house and so on, even in the far distance. In winter it's very brown or grey, and if you go in spring it's bright green – the colours are variable. (Gillian)

We are, as suggested earlier, not alone in this. For example as Marchant (2003: 24) says: 'On all often-taken journeys, there is a familiar marker which tells you that you are leaving home … But it was when we crossed the Thames by Battersea Power Station that my romantic juices started to flow. I loved the sight of London from the railway bridge.' Many of those whom we have spoken to and corresponded with were keen to detail their own feelings of affection. Some expressed curiosity and wanderlust:

> I have been interested in public transport (trains, buses, boats, planes) for as long as I can remember – perhaps starting from wondering where all those people were going and why couldn't I go there too! (Adam – USA)

> I grew up in a Midwestern town with abundant freight service, and the sight of those trains heading into the cornfields always made me wonder about and yearn for the greater world beyond. (Gerry – USA)

For others an interest in rail paraphernalia stimulated their interest:

> I loved trains from the moment I saw one at around age three or four. I liked the tunnels and bridges and coal mines in the area I live. My mom encouraged this by sometimes waiting for trains at crossings or stopping to see them when we were near the rail lines. (Reg – USA)

> When I was about four or five I received a model railway set for Christmas and played with it nonstop. My parents realized they were onto something good! (Martyn – Canada)

> My father had a model railway, although it was gone before I was born. He had photos of it and used to take the kids downtown to the train station to watch them go by. When I was about ten, we moved to a house near a rail line (light traffic, one or two trains a day). It had a basement where we ran some Lionel trains someone had given us. (Dan – USA)

In addition to family gifts, family history was significant for some:

> I have been interested in trains since I was a small child in the late 1940s, simply because my parents had built a house where I could see the railway line. My father was a bit of a railfan ... and [he] often told me stories of his travel ... My mother's family had a strong railway background, and I often visited a great uncle who held a senior position in the railways. He retired alongside the railway line, and because I was the only nephew who was remotely interested in trains he would spend hours telling me stories of his time on the railway, and of his beloved cricket in which I had no interest whatsoever. (Owen – New Zealand)

> My family tree includes railwayers, railway executives, a railfan and severe cases of wanderlust. I think all of these add up to my passion for trains. (Nick – USA)

Whereas, for others, issues of technology and size were the main enticement:

> When I was about five my father would take me to see steam train excursions in and around the City of Ottawa. Many times my heart would pound as the train advanced towards us. (Baz – Canada)

> I guess I have been interested in trains as long as I can remember. Now at seventy-one years of age, I suppose that the interest covers about sixty-eight years ... Mother used to take my sister and me to visit an aunt who lived on a farm about twelve miles away and right next to the railway line where I

could hang over the gate and watch the double headed locomotives on the express. When I was nine, the family went on holiday to our capital city, Wellington, and almost the whole of my vacation was spent on the railway platform watching trains coming and going. (Grant – New Zealand)

I'm not sure about what sparked my interest, but I believe it has something to do with the fascination of big things. When I am up close to the train and at track level, there is something appealing about a big cohesive unit rolling by. I suppose the only words that I could come up with are, 'majestic', and 'powerful'. Even though trains may be filthy and/or full of graffiti, I still believe that they deserve to be called majestic. (Eugene – Canada)

My earliest memory [of trains] is of standing close to a steam locomotive drive wheel about twice as tall as myself in a station and being startled when it slowly began moving with a loud bark of steam exhaust. (Ron – USA)

So enthusiastic were some of our respondents – namely Eugene Wong and Henry Lewis – that they asked particularly to be referred to by their own names throughout, rather than by the pseudonym we promised. This affection is also reflected in the interest of the colleagues, friends and acquaintances who, when they hear about our work, happily tell us their favourite railway history. But the stories are not all affectionate; frustration too is often part of the tale. Alongside happy memories of good journeys and great engines, people complain about the focus on consumerism and the lack of quality in relation to trains and train travel today. Our own experience is relevant here too in that one of our initial motivations to undertake this work was the annoyance we felt following a new public train announcement that first class was a good place for the business traveller. As we both regularly engage in work activity on the train, our concern to argue that the train was a space and a place in its own right began here, not least because we know that this type of work began long before our time:

Trollope was, among Victorian novelists, the one who came closest to Dickens in the frequency and extent of his railway journeying, as a servant of the Post Office and as a hunting man in pursuit of his sport. Railways began to appear in his novels in 1857–8; Barchester Towers and The Three Clerks were both written then – largely in trains, with the aid of a simple device he fashioned for the purpose. (Simmons 1991a: 201–2)

There are of course other frustrations:

… at Victoria, [I] pass ranks of stuffed penguins gawping like zombies up at the departures board, waiting for 'The Word' – the platform from which their train might depart. Why do we accept this ridiculous situation as natural? Our country must be the only one in which passengers never know from which platform their trains will leave, if they leave at all ...

I take the District Line and change to the Piccadilly Line at Hammersmith by simply crossing the platform. I feel a little glow of satisfaction, as if I have won a little victory. If I had changed at Earls Court, I would have faced an assault course devised for an SAS training exercise.

I am on my way to Japan where the Shinkansen bullet train will whisk me effortlessly at high speed almost anywhere, never late – and also never early ...

After a week in Tokyo, travelling each day by underground, I can report that every escalator was working ... One does get the impression that no London Underground station ever has all its escalators operating at the same time. (Harry Kroto 2003)

And of course there are those who do not share our interest, either of affection or frustration, as a conversation between Ian Marchant and a taxi-driver in York nicely demonstrates: '"What brings you to York, mate?' ... "To visit the National Railway Museum" ... "Trainspotter, are you?" ... "No, I'm researching for a book about trains" ... "You want to try writing about something interesting, mate"' (Marchant 2003: 41). We have never, as two women, felt that we have had to justify our interest, even though it seems that we are somewhat rare:

Railway literature (actually I should say 'railway books', because there is precious little actual literature on the subject) is excessively interested in steam locomotives. This is understandable, because they are big and smoky and fast, all the things that boys like. There must be a book by a woman in the thousands of titles I have seen, but I have never found it. (Marchant 2003: 43)

Admittedly our book is about social and cultural aspects of the train and train travel and not 'just' about the so-called masculine face of technology but, as Margaret Walsh (2002: 1) argues, 'taking gender seriously produces different perspectives on transport history'. Although historically written primarily by men for a male audience, and focusing on machinery, technology and the operation of transport companies, recent research and writing on transport and travel written by both men and women has begun to consider the gendered nature of public and private life in relation to transport and travel (e.g. Walsh 2002; Whitelegg 2002; Strangleman 2004).

Methods

In preparing for and writing this book we have drawn on a mixture of primary and secondary sources. Thus, in addition to being multi-disciplinary, our work draws on multiple methods and our analysis is grounded in this triangulation. In detailing our methods, we acknowledge the opportunistic nature of those that we have used. In particular, we do not mean to suggest any hierarchical status of different methods.

Secondary Analysis
As Shulamit Reinharz (1992: 146) notes, content analyses of cultural artefacts (documents that are produced by people) can come from every aspect of human life, including the writings of an individual and also 'high' culture, popular culture and organizational life. She adds that the only limit to what can be considered as a cultural artefact is the researcher's imagination. These types of documents are of course not written or produced for the purpose of the research, so June Purvis's (1994) description of analysing historical documents is relevant more generally to the analysis of other cultural artefacts. Purvis (1994) suggests that what the researcher tries to do is immerse herself in the sources, get a 'feel' for the time and place, and then engage in descriptive analysis, comparing the descriptions of life offered in one account with others and other printed analyses. She adds that it is important to find out as much as possible about how the personal documents were produced, who wrote and created them and why, and what sources of information were drawn upon. We have attempted to do this with the films, books, poems and other 'documents' on which we draw.

Primary Data Collection
Our primary data were collected qualitatively through semi-structured interviews, interviewer-led focus group discussions, open-ended email and paper questionnaires. Qualitative methods are valuable for our purposes as they allow researchers to explore issues in greater depth than would be possible with larger groups (Gilbert 1993). These methods are also valuable as they enable respondents to detail their experiences in their own words and to thus influence the direction of the research (Stanley and Wise 1993). In engaging with feminist philosophies that seek to equalize research relationships as much as possible, we acknowledge that there are points at which we refrain from commentary and allow respondents to have the 'last word'.

The accounts of a large number of respondents – in excess of 100 (some of whom responded very briefly and one or two of whom were hoaxes) – from the UK, Canada, the USA and New Zealand are reported in this book, both men and women, aged from six to over eighty. Although our respondent group includes more adults than children and more men than women, we have been able to undertake a gendered analysis across the life course. Our group is less representative in terms of class, ethnicity and dis/ability, with the majority of our respondents having middle-class occupations and lifestyles and the vast majority being white and non-disabled. As previously noted, our respondents include railway workers, rail enthusiasts (sometimes referred to as rail fans and a group which includes – but not exclusively – train-spotters/watchers) and rail users. It includes individuals who worked on the railway for years and others with just a short history of railway work; it includes self-confessed 'obsessive' fans and those who watch the train on occasion and regular and infrequent rail users. It is not always possible, however, to categorize an individual's identity when quoting them here. People who work on trains, for example, may also be rail users. Some rail users – and indeed some railway workers – are also rail enthusiasts.

We have not interviewed/corresponded with people who have no relationship with trains, and, despite some irritations and frustrations, the vast majority of our respondents feel some affection for the train. Our international respondent group explains the variable use of language. As Simmons (1991b) notes, even the word 'railway' is important for it describes what is distinctive in the thing itself. Although in the nineteenth century 'railway' became normal in Britain and 'railroad' in USA, that distinction was not rigid. In this book there are differences between the way people describe the journey – e.g. travelling or riding – and the way they describe parts of the vehicle – e.g. compartment or car. The reasons for travel and the use of train space are also variable. For example, in terms of travelling from A to B our rail users included:

- individuals who travel as part of their work, which is sometimes but not always paid for by their employer (e.g. meetings, in-house training, conferences, etc.);
- those who travel to and from work on the train regularly;
- those that use the train only to go on holiday and/or for day-trips;
- those that do all of the above.

Further, in terms of use of train space (i.e. what goes on on the train) we have respondents who:

- engage in work activities on the train;
- engage in leisure activities on the train;

● use the train for sightseeing the passing scenery;
● do all of these; for example:

> I write letters and references and … I always break up the journey by looking out for the sea. I give myself a little bit of a stretch by looking at the sea when we hit that part of the journey … I'll read a novel or just stare out of the window, which I do find very pleasurable, particularly at certain points on the journey. (Rhian – UK)

Extending the autobiographical, we are ourselves included in the respondent group, explicitly making use of the fact that all research is in some ways auto/biographical (e.g. see Stanley 1993; Mykhalovskiy 1996). We have attempted a grounded analysis that, of course, is influenced by our own experiences and views, both as respondents and as researchers. As such, we acknowledge the intellectual and personal presence of the researcher at all stages of the research process (Stanley and Wise 1990; Cotterill and Letherby 1993). All respondents except ourselves, Eugene and Henry, have been given pseudonyms.

As with all research, our study is time-specific. The particular political debate concerning the 'state of the railways' as well as the current focus on nostalgia and consumerism and quality (see pp. 3–4) are likely to have structured our data. Had our work been undertaken at a different time, our data might have been very different. At times in the book we reflect on this. In single and focus group interviews, in questionnaires and email discussions our focus was on the following:

● respondents' interest in trains and train travel;
● respondents' like and dislike of trains and train travel;
● respondents' experience of work and leisure on the train.

We draw on respondents' accounts variously in each chapter: in some, respondent voices are dominant; in others, less so. We also at times draw on observational data, on our experiences together and alone on the train, at railway stations and at the National Railway Museum Library at York, where we collected appropriate references and quotes. It seems to us that, when researching trains and train travel, everywhere we go we meet someone who has a relevant story to tell. Thus, although we do not claim that our work can be generalized to all people and situations – the economic and political analyses, for example, are limited to the UK – it is likely to have relevance and meaning for anyone who has any relationship with trains and train travel, both in the UK and in other industrialized or postindustrial cultures.

–1–

Points and Branch Lines
Locating the Train in Time, Place and Space

Introduction

In this chapter we explore the train and train travel in the context of social theory. We draw on a range of disciplines to inform our analysis. The discipline of sociology provides the more abstract theoretical concepts of modernity, post- (or late) modernity and urbanization, as well as the more interpersonal themes of identity (especially those emerging from feminist thinking). The discipline of history enables us to explore trains and train travel from the perspective of industrialization and colonialism. Philosophy helps us to contextualize the concept of time, whilst social geography offers the crucial concepts of place and space.

Throughout the chapter, embedded in the overarching concept of 'Grand Historical Time', there is occasional conceptual movement from the 'outside' of trains to the 'inside' and back again. This is symbolic and characteristic of the management of the subject-matter in relation to 'space'. We are concerned with social interaction within trains, and trains carry this interaction on railways through time, and between a multitude of other spaces and places. In the same time/space of 'Grand Historical Time', railways and trains themselves have evolved into spaces and places with different forms. All these different aspects of trains and train travel are not separate; they are interwoven in subtle and complex ways.

Changing Forms through Grand Historical Time

In the context of Grand Historical Time, the story of railways begins at the end of a long era in which the main material used for energy and technology had been wood. During the eighteenth century wood had lost its universal function: 'Iron became the new industrial building material, coal the new combustible. In the steam engine, the prime mover of industry, these two combined to produce energy in theoretically unlimited amounts' (Schivelbusch 1986: 2).

From the beginning, therefore, the evolution of the railways in Britain has reflected the evolution of capitalism in Britain. Beginning with the first railway company to carry passengers – the Liverpool and Manchester – networks of railways grew rapidly, even from the early nineteenth century. We can perceive the development as a battleground in historical time in which the *nouveaux riches* entrepreneurs were seeking, with the help of Parliament, to wrest land – places and spaces – from the traditional propertied classes (Wolmar 2001: 20). The development took place in a haphazard way; neither government nor anybody else sought to coordinate it (Hamilton and Potter 1985: 8). This Victorian culture of *laissez-faire* was a matter of political dogma. The beginning of the twentieth century saw the virtual end of 'iron road' construction; the competition for lines on limited territorial space had reached almost saturation point, and the smaller lines had not yet proved profitable.

During the First World War, experience of cooperation between railway companies led people to believe that a return to the pre-war attitude of cut-and-thrust competition would be disastrous. The 1921 Railways Act sought to increase the national efficiency of the railway. As the motor car emerged as a major competitor, the government – helped by the national standardization of track width – rationalized the network of railways into four administrative groups: Southern; London Midland, Scottish; London North-Eastern; and Great Western. This more cooperative 'Big Four' would remain until and beyond nationalization.

The interwar years were – and are – seen by many as the 'golden age' of railway. Public relations departments of the Big Four created an image of prestige streamlined 'romantic' trains that remains even today (see Chapter 3). The Labour government elected in 1945 was committed to bringing all the principal utilities under national ownership. Like the Victorian *laissez-faire* and the privatization to come more than forty years later, nationalization was an act of political dogma (see Chapter 2). At the beginning of 1948, British Railways was charged with providing '"an efficient, adequate, economical and properly integrated system of public inland transport" with the aim of breaking even … The nationalised sector, therefore, was never set the task of profit maximisation, but rather a far more ambiguous target of serving the public good. At nationalisation the railways were in a mess' (Strangleman 2002b: 2.15). Jessica, a rail user and one of our older respondents, remembers that:

After the war Europe was such a shambles, they had to completely rebuild it, which meant that all its big industries were rebuilt to modern standards. Ours weren't – we just rebuilt the ones that had been bombed. It was the same with the railways. They didn't spend money on our railways, we still kept going with the old Victorian system ... So all the European ones were built new, you see, so they had an advantage there. (Jessica – UK)

As with the economy as a whole, the economic health of British Railways did not improve significantly, and the next proposal for change came in the Modernization Plan of 1955. This was designed to renew the infrastructure and equipment of the industry; one of its key features was the complete eradication of steam locomotives (Strangleman 1999: 743). If the coming of the railway had signalled the end of the Middle Ages almost overnight, then the passing of the steam era in the 1960s signalled the end of the Industrial Age in Britain:

> Without steam engines to keep fuelled, the coal industry lost its best customer and much of its strength. The railwaymen and the miners had always stood shoulder to shoulder, a vast army of men who understood the vital chemistry of fire and water. But the bond of mutual dependence had been broken and the hum and clatter of industry would never be quite as cheerful. (Whittaker 1995: 89)

Shortly after publishing the Modernization Plan, government announced a multi-million pound scheme to 'modernize' the road network as well. The Modernization Plan had overlooked a problem: 'Since entering the car ownership club was the ultimate ambition, and becoming feasible for the average family, there was little incentive to walk a mile to a scruffy BR station to wait an hour for the slow train that bore no resemblance to what the government was promising in its modernization manifesto' (Wolmar 2001: 41). As Christian Wolmar further notes, it is very difficult in hindsight to understand just how strong the faith was that the car represented the future. There was simply no conception that high-speed trains could possibly be the preferred mode of travel for longer journeys. And the car and road lobby was a growing political force both inside and outside the place and spaces of Parliament:

> In 1959 the rise of the road lobby was crowned by the appointment of Ernest Marples as Minister of Transport. Marples was the greatest self-publicist ever to hold this post and his background was entirely in the road industry ... Being the Minister of Transport ... [he] was not permitted to retain the ownership of his road construction company ... He passed his shareholdings to his wife, which apparently he viewed as eliminating any personal interest or gain in his being responsible for Britain's roadbuilding programme! (Hamilton and Potter 1985: 50–52)

Determined to have a rail industry that was subordinate to the roads –
and with the Modernization Plan only half implemented (Murray 2002:
7) – Marples used a highly critical report to influence the Transport Act
of 1962, which effectively fragmented the rail industry, while keeping it
still under government control. He appointed Dr Richard Beeching –
whose presence on the team working on the report was almost his only
experience of the rail industry – as the first chairman of the British
Railways Board. With the passage of time, the report was perceived as
deeply flawed and the result of 'powerful vested interests manipulating
government and railway management such that the only option they
would consider was cuts' (Hamilton and Potter 1985: 62). 'Beeching's
cuts were never going to save much money ... It was that faith in road
transport which underpinned Beeching's thinking and led to the massive
closures, even of lines that carried large numbers of people' (Wolmar
2001: 48).

As the railway journalist Patrick Whitehouse observed as early as
1962, 'the English are curiously sentimental about their railways. Let the
most unprofitable branch line close or even be threatened with closure
and protest will follow as a matter of course' (Payton 1997: 17).
Whitehouse, argues Payton, saw the postwar enthusiasm for rural railways as the 'urge of the city dweller to escape the roar of the traffic, the
smoke haze and the rat-race to find the relative peace and quiet of the
countryside'. In the succeeding half-century, the reasons for enthusiasm
have largely reversed. As people moved out of the towns to cheaper
housing, but employment remained within the spaces of cities and towns,
this apparent 'sentimentality' has since become more concerned with
economy and ecology than with escape.

Under consecutive governments, investment in the railways dropped to
less than 10 per cent of costs, comparing badly with France and West
Germany. Despite this, some parts of the industry actually began to show
a profit and the travelling public were eventually covering nearly three-
quarters of the costs (Murray 2002: 8). But, with vastly changing political cultures during the 1970s and 1980s in Britain, this improved
efficiency was simply seen as making the industry ripe for profit-making
privatization: 'Selling off the railways was an idea first hatched in the
hard right circles of the Conservative think-tanks ... [T]he scheme for
privatization finally laid before parliament in 1992 was extraordinary ...
around 100 different pieces [to be sold] to somebody different ... It was
a scheme only a lawyer could love' (Murray 2002: 12–15).

The Railways Act of 1993 broke up British Rail and privatized the
entire industry in the name of competition and market forces: a further act
of political dogma. As has been well documented in other arenas,

however, privatization actually unleashed not competition, but a new 'stampede' towards monopolies, particularly those of existing bus monopolies. Based largely on the discredited pattern of bus deregulation in the 1980s, the picture of the railways in 2001 revealed 'four bus companies dominating train operation, one track monopoly showering its shareholders with taxpayers' cash, a few construction firms bringing the practices of the building site to railway maintenance, and three banks owning all our trains' (Murray 2002: 22). Two of our respondents – both of them railway workers and rail enthusiasts – were particularly keen to comment on this:

> I just fail to see how splitting something up can give you a better joined-up transport service. But p'raps I'm naïve. (Jim – UK)
>
> There's four different railway companies based at Crewe ... now [name of train operator] are on about opening up a depot there for the Holyhead line, but I don't know if they will or not. You've got three different companies at Manchester as well ... I do sincerely believe that it was the fragmentation of the railways that has caused a lot of the problems. (Ben – UK)

Radical privatization of railway and train space, however, is not the end of the story. In October 2001, one government announcement will be remembered as a landmark in British railway industry. Stephen Byers, the Transport Secretary, announced that he was appointing administrators to take over the affairs of Railtrack (the company with responsibility for track maintenance); the government had decided the company at the heart of Britain's privatized railway system was effectively bankrupt. In retrospect, Railtrack's fate had been sealed a year before, when a train was derailed near Hatfield in Hertfordshire. It was a relatively minor accident but it brought Britain's railways to a near halt, and exposed deep flaws in the way in which they had been privatized (Wolmar 2001).

> I think the main failure of privatization has been on costs of doing things and a lack of control over the costs, ironically. Particularly with infrastructure work, Railtrack as was, were taken to the cleaners by contractors. (Tony – UK)

In time, suggests Wolmar (2001), the privatization of British Rail will be seen as a crazy experiment led by ideological politicians and supported by equally messianic civil servants. Some public services, he argues, simply cannot be commodified and bundled up in such a way as to make them suitable for the private sector.

In Britain of 2004 the structural form of railways has come almost full circle to the original haphazard system of the nineteenth century. The main difference is that, following a series of major crises in perceived dependability, safety standards, track maintenance and extreme weather conditions – and (therefore) public and market confidence – most investment in railways 'continues to come from the taxpayer, including nearly all the money for major new projects' (Murray 2002: 19). This is despite an eleven per cent increase in profits for bus companies such as National Express, which owns Midland Mainline and Central Trains (*Derby Evening Telegraph* 2003).

Up to this point we have considered the changing forms of railways through Grand Historical Time. Now we begin to explore the more abstract themes of time, place and space as they can be applied to railways and trains.

Other 'Times'

Time, as Barbara Adam (1990: 1) points out, is a fact of life. All too often it is perceived as natural, fixed and unproblematic. Helga Nowotny (1994: 113–14) notes that any discussion of the subject of time actually never deals with time alone, but also with the ways in which we allocate time. We do this in various political arenas:

> So much time for ourselves: so much time for others; so much time for work (paid): so much time for work (unpaid); so much time for buying: so much time for making; so much time for fundamental needs: so much time for luxury; so much time for waiting: so much time for getting things done … Every categorization says something about the content and its quality at the same time, since the assessment results from the relation with the remaining pattern of allocation.

In this book – and in the empirical research that preceded it – time itself is constructed in a number of different ways. We have already explored the railways through Grand Historical Time. Other constructions of time in this context include:

- 'clock' time, which is especially relevant to work practices, work to be done and journey times (including departure and arrival times);
- 'leisure' time, as it relates to spaces both within and outside the train;
- 'everyday' time – the time of desired quality to carry out life activities;
- 'train' time within the train, during which places are constructed and different spaces used;

- 'embodied' time – the relationship between bio-time, train time and the reason for the journey and
- 'empirical' time – the 'moment' in which the research took place, which had a strong bearing on the emergent issues.

We can immediately perceive the logic that time measured by the clock is incomplete because it is divided arbitrarily from the outside. Although we cannot reject the significance of clock measurement as simply false, we can see that it differs from subjective experience: 'Our experience of time rarely, if ever, coincides with what the clock tells us' (Melucci 1996: 11).

As we have noted, the invention of railways and trains occurred at a specific point in Grand Historical Time. But railways also have a deep meaning for our individual sense of time and memory. 'Railways are leys; lines of connection. They connect places, and they connect us with time, and the ghosts of time. The railway is a road of memory' (Marchant 2003: 304). Just as Hogwarts Express, leaving from Platform Nine and Three Quarters at King's Cross station, carries the fictional character Harry Potter from the place of the Muggle to the place of magic (e.g. Rowling 1997), so railways and railway archaeology carry our temporal and spatial consciousness all the way from our postindustrial present back to the Roman occupation of Britain:

> The Newcastle roads were built in the seventeenth and eighteenth century to accommodate a wide range of wagons which were already in use. It was natural that the rails were so far apart as to accommodate the average axle-width of a seventeenth-century farm cart. The average width was about four feet eight and a half inches. The wheels on carts were this far apart, so that they could fit in the ruts of the ordinary late medieval and early modern roads. These roads had not been improved since they were built by the Romans. The wagons were running in very old grooves, grooves that had been cut by the Romans' chariots. The average size of Roman military horses' arses meant that the average distance between the chariot wheels was about four feet, eight and a half inches. (Marchant 2003: 180)

In a very real and material sense the coming of the railways meant that 'clock' time – previously based on the place of the 'locale' – was standardized and thus destroyed: 'London time ran four minutes ahead of time in Reading, seven minutes and thirty seconds ahead of Cirencester time, fourteen minutes ahead of Bridgwater time ... Greenwich time was (eventually) introduced as the standard time, valid on all the lines' (Schivelbusch 1986: 42–3). The travelling public were informed that 'passengers who are as far west as Bristol should be aware that this makes

Figure 3 'Clock' time or 'York' time? Station clocks at York. Copyright: Gillian Reynolds. By permission.

a difference between the geographically local time and the railway time of nearly twelve minutes' (Williams, 1877, quoted by Povey 1974: 61).

Station clocks are thus intimately connected with both the place of the railway station and the influence of railways on time itself. They represent in an iconic fashion the coming together of time and place in the context of railways and trains (see Fig. 3).

Locating Place/s

Henri Lefebvre (1981) theorizes a three-dimensional metaphor of the concept of 'place'. It requires three facets: imagined representations of space; representation of space such as those mediated through advertising, and the experienced 'real' space. These three dimensions come together to construct a 'place'. They thus provide us with a grounded understanding of space without losing sight of the symbolic meaning of place (Harvey 1993):

> Place is a deceptively simple concept in geographical thought; we want to make it difficult, uneasy. We want to show that places do not exist in a sense other than culturally, and as a result that they can appear and disappear, change in size and character, and even move about according to the way in which people construct them. Places then have no objective reality, only intersubjective ones. (Shurmer-Smith and Hannam 1994: 13)

Some theorists prefer to describe roads, railway lines, motorway service stations and airports as 'not quite/almost places' (e.g. Thrift 1996: 299). For Wolfgang Schivelbusch (1986) the development of the railway and the subsequent 'annihilation of space and time' meant that only departure and arrival were 'real' events. These views represent the train as a space but not a place in and of itself. We would suggest that, because social interaction routinely takes place on a train, the train constitutes not only a 'space' created, defined and influenced by social relations of power, but also a 'place' that exists within the minds of individuals and groups. As human beings, we transform spaces into places through language and meaning (Richardson 1989).

In the second half of the nineteenth century, London constituted another meaningful experience of place. The coming of the railways had a particularly devastating effect on residents as the companies drove their tracks through already built-up areas in order to get their termini near to the centre (Hamilton and Potter 1985). Between 1859 and 1867 some 36,000 London citizens were moved from their homes because of railway construction, and the building of St Pancras station alone caused 4,000 houses to be demolished (Rallis 1977). The effects were exacerbated because before 1880 no railway company was obliged to rehouse those evicted for railway construction.

More and more people left the land, moved into towns and became labourers for railways, mills and mines (Gourvish 1980), dependent upon others for the supply of food; London, for example, trebled its size during the nineteenth century (Crouch 2000). Food shortages were (at least in theory) ameliorated by the fact that more than a million horses, previously kept for transport, were made redundant by the railway networks. The foodstuffs (e.g. oats) released by their redundancy could potentially feed more than eight million labourers. The steam engine took over as the new 'horsepower'; the 'last gasp of the Middle Ages was lost in a puff of steam' (Marchant 2003: 141).

Although a number of other factors contributed to the development of urban places from the seventeenth century onwards, the railways were dynamic in changing the very structure of social life. As well as facilitating travel between existing towns, the railway companies exerted their own direct influence on urbanization. Crewe, Derby, Swindon and Middlesbrough, for example, all began or grew as a result of railway technology and employment. In Buckinghamshire, Wolverton grew from virtually nothing to a population of 9,000: 'built by order of a Railway Board, at a railway station, by a railway contractor, for railway men, railway women and railway children; in short, the round cast-iron plate over the door of every house, bearing the letters LNWR, is the generic symbol of the town' (a visitor to the town in 1850, quoted by Hamilton and Potter 1985: 10).

Railways provided the conduits through which foodstuffs and other necessities made mass living a possibility in urban places. According to John Francis, the nineteenth-century commentator and strong advocate of railways, in 1831 an initiative to build a railway between London and Essex was seen by some as greatly beneficial in improving the life of Londoners: 'The whole country will become contributory to the London market, the first necessaries of life will be supplied in greater abundance' (Francis 1967: 242). But it was not only city markets that were to benefit from the railway. Individual entrepreneurs were permitted to build branch lines, connecting their own estates to a main line railway.

The movement of populations towards market towns also gathered momentum as money became the standardized medium of exchange through which social relations were expressed: 'In addition to the social advantages which accrued from increased communication ... was the development of commerce, the increased importance of the various places through which it passed ... The Stockton and Darlington railway turned the shop-keeper into a merchant; erected an exchange; gave bread to hundreds; and conferred happiness on thousands' (Francis 1967: 56–7).

'Competition was carried into villages hitherto contented with all which had contented their rude forefathers. The smaller towns exhibited an unwonted business and bustle' (Francis 1967: 294). Urban social life, argues Anthony Giddens (1991: 33–34), 'breaks down the protective framework of the small community and of tradition, replacing these with much larger, impersonal organizations. The individual feels bereft and alone in a world in which she or he lacks the psychological supports and the sense of security provided by more traditional settings.' Essentially, the character of urban living involves impersonal relationships, distance, loosening of traditional authorities and control, interaction with strangers and a money economy as the sole means of exchange.

In writing of the fragmentation of personal experience in conditions of modern urban life, Giddens echoes Georg Simmel. Simmel (Frisby 1992) argues that our freedom of action is seriously limited by both the require-ment for punctuality and the impersonal transactions demanded by the ethos of the place and its money economy. However, on the positive side – unlike the social relations of small traditional communities – the defence mechanism of reserve creates a new freedom of action for indi-viduals. There is a constant possibility that strangers could form closer relationships (Levine 1991). Places affect social relations as people migrate (commute) in and out of them on a daily, weekly, annual or semi-permanent basis.

Such theories of the metropolis can also, for our purposes, be applied to the concept of rail travel. As in a city, the population travelling on a train is an ever-changing world of strangers – each one a potential social relationship. The 'place' on the train – as in a city – is reconstructed as the spaces are 'redeveloped' by people who get on or off the train. As in a city, even the empty spaces (seats, standing areas) of the train are of social significance (see Chapters 5 and 6). Such spaces are assessed, contested and redesigned as new places. Thus – like a city – the train is a space in which place is constructed.

Railways in Global Spaces

The concept of space (in all its complexities) is fundamental to our analy-sis. Here we try to simplify it without losing the vital threads of the complexities. At the same time we acknowledge the intricate connection of 'space' with 'time' and 'place'. 'Space' was traditionally thought of as simply a 'three-dimensional void': things were held to exist only if they occupied a particular space (Shields 1997: 194).

A number of varying definitions of the concept have emerged, some-times in contradiction to each other (Massey 1993): over the last fifty years it has been variously described as the anxiety of our era (Foucault 1972); an axis of experience and conceptualization (Massey 1993); a route to truth and 'reality' or 'cultural artefact' (Shields 1997). In spite of – or perhaps because of – such valorization of the concept, however:

> space becomes multiple and discontinuous and we are compelled to change our yardsticks, to combine quantity and quality, to position ourselves, and to move with great flexibility … [W]e still inhabit a physical space, we still

handle objects endowed with physical dimensions, we still have to cover distances physically…We are constantly on the move, we travel much more than we ever used to … but we often do so aimlessly and unaware of where we really are. (Melucci 1996: 17)

Alberto Melucci is referring to the present time and cultural context, but his words could also have been true of the beginnings of the railways. As people experienced rail travel, they also experienced overnight, as it were, a fundamental change in perception of space and time:

The following day, 140 passengers were waiting for the first scheduled train to Manchester. Eleven years after Peterloo and two years before the Reform Bill, modernity had been born. Henry Booth … saw what had happened … [commenting] *Perhaps the most striking result produced by the completion of this Railway, is the sudden and marvellous change which has been effected in our ideas of time and space. Notions which we have received from our ancestors and verified by our experience are overthrown in a day, and a new standard erected, by which to form our ideas for the future.* (Marchant 2003: 61, original emphasis)

As Nigel Thrift notes, it is unsurprising that the 'annihilation' of time and space was a favourite subject of writing for Victorians. By 1830 movement between the major towns was some four or five times faster than in 1750: 'The subsequent growth of the railway network made for even more dramatic leaps in speed, frequency and access … The effects were all the more arresting because they came to be experienced by so many people' (Thrift 1996: 264).

To restate a truism, trains – as spaces – use time to pass through, by and between other places and spaces. This movement is noted not just by those travelling on the train – from whence 'the world is presented as seen from within a moving platform, as a passing momentary spectacle to be glimpsed and consumed' (Thrift 1996: 265) – but also by passers-by and rail enthusiasts who are on the outside, looking in or at the train. Depending on where we are situated, what we see can look very different: 'From an aeroplane flying thousands of feet up above the ground at great speed, the ground can appear to be a stable image, yet looking out of a train travelling rapidly along its tracks, but considerably slower than the plane, we are very conscious of our movement through the landscape and a tendency for closer images to blur' (Rodaway 1994: 124).

For the traveller, this landscape was filtered through a 'machine ensemble' (Schivelbusch 1986). The character of both the 'machine ensemble' and the landscape was one of highly disciplined technology and space. The most visual imagery of this discipline took the form of telegraph wires and poles – resulting from the strong links between the railway companies, the mail, the electric telegraph and the government of the day (Schivelbusch 1986; Wolmar 2001). The telegraph poles became the gauge by which travellers determined the speed of the train:

> I can remember as children we were told to use the telegraph poles to work out how fast we were going, and so improve our maths – something to 'keep us from being bored' while travelling on trains. How I hated it! (Gillian – UK)

'Disciplined' space, however, is not synonymous with 'stable'. In reality, the only stable element of any landscape is that it 'is never inert, people engage with it, rework it, appropriate it and contest it. It is part of the way in which identities are created and disputed, whether as individual, group, or nation-state' (Bender 1993: 3, quoted by Aitchison 1999: 33). The landscape represents a social and cultural 'geography of the imagination' (Aitchison 1999: 31). It follows, therefore, that any landscape is also a political space.

It is hard from the twenty-first century to conceive of the effects that rail travel had upon the vision, perception and experience of early nineteenth-century rail travellers. Travel was no longer dependent on the natural contours and landscapes of spaces and places. The builders of the railway lines aspired to the perfect road: hard, smooth, level and straight. But such features were achieved only by totally changing the spatial landscape with cuttings, embankments, tunnels and viaducts. This happened in Britain because labour came at a cheaper rate than scarce land: railway development in the USA would take a different route – scarce labour came at a premium rate, but available land seemed almost limitless (Schivelbusch 1986). These features would permanently influence the differing experiences of rail travel between the two countries.

For most of the nineteenth century railways were not perceived as scarring space but as improving it. Tunnels, cuttings and so on were all celebrated as part of exciting Progress. Even by the mid-nineteenth century the 'new geography' created by the railways had already become a new 'natural' terrain (Schivelbusch 1986). Concern only began to emerge towards the end of the century as part of a more general intellectual reaction to industrialization (for example, in the founding of the National Trust). Industrialization had, by that time, been around long enough to encourage a conscious nostalgia for the past (Crouch 2000). From the twenty-first century we not only see this created and contested landscape as 'natural', but even as representative, and symbolic of a nostalgic past. Jeremy – a rail user – notes:

a lot of bus journeys are through urban areas ... it's much more changeable on the bus. There's a kind of feeling of tradition about taking a train journey – in the sense that it's not as changeable, it doesn't change as much. (Jeremy – UK)

Movement through these spaces and places, however, is not a free-for-all. It is 'guided by networks etched on the ground, by our corridors, by frequencies, by maps, by itineraries, even by parking restrictions' (Thrift 1996: 304). And the landscape is not only perceived in visual or written form – in the early nineteenth century, railway companies published leaflets that gave a broad description of their routes. This was often accompanied by a map, showing the stops *en route*, and claims that their route was 'the most picturesque' (Anderson and Swinglehurst 1981).

In the twenty-first century, however, rail travel is not seen by designers of trains as a way of 'sightseeing'. Windows of newer trains tend to be smaller, and increasing speed makes some people feel that only the points of departure and the destination are supposed to be relevant to a journey:

> (A)part from what I glimpsed at Coventry or Rugby, it all flashed past so quickly – a thump of squashed air against the window and a blur of blue and white livery – there was no hope of getting any numbers. Someone had shifted the gears and moved train-spotting into the fast lane. But this speed wasn't there to thrill train-spotters, its purpose was to blur, to marginalize everything between A and B. These trains had windows, but you weren't really supposed to be that interested in the outside world, businessmen supposedly had better things to do than look at sheep and canal boats. (Whittaker 1995: 138)

Coventry, like Dawlish and the Fens (see Introduction, Chapter 3 and Chapter 4), is significant to our own personal histories (see Fig. 4). Gayle has worked full-time at Coventry University since 1994 and Gillian part-time since 2002. Coventry, rather like Stoke-on-Trent, where both of us have studied and lived, is subject to much not-so-playful derision. However, Coventry, as the summer 2004 Virgin Trains magazine assures us, is 'up and coming':

GHOST TOWN
Famed mainly for The Specials and getting flattened in the war, Coventry hasn't been high on most people's 'must see' list.
No longer ...
Dramatic change is afoot in Coventry. Famously razed by bombs during the Second World War and then subjected to one of the blandest post-war

redevelopments of the 50s and 60s, the city is finally fighting back and shaking off its gloomy image to emerge as one of the most exciting inner city developments in recent years.

Now, for the first time, you can see the fruits of the £50 million Phoenix initiative, which has been some seven years in the making. (Locke 2004: 38)

Thus, space, as argued by radical geographers of the 1970s, is socially constructed, and social life is spatially constructed. This complex construction also takes place within a multiplicity of dimensions: 'space is essentially disrupted. It is, indeed, "dislocated" and necessarily so' (Massey 1993: 157). This means, in turn, that space is not only of political interest, but is itself open to politics. 'Distance' in space is also of political interest. Such politics apply not only to social relations on the inside of the train space, but also to the relations between the train and the places or spaces through which it travels. In built-up areas, for example, we gaze upon private spaces such as back gardens, or catch glimpses into people's homes. In this way, we use the windows on trains to view and analyse the spaces outside; and people on the outside relate to the train as a visual object of leisure or irritation (see Chapter 4):

Figure 4 Coventry railway station. Copyright: Gillian Reynolds. By permission.

Close-up there is a surrounding space that is touched ... a space where people can be met. Far off, there may be a distant view, maybe through a window, spaces reached only in vision or sound ... [The] space grasped immediately around the body and the one reached only in vision are not separate. Instead they interact, are acknowledged together ... Near and far spaces are not separate, nor are the metaphors and materiality of the space and experience. (Crouch 2000: 65)

Both landscape and map – even railway maps, which barely resemble anything approaching a recognizable representation of reality – emerge 'as concepts, tools or visual strategies in forms which contemporary users would recognize them ... Landscapes and maps, therefore, are culturally specific visual strategies, ones which have evolved over time' (Rodaway 1994: 126). In order to recognize these 'culturally specific' strategies, we need also to understand spatial changes in Western culture itself.

It is almost impossible to overestimate the impact of the railways upon the 'spaces' of British economy and lifestyle during the nineteenth century: urban living, agriculture, labour, tourism – even fish and chip shops – were all deeply influenced by their existence (Wolmar 2001: 22). The railways epitomized technological development and stimulated mobility of the population, both symbolically and in life experiences: 'the Victorians equated the railways with progress and civilization. Their coming was hymned in art and literature on a scale of imagination and power which the steam train's unromantic supplanter, the motor car, wholly failed to inspire' (Richards and MacKenzie 1986: viii). For the Victorians, this belief in progress incorporated an image of a future utopian space as the outcome of an evolutionary process. In the twenty-first century, technology seems less benign; fears of catastrophic spaces are linked to a more general sense of powerlessness and insecurity (Levitas 2000).

Elements of the Victorian attitude to railways clung to the system for many years and (arguably) are still there for some people, as we shall see. The truism is worth noting, however, that all the technological progress was made, not by the technology itself, but by human beings, who were themselves caught up in the romantic and utopian spirit of their time and space: '[t]he railway couldn't be built by cynics. Our romantic feelings about it arise partly because it was built by romantics ... The pioneers were all starry-eyed about what the railways might bring' (Marchant 2003: 24–31).

The ways in which railways and rail travel were introduced, developed and used cannot be divorced from the politics, economics and culture of the Victorian era onwards. We have already seen that space is political and there is a spatial dimension to politics. In relation to politics here, we discuss the involvement of the State. Although colonialism has as much to do with politics and economics as spaces, this book is not the place to argue over such distinctions. In relation to the railways, we prefer to limit our discussion to the economic and spatial aspect of the phenomenon. Under the heading of Space and Form in Trains we speak of the class system and the way this connects with identity and relations between private bodies in public spaces.

Politics and State Involvement

For our purposes here, we use a relatively broad definition of 'State': that is, the concept includes government itself and the mechanisms, systems and apparatus that act to support a particular method of control or government of a given territory (for example, liberal capitalism). Politics and State involvement are practised in 'real' places and spaces: interestingly, the 'railway interest' in Parliament was estimated at different times to be between fifty and one hundred and fifty MPs – enough to topple a government and therefore a powerful force (Hamilton and Potter 1985: 8).

As Stephen Glaister and Tony Travers (1993) note, the power of the State has been a major issue throughout the history of the railways: 'The opening of the Liverpool and Manchester Railway was set for 15 September 1830. The company had run out of money during the building of the project, and the Exchequer had coughed up to the tune of £100,000' (Marchant 2003: 60). Indeed, Parliament's necessary part included permission for the compulsory purchase of land for the railway to be built (Hamilton and Potter 1985: 8). The costs of railway ventures were discussed ad nauseam by both Houses of Parliament, and there was much criticism of, as well as adulation for, the new technology.

Criticism focused on a wide range of actual and perceived difficulties such as smoking on trains, animal welfare, working at night, loss of employment, and geological consequences, as well as the issue of finance. The potential for profit (rarely fully realized) was unparalleled in history, even though the railway's 'unpopularity with the ignorant can scarcely be described; the horrors of the infernal regions [hell] were figured by it' (Francis 1967: 4). In 1832 the government imposed a tax on rail travel. There was to be no distinction in taxation levels between the different classifications of ticket. The poorest groups among the travelling public thereby paid proportionately more tax for their travel than first-class passengers.

There was also concern about national communication. The success of the first railways had made stagecoaches largely redundant, and this caused difficulties for the Post Office because people could not be persuaded to carry mail to different places except at exorbitant rates. A Parliamentary Committee concluded that the railway companies had power to prevent movement of mail, so they should be compelled to perform any services required by the postmaster general. These services included a right for the Post Office to run their own train – their own space – free of charge at any time they chose, and also a right to use the labour of railway employees (Francis 1967).

In the relationship of the State to the railways, it is important to note that – although the state was 'as eager to claim its services, as it was willing to influence its destinies' (Francis 1967: 18) – neither the government nor the railway promoters wanted to take responsibility for the actual spatial transportation of the public:

> When the railway was first sanctioned, it was scarcely understood; and, considering it in the light of a canal, the way was left open for all. To this the promoters not only consented, but declared it was not their wish ... to convey passengers or goods and that they were only anxious to be toll proprietors. The legislature had, therefore, enacted that any person might run his own trains by paying certain tolls. Owners and occupiers of adjoining lands also were empowered to make branch lines and have free access to the railway. (Francis 1967: 9)

In the early to mid-nineteenth century, everyone with capital to spare had invested heavily in the railway companies, often at the expense of other investment opportunities: 'at its pinnacle, it is estimated that railway investment in Britain amounted to 45 per cent of the national total' (Murray 2002: 2). The spaces inhabited by the middle-class population were saturated with railway mania. They 'saw their neighbour's establishment increasing; they heard the cry of the railways at every turn; they listened to speeches at dinners, uttered by solemn, solid men upon the glories of the rail ... Their clerks left them to become railway jobbers. Their domestic servants studied railway journals. Men were pointed out in the street who had made their tens of thousands' (Francis 1967: 144).

Eventually, after such frenzied investment activity and in the face of enormous and unacceptable levels of fraudulent dealing, the government responded by raising interest rates. Writing in 1851, John Francis records that this action precipitated a deep fiscal crisis because so many people responded by selling shares and disowning railways. In that wonderful flowery language of the nineteenth century, he notes that 'no other panic was ever so fatal to the middle classes' (Francis 1967: 195).

We can see, then, that, in terms of space, the State and politics were crucial. Debates and decisions by Parliament directly limited or enabled the development of railway spaces. There were, however, less direct – but equally important – ways in which the culture of the time had an impact on the nature of space.

Imperialism and Spaces of War

Railways were perceived by some in the nineteenth century to be 'the triumph of a period of peace' (Francis 1967: 140), but they are neverthe-less inextricably connected to Victorian imperialism, colonialism and wars. The Crimean War was one of the first major conflicts in which rail-ways played a significant role. A determining factor in this may well have been the self-confidence of railwaymen at the time that 'almost any problem could be solved by the building of a suitable railway in the right place at the right time' (Cooke 1990: 20). The places and spaces of war were vital to the development of the railway (Marchant 2003).

The railway companies also utilized imperialism, exporting capital, machinery and skilled engineers to all parts of the globe. It made the rail-ways 'pioneers not merely of British money but of the British Empire and its traditions as well' (Murray 2002: 3). Fuelled by capital from Britain, such investment sometimes encouraged colonialist places, as in Canada, whereas – at least, initially – in South Africa (despite the efforts of Cecil Rhodes) private investment strengthened republican sentiments. Once such republicanism had been 'dealt with', the perceived need for a centralized railway and customs system was a strong compulsion driving both victors and vanquished into imperial union (Robinson 1991). By 1913, London had invested more than £850 million in Canada and South Africa alone, the bulk of which had gone into the railways:

> Drawn into more or less profitable partnerships with London's financial and commercial empire, their politics were correspondingly biased in favor of cooperating with British free-trade imperialism. Railways, moreover, attracted a flood of new immigrants; at the peak of British investment in Canada, between 1900 and 1914, for example, over a million people emigrated from Britain to the Dominion. This migratory effect of railway investment also did much to reinforce imperial loyalty in self-governing colonies. (Robinson 1991: 184)

Other political battles nearer to home influenced the growth of railways within Britain. After the Act of Union between Great Britain and Ireland in 1801, for example, Irish Members of Parliament sat at Westminster for the first time. Because of the need for efficient travel and the political difficulties in Ireland, 'it became expedient to be able to move large numbers of troops up to the Irish ports, quickly and efficiently' (Marchant 2003: 187).

During the First World War the railways were expected to shoulder the burden of transporting men, munitions and materials to, and around, the spaces of conflict (Wolmar 2001: 27). The need for transport was so great that more than 80,000 wagons were requisitioned from the railway companies for the Western front. The high death toll in the (in)famous battle spaces (which subsequently became 'places') of this conflict was made possible largely by using trains to move such massive numbers up to the front line. The conflict:

> imposed great demands on the railway network, caught up as it was in the first great mobilization of the nation-state in the twentieth century…The government took control of the railways during the war, establishing a Railway Executive Committee … This form of quasi-nationalisation was ended in 1921, when the railways were returned to private control, with a £60 million dowry from the Treasury as compensation for the years of state supervision. (Murray 2002: 4)

In the Second World War, as in the previous conflict, trains played a significant role as spaces of war, both as a tool to carry millions of tons of munitions, construction materials for airfields and fuel and bombs for aircraft (Wolmar 2001) and as 'heroic saviour'. At Dunkirk, for example, three hundred thousand troops were picked off beaches and transported across to the Channel ports where over one hundred and eighty trains waited to move them to reception camps all over southern England. No advance information was available of how many men were involved or when or where the trains would be required; yet the operation was largely successful (Hamilton and Potter 1985). Similarly, trains played a crucial role in the evacuation of children from major cities.

The part played by railways and trains in conflict and the building of the spaces of the Empire was reflected and symbolized in a legacy of naming locomotives:

> I wanted to see engines at their best and was unashamedly looking for diesels now, for Warships and Westerns and Hymeks … .It was a waste of good spotting time to be too standoffish about dieselization … Yes, the Warships were named after the same warships that upheld the British rule, but at least they were colourful and ambivalent and free from the smell of schoolbooks. (Whittaker 1995: 63)

Even the apparently innocent leisure space of train-spotting was thereby colonized, a form of propaganda on wheels: 'we had an endless list of writers and admirals and victories to celebrate, hundreds of stately homes and colonies, and when steam was gone the notion was simply transferred to the diesels' (Whittaker 1995: 243).

From the beginning, rail travel had encapsulated a sense of violence and potential destruction. This was symbolized in the metaphor of the train as a projectile shot through space (Schivelbusch 1986). We see the epitome of this symbolic similitude to war in the well-known modern concept of a 'bullet train'. It is clear that the culture of imperialism had a massive impact upon space throughout much of the world. Railway technology was both enabler and weapon of such economic, militaristic and symbolic colonization of space.

Space and Form in Trains

So far we have focused our attention on the impact of railways on spaces 'outside' the train. Now we turn our attention to the space of the train: we 'climb aboard', as it were. The first section here may be described as peculiarly British, highlighting, as it does, aspects of British historical and cultural identity and their effect on development of the railways. In reciprocal fashion, the form of train provision in Britain reflects back an image of British culture that, to many people, seems an outdated (and, to some, nauseating) relic of history. Readers from, or among, other cultures may find it useful to compare our analysis with their own experiences of cultural identity within the spaces of trains.

Identity and Class

Fundamental to the place and space of the railway in Britain, and often in the spaces of colonialism, is the concept of class. The Victorian era witnessed the rise of the middle classes in relation to both the aristocracy and the 'masses' or labouring classes.

Much of the financial impetus behind the establishment of railway lines was the belief that goods traffic would increase substantially. But, in the event, the upsurge in passenger traffic was even more staggering … In fact the railway companies of the 1830s (not unlike the airline companies of the 1950s) were originally unaware of the economic potential of a mass, low-income passenger market and they concentrated instead on more prosperous travellers. It is characteristic and significant that when the directors of railway companies put their minds to the task of providing more comprehensive passenger facilities, they ordered their rolling stock, prices and passengers by class. The railways exemplified the degree to which the language of class permeated English society. (Walvin 1978: 36–7)

Under certain circumstances and in certain times and spaces, middle-class interests coincide with those of the aristocracy but are antithetical to the interests of the working classes. The coincidence of middle-class and aristocratic interest was exemplified in the spaces of first-class rail travel – although, according to Jack Simmons (1991b), it was originally the trains, not the carriages or travellers, which were classified. 'First-class' trains were related to time rather than space – they were simply faster. But by the mid-nineteenth century, we can recognize the familiar social classification of carriages. Francis notes that in 1712, for example, the spaces of transport had meant that '[t]he peer and the "parvenu" were kept at their relative distances … It contrasts so strangely with the noble of the present day stepping into the first-class carriage with no more attention than is paid to a first-class passenger, mixing with the tradesman and the merchant, and joining with the architect or the attorney in familiar conversation' (Francis 1967: 19).

It is informative that Francis notes the presence of the tradesman, the merchant, the architect and the attorney – all members of the growing middle classes. The travelling spaces of the labouring classes, who used third- (or even fourth-) class carriages, incorporated markedly different experiences. Whilst some companies provided trucks that were open to all weathers, other companies – Great Western, for example – did not even allow its third-class passengers to look at the countryside spaces through which they were passing; they were encased in a box without windows (Wolmar 2001). Despite Gladstone's 'Penny Trains' Act of 1844, it was only towards the end of the century that the railways really began to come within the reach of ordinary people – 'the working class still got around on foot' (Hamilton and Potter 1985: 11). In 1854 *Punch* magazine critically reported on the then-accepted standard of third-class travel:

The mode in which our third-class travellers are treated is a scandal to an age which legislates for the comfort of a cab-horse and places water-troughs along the Strand for the benefit of any lost sheep or idle dog … It is certainly as cruel to expose a number of thinly-clad women and children to rain and wind for several hours on a railway train, as it is to exact from an unhappy donkey more than a fair day's work for a fair day's thistles. (*Punch* 1854, vol. 26: 133, quoted in Simmons 1991a: 97)

The design of carriages contributes to the experience of social relations within that space (Schivelbusch 1986). In first-class carriages, for example, reading became immensely popular. Lending libraries and bookstalls all initially catered exclusively for rail travellers. W.H. Smith printed booklets especially to 'accompany' people on their railway journeys. One such booklet – *The Illustrated Railway Anecdote Book: a Collection of the Best and Newest Anecdotes and Tales to the Present Day, Selected for the Reading of Railway Passengers* – begins with the wonderfully pompous words:

> Anecdotes have enjoyed so wide a range of public favour, that it is trusted the present attempt to apply them to beguile the monotony of a Railway journey, may be received with like indulgence. As conveying the conversational opinions and peculiarities of many celebrated individuals, the present assemblage, from the variety and assemblage of its sources, will, it is believed, be found to possess attractions of no common order; and with this brief letter of introduction, we proceed to the more pleasurable duty of a Companion to the Railway Carriage. (W.H. Smith, nineteenth century, undated: 3)

First-class travellers came from those social groups who were culturally accustomed to using formal conversation to negotiate spatial relations in public places, and then only when one had been introduced by a third party. Reading became a surrogate for conversation, and an escape from the embarrassment of not speaking to unfamiliar travelling companions. The railway users of other classes experienced a very different kind of space, one which encouraged continuous communication (Schivelbusch 1986). 'It is foolish ever to travel in the first-class carriages except with ladies in charge. Nothing is to be seen or learnt there; nobody to be seen except civil and silent gentlemen, sitting on their cushioned dignities. In the second class, it is very different' (Hawthorne 1855, quoted in Simmons 1991a: 97).

As the network developed and rail travel became a part of common (if not everyday) life, the rolling stock was rationalized. Fourth-class travel was phased out and the small distinctions in design between second- and third-class travel may have rendered second-class travel unsustainable: 'Whereas second-class seats were formed so that one's buttocks did not have to touch those of a stranger's, third-class seats were flat ... This was too silly even for England. Something had to go ... It was third class which was the most popular, and second class which died' (Marchant 2003: 53–54).

In reality, it is less likely to have been the popularity of third-class travel than the increasing affluence of the middle classes, and their aspirations to travel first class, which encouraged the removal of second-class rolling stock. Not until the mid-twentieth century, however, was the title of third class changed to second class. In the 1980s even the title of 'second class' was changed in favour of the less politically laden classification of 'standard class'. Twenty years later, however, many people – especially those who are forced to travel at peak times – still refer to 'second-class' travel, even though contemporary perception of distinctions between standard- and first-class travel owe more to space (overcrowdedness and availability of a seat – any seat!) than anything else. Experiences of the spatial quality of travel are clearly influenced by the time of travel, when Whittaker can comment: 'Today's standard class is comfortable enough for any reasonable human being. First doesn't have that much to offer ... what really gives the first-class passenger a buzz is the legroom and the status ... There's no style, no mystery, and subsequently the truth is that today's first class is a sad anachronism' (Whittaker 1995: 192).

Spaces for first-class travel may be anachronistic in terms of traditional social status, but it is unlikely to disappear, if only because the continued existence is mainly supply-led, aimed at stimulating – forcing – a demand: in other words, if travelling is made uncomfortable enough, for long enough, in standard-class travel, then more people will pay for first-class travel. Trains going to the capital, for example, can consist of up to 50 per cent first-class carriages, even though these may be less than half full. Passengers in standard class, meanwhile, may struggle to find even standing room at peak times. Politicians, and others, seen on TV news bulletins taking trains are invariably featured with the words 'first class' written somewhere in the picture. For many travellers, though, the phenomenon of first class simply elicits a sense of cynicism, injustice and anger (see Chapters 5 and 6).

Identity and Private Bodies in Public Spaces

Within this book we consider the relationship between 'body' and 'space': 'bodies matter, and they matter enough to form the "hidden" base of many sociological studies ... [but] sociologists have [traditionally] shied away from specific analyses of the body' (Shilling 1993: 20). The body lies at the fulcrum of many debates concerning the theoretical dichotomies proposed in sociology: biology and society; nature and nurture; individual and State; male and female; masculine and feminine; private and public; and space and time. Bodies, body techniques and body management vary across cultural space and historical time. Living within our bodies is both enabling and restricting: our daily experiences of living are inextricably bound up with experiencing and managing our own and other people's bodies (Shilling 1993).

As Erving Goffman (1969) demonstrated, our very ability to engage in social life depends upon the managing of our bodies in both time and space. Crucially, there are both female bodies and male bodies which are situated within time, place and space. There is also a well-articulated literature within geography that examines the 'gendered nature of space, place and landscape' (Aitchison 1999: 24). Time, space and place, then, are all gendered: that is, they are experienced in a different way by women and men. This is because – among other differences (see Chapter 6) – men's and women's bodies are perceived differently not only within a predominant culture but also by those whose task is to analyse that culture: 'Critical readings of the textual strategies of sociology should alert us not only to how women have been over-invested with corporeality and under-invested with sociality, but also how men have invested themselves with sociality while divesting themselves of their corporeality' (Witz 2000: 10).

One of the many changes brought about, or influenced, by the railways was an increasing sense of the body as 'an anonymised parcel of flesh which is shunted from place to place, just like other goods. Each of these bodies passively avoided others' (Thrift 1996: 266). Simmel (Frisby 1992) argues that no social interaction can be fully understood without taking into account the spatial context and the use of the space. Particularly relevant to our discussion here is his contention that we (especially in the developed world) require control over – and often exclusive occupation of – our 'personal space'. Simmel suggests that the modern, objective way of dealing with space is 'reflected in a code that structures action at the microlevel, for example, in the maintenance of privacy and affective control to preserve "personal space", as well as at the macrolevel where the state and the metropolis must treat citizens in a more impersonal, reserved fashion' (Lechner 1991: 199).

Sociology, as Stacey (1981) argues, began at a time when there was a separation of industry from home and sociological attention was on the factory, the market-place, the state, the public domain: 'the sphere where history is made' (Smith 1974: 6). Stacey (1981: 189) adds that this theoretical and empirical concentration on the public domain has led to a 'conceptual straitjacket of understanding within which attempts to understand the total society are severely constrained'. Even when the 'private' sphere was the subject of theoretical interest, it was its 'function' in relation to the public world that was important. Functionalist sociologists, for example, considered the nuclear family to be ideally suited to modern industrial society, and drew on social Darwinism to justify strict gender roles, arguing that women were naturally expressive (caring and nurturing) and men naturally instrumental (Parsons and Bales 1955). There was no consideration of different family types or individuals who did not meet this 'norm' (Bertilsson 1991). Thus, from this perspective, the home – the private sphere – is of little political and theoretical importance as it is merely a place of retreat from the public world (see Letherby 2003 for further discussion). Yet, surely, as Edwards (1993: 28) argues: 'The public/private split can be used in a revealing way ... provided it is recognized that the divisions and boundaries between the two are not only not constant, but are to some extent different for each person according to structural and other factors operating on or in their lives.'

We can see, therefore, that the issue of space in relation to trains and railways is supremely multidimensional. It takes into account the parts played by changing cultural understandings and perceptions of space, geographical and geological changes to the landscape, the extension of political power (both nationally and internationally), and some of the ways in which Victorian culture colonized the railways (through issues of class) as much as the railways colonized Victorian culture. In short, the railways were crucial in developing an understanding of what it was to 'be British' in Victorian times.

Analysing Railways in Spaces and Places of the Twentieth Century

How do the concepts of time, place and space together have an impact upon the development of railways and rail travel – and vice versa – throughout the twentieth century? The response to such a question must include brief reference to ways in which the culture itself has changed over the space and time of a hundred years. The debates about the 'shape' of the contemporary Western world revolve around suggestions that:

> it is undergoing processes of transformation which have moved it from a state of modernity [large, differentiated populations; industrialization; capitalist market economy; scientific and technological nation-states] to one of post-modernity [a 'globalized' world of media-oriented consumption; diverse cultures, values and lifestyles; rejection of traditional forms of authority and power; fragmented society] ... Just as modernity constituted a radical departure from traditional societies, so postmodernity, it is argued, represents a fundamental disjunction with modernity. (Thomas and Walsh 1998: 363–4)

Forms of knowledge, universal standards and values and ideas of consensus have all been challenged, undermined and fragmented, providing a vacuum in which self-identity and self-reference are the 'new' authority. The Western world has become literally self-centred: 'What we learn through our bodies is no longer validated in the way it used to be, and this is why "experience" is popularized as individual, unique. It is also why a general sense of fragmentation and flux is characteristic of the modern condition' (Mellor and Shilling 1997: 24).

Because the 'post-modernist movement' within the social sciences emerged largely out of the protest movements of the 1960s, however, some theorists view it as no more than a transitional way of thinking as people seek to understand the current changes from 'modernity' to – something else (Giddens 1991; Beck 1992; Lyon 1994). Indeed, some writers refuse to use the term 'post-modernity' altogether, preferring instead that of 'late' or 'high' modernity. Others suggest that the fragmentation is only 'apparent' and not 'real': Fredric Jameson (1984) argued that the 'interesting, and then unasked question about postmodernism, was not why was the world fragmentary and contradictory, but why it appeared to be so' (Levitas 2000: 209).

One major consequential change to such a culture has been that, because as individuals we have largely become our own reference points, we have also shouldered the responsibility for making correct choices in our everyday lives, based on information available. As Giddens (1991) notes, we have no choice but to choose – small decisions, large decisions – every waking moment, and this leads to a state of 'existential anxiety'. Other theorists have begun to describe this kind of culture as a 'risk society' (e.g. Beck 1992). Whilst debates continue as to the qualitative shape and form of such a society, it is clear that 'risk analysis' has become a fundamental part of the individual Western psyche: 'risk has become an increasingly pervasive concept of human existence in western society; risk is a central aspect of human subjectivity; risk is seen as something that can be managed through human intervention; and risk is associated with notions of choice, responsibility and blame' (Lupton 1999: 32).

In relation to railways and trains, of course, risk is not merely an individual dilemma. As we noted earlier, for example, our research for this book took place mainly during a time of greater perceived risks in connection with railways, and this will have had an effect upon our data. Some of our anxiety arises because, as 'lay people', we lack an overview of the railway system and so are unable to make judgements regarding risks. But 'expert' knowledge is also mediated through the mass media as through a prism, and we have largely ceased to put our faith in scientists: 'Most theorists agree that post or late modernity is characterized by a growing sense of the failed promises of early or "simple" modernity and a tendency to challenge key assumptions of this period, particularly those that unproblematically view science and medicine as the vanguards of progress' (Lupton 1999: 11).

What has this theorizing to do with a study of trains and rail travel? It is because these concepts are important in any analysis of the modern move to urban and city spaces. City life, in turn, is crucial to understanding not only the historical influence of the railway, but also 'public' (social) life and social interaction within the space and place of a train, even though our destination on that train may not be a city.

The complexity of time, place and space itself – and the even more complicated ways in which these concepts interact with each other – means that there are many ways to read a 'text' (Filmer 1998). Our analysis in this chapter, as always, is embedded in our own cultural, social and economic background and experiences. One of our email respondents wrote to us with his own philosophical comments on rail travel:

> When I took a ride of 'The Canadian' of Via Rail, I felt that I was experiencing history, as well as being a part of history. Seeing the scenery helped me to picture what the builders of the railway and earlier passengers experienced. Talking with others helps in the same way. Many of the people I met have important ties to the railway in that they worked for the railway or their friends and/or relatives worked for the railway … It would be kind of neat if rail companies could let passengers find a way of journaling their experiences, and then compile them all onto a website or something else. Even if the experiences were sad, I would still like to see them, because it tends to make rail a bigger part of our lives. I don't understand how to explain it. When a former prime minister died in Canada, he was taken by train from one place to another. This will be a part of our history, and I think that that event is important. (Eugene)

We can see from these comments how intricately woven together are the concepts of time, place and space. The sense of Grand Historical Time is there, in 'experiencing' and 'being a part of' history. 'Train' time is also mentioned, in the activities on the train, such as conversations with interesting people. 'Place' is present, not only in the shape of Canada itself and the travels of the deceased prime minister's body, but also in the ways in which the train itself became a place of reminiscing, of reconstructing historical time. The great 'spaces' of Canada – the 'scenery' and landscape, and the thoughts provoked by it – are fundamental to the very existence of the train, even symbolized in its name. The virtual spaces of the Internet, meanwhile, represent relatively new spaces of colonization, which have a further impact upon our perceptions of Grand Historical Time.

Reflections

When you are sitting (or standing) on a train, journeying from A to B, perhaps delayed – yet again – and wondering how you are going to explain your absence – yet again – from that crucial meeting, it is difficult to be philosophical about the location of railways and trains in time, place and space. You are probably more concerned with 'train' time or 'embodied' time than with Grand Historical Time; more concerned with reaching your destination than with the amazing influence of the railway on that metropolis as a centre of capitalism; more concerned with the 'weirdness' of the person sitting opposite you than with digesting the abstract conundrum of private bodies negotiating public (moving) space. Perhaps you have even sat next to us – Gayle and Gillian – as we have debated the differences between 'place' and 'space' and got excited by each other's thoughts and reflections. The newspapers might have been full of dire warnings about the state of the infrastructure, but maybe we were more intrigued by the immaculately dressed businesswomen recording sales of their beauty products on their laptop as they were travelling from one trade fair to another.

Often, putting an ultra-ordinary phenomenon (which is what rail travel now is) into a theoretical context requires distance (space), a step backwards from the everyday issues of punctuality, reliability and reasonable provision of a service. This is what we have sought to achieve in this chapter: how trains fit into time, place and space; and how time, place and space have all been changed or influenced by railways and train travel. We have discussed ways in which railways have changed landscapes and human perception, changed the ways in which we live and move and experience our lifestyles. We have looked at the part that railways have taken in encouraging such changes around the world, as both an enabler and a weapon of imperialism, war and colonialism, and how such culture has symbolically colonized the interest in trains.

The chapter very much reflects our own interests in rail travel and where to locate it sociologically within the all-important concepts. It is, in effect, our own discourse, or chosen field of discussion, of trains as they have an impact upon, or are influenced by, the social condition. In Chapter 2 we continue the theme of discourse but from the perspectives of other groups' interests. This will help us to locate rail travel within the public politics of UK culture.

–2–

Leaves on the Line
Current Discourses of the Train

Introduction

In this chapter we begin an analysis of some public discourses of rail travel in Western culture. First, however, a word about 'culture' and 'discourse'. The ancient word 'culture' has embodied different meanings in different eras. A current dictionary definition, for example, is a 'particular form, stage, or type of intellectual development or civilization' (*Concise Oxford Dictionary* 1982: 231). In a social science context, however, it is more often used to refer to 'whatever is distinctive about the "way of life" of a people, community, nation or social group' (Hall 1997: 2). In other words, it is a set of practices based on mutually shared understandings. These shared understandings are based in language.

Language itself illustrates a combination of signs and symbols to provide meanings: thus, it represents and embodies ideas, feelings and beliefs that symbolize a shared identity and way of life. We noted in our Introduction that discourse reveals a historical context of power relations (Foucault 1972). It helps us to understand how what is said (or written or represented) 'fits into a network that has its own history and conditions of existence' (Barrett 1991: 126). 'Discourse', in this context, then, is more than simply the way that particular groups discuss a phenomenon such as rail travel.

As we have argued, there are discourses (both public and private) that are seen as 'authoritative', some that are 'dominant' and others that are 'dominated'. Consumer discourses, for example, are often perceived as 'authoritative' in some contexts but as 'dominated' in others. The validity of the context, meanwhile, is bounded by 'dominant' discourses. In this chapter railway workers and consumers (rail users, rail enthusiasts) 'transgress' some of those bounded contexts, as they and we explore some of the contemporary difficulties of – and for – the railway system. We work towards an analysis of the different discourses, or ways in which people actually talk about trains, and consider what this means in terms of personal or public politics. The ways in which different political and social groups discuss risks – in the course of the train journey, in financial terms, in the relationship of the train to environmental issues, and through the lens of nostalgia – enable us to understand more critically the forms of both social control and social possibilities opened up to us. But we, Gayle and Gillian, cannot legitimately separate ourselves from the contextual and historical milieu: we are also 'in' this chapter. We too are influenced by nostalgic memories of trains and rail travel in our childhoods. We too are susceptible to the 'golden era' of railway promotional art. We too use the contemporary railway, and experience the consequences of government policies. Our understandings, as we noted in our Introduction, are located within – and emerge from – our own life experiences.

Discourse of Humour

Anyone mildly interested in the British railway system of the early twenty-first century will know that the expression 'leaves on the line' is a source of cynical humour aimed at the state of the railways: 'it's like a bad comedy sketch' (*Panorama* 2003). It has become a joke largely because people simply cannot understand how a small leaf can make a heavy train late (see Fig. 5). Network Rail, wrestling annually with the problem, point out:

> Each Autumn thousands of tons of leaves fall on the railway. These leaves, compressed by passing trains, yield an organic oily residue that can spread

Figure 5 Leaves on the line? Copyright: line drawing by David Bill (Billy). By permission.

for miles along the tracks causing rails to become slippery. This residue is like black ice on the roads with the same potential for wheel slip. Wheel slip can cause damage to the railway line and to train wheels leading to train service disruption ... Every year Network Rail spend a considerable amount of money to cut back vegetation, to clear leaves from the line, to erect leaf catching fences and to lay gritting paste on lines in problem areas. (Pennington 2003: 1)

So why does Britain alone appear to have such an intractable problem with leaves on the line? The answer, it seems, is varied: we have a greater percentage of deciduous trees (Kampfner 2003); the nature of autumn in Britain's climate (Wolmar 2001); conservation of the line side (Sargent 1984; McNab and Price 1987); and design of rolling-stock (Ransom 2001). One of our respondents, a train driver, reinforces Ransom's explanation:

We will be asked sometimes, if we're late ... I might say well the locomotive wasn't a very good locomotive, the track conditions weren't very good with what we call slipping a lot, no rail adhesion – that's when we get the *leaves on the line* [laughter]. We know it's a joke, but it isn't really, especially when we've got a heavy train...it's in the Autumn time ... .the steam engines and the coaching stock in them days, and the first generation diesels, had got brake blocks on the wheels, so the wheels were scrubbed. So any leaves that adhered to the wheels would get scrubbed off on the brake blocks. (Ben – UK)

Jokes are an integral part of cultural discourse. They have certainly always been an element of the relationship between the travelling public and the institutionalized railway. In the past, the British Railways rock-cake (more rock than cake) and the British Rail sandwich (damp bread, rubber cheese) have been major weapons of humour, part of the cultural discourse around a cultural icon. This is ironic when we look back: 'Nobody realized then that damp bread and stiff cheese was really a most trivial complaint. Nobody appreciated the managerial and technical skill that lay behind keeping a safe train on the tracks. Nobody understood how chaotic and lethal a badly run railway could be. Now we know these things' (Jack 2003: 20).

A focus on leaves on the line as a joke represents a movement away from these 'trivial' concerns. Here we use it as a metaphor for all that could (or does) go wrong on or with a railway system – an acknowledgement of the myriad risks and crises encountered, suffered, audited and managed. In 2001 a Railtrack spokesperson commented: 'We had perfectly decent standards for wheels, perfectly decent standards for rail, but where the two touch perhaps hasn't had the attention it might have done' (quoted in Murray 2002: foreword). Leaves are just one of kind of 'risky' matter which comes between the wheels and the track (others include rocks or trees, non-sticky snow, supermarket trolleys, motor bikes, old sleepers and animal or human bodies).

Discourses of the Journey: Reliability and Safety

Apart from daily commuting, comparatively few of our rail journeys comprise one single train all the way from beginning to end. One of the main features of an efficient railway system, therefore, is a reasonably smooth transition from one train to a connecting train. As Ian Marchant (2003: 214–15) points out:

> In the good old days, if you had two minutes to make your connection, you wouldn't have worried. You would know that the station-master would hold the connecting train until your train got in. But since privatization, this is a common courtesy which has gone out of the window. The Train Operating Companies get fined every time one of their trains is late. So they never hold up connections under any circumstances ... . You see ... [people] fuming at station staff who've watched the last train happily set off, dead on time, two minutes before the train from London gets in. Then after a lot of shouting, the staff arrange taxis for the sixty-mile road journey to Barrow. This, of course, is insane, the product of a disordered mind.

The importance of making connections between two trains appears to have been ignored during the privatization process. Yet the problems incurred in this respect are inextricably interwoven with the nature of competition between companies:

> They keep on about they want integrated public transport i.e. between the buses and the trains but you can't even get integrated transport between the different railway companies ... Whereas under BR they used to wait, they'd have so many minutes waiting time. All that's gone now ... it's because of privatization ... because it all boils down to money as well now and time is money to all these railway companies. One minute's delay equates to about a thousand pound. (Ben – UK)

Although a railway worker, Ben no longer travels by train, even with the benefit of free passes. He describes his experience of trying to make connections:

> The last time I travelled by train for any distance was to go to a funeral down on the East coast ... Coming back in the evening I actually got into London

and the last train to Crewe had gone. Now me being on the railway, I know one or two little dodges – and I knew that there were trains out of Euston that stop at Crewe but are not booked to passengers to stop at Crewe – maybe to change drivers or something like that. So I got on one of these trains, but the normal passengers wouldn't have known that. I happen to know these little things so it's probably easier for me to travel on the trains than the normal passengers.

Being able to pick up a second (or third) train on a journey depends in part on the speed and reliability of the previous train. Ben describes the difficulties inherent in this:

Unless you can get freight running at a higher speed, you're always going to get problems. Freight trains tend to have a higher failure rate than passenger trains, you get problems with the locomotive failing, you get problems with the wagons, brake problems and so on ... We do get lots of brake problems on them, and if you've got a freight train half a mile long, and there's only the one person on them, the driver, and inevitably you get your problems near the back end of the train, you don't sort it out within two or three minutes. It's at least half an hour to sort anything out. (Ben – UK)

Another (mainly rail user) respondent, Henry, felt that the travelling public are less concerned about safety issues relating to trains than with similar issues on air travel:

But the interesting thing is that if an aeroplane is two hours late, you don't complain nearly as much as if a train is half an hour late, a plane is allowed to be late because it is about safety and we have a different attitude to flying. But a train mustn't be late to that extent ... we don't have to worry about the safety issue, whereas with a plane – 'oh please take five hours because we don't want a faulty engine, please send away to Boeing for a new engine and then we'll be happy'. (Henry – UK)

The subject of speed is currently part of the discourse of trains, as main lines get upgraded to take new 'tilting' trains, designed to negotiate bends at higher speeds. But how fast is 'too fast'? Some respondents feel that greater speed is, in general, unnecessary except in long-distance competition with airlines:

I can't see the purpose of – it's certainly not for me. Going that fast – reaching London ten minutes earlier, doesn't seem at all necessary. But I could see that London from Glasgow could be more important, they might get to London forty-five minutes earlier or something. (Joseph – UK)

Stuart – a regular commuter – points out that speed must be balanced out not only with a perception of safety, but also with passenger comfort and being able to continue intellectual and social activity:

> Provided that it was safe, I am quite happy for them to go a bit faster – provided it *felt* safe as well … I wouldn't like to be going faster if I was thrown around, I'd rather go a little bit slower and feel comfortable so I can get on with reading or working or talking … and not be conscious of the fact that I am travelling. I mean that is one of the advantages of the train, that when it is at its best, it's like sitting here in my armchair … we've either got to travel slower or we are going to be thrown around a bit.

Others acknowledge that speed is more an issue for the train operating companies, but through public discourse it is manipulated into a marketing tool:

> If the trains go faster, they get more journeys out of their train in a working day, and so they get more value out of their assets … if you remove five minutes from a journey time, added up during the day, you might be able to get an extra London/Glasgow and back instead of a London/Liverpool and back. And so you get more value out of your assets. It's all to do with business and making use of the assets … .obviously they market it as being for the benefit of the passengers. (Jim – UK)

Stanley Hall (1999: 126–7) suggests that privatization is particularly convenient for governments, especially when delays are frequent:

> If any proof were needed of the Government's inability to understand the inherent long-term nature of the railway, consider the criticism that is being levelled at the Train Operating Companies for their failure to produce instant improvements in performance. The attack on Virgin for what is admittedly an unsatisfactory standard on the West Coast main line is a little unfair. Punctuality on that line was unsatisfactory when it was in BR's hands, and will only be improved after massive investment in both the infrastructure and the rolling stock. BR recognized this ten years ago and produced plans for improvement, but the government of the day failed to provide the funds … .The railways, despite being privatized, are still a political football.

Rail users are, in the main, aware of problems in the system and tend to be more balanced in their discourse than either Parliament or the media. As Stuart says:

I am always much happier when the train is moving, when it is rolling at a reasonable speed and you know that you are going to get to your destination. I think it's about being in control, just liking to know where you are at … It's not unsafe – it's just that you don't know whether you're going to get to work this morning or not … I mean they say that more trains are late this year than last but of course they are if they're doing all this maintenance work – they are bound to be late aren't they? So you can't sort of hold it against them that there are delays … I mean you can't blame [name of train operator] if the signals aren't working can you? Or if the track is faulty? You can blame [name of train operator] if the driver doesn't turn up … or they got the engine out of the shed and it wasn't working so they had to go and find another one.

At the time when debates about privatization were taking place, some of the political discourse in support of it included criticism of the nationalized railway's unresponsiveness to consumer demand. In the early 1990s, for example, the then Transport Secretary John McGregor stressed British Rail still: 'combined the classic shortcomings of the traditional nationalized industry. It is an entrenched monopoly. That means too little responsiveness to customer needs' (Bagwell 1996: 139, quoted in Strangleman 2002b: 2.20). Two years later, charges were still being made, this time by another minister involved in the privatization process, Brian Mawhinney, that it 'was the same old nationalized industry story … The command economy with a vengeance' (Department of Transport 1994: 4, quoted in Strangleman 2002b: 2.21).

A key development of the late twentieth century in managing production has been the principle of 'just-in-time' (Lubben 1988). This is a philosophy in which assets are used more efficiently to provide just what is needed when it is required. Subsequently the concept has been broadened, especially by academics, to include food production (Moscowitz 1994), the construction industry (Low and Chan 1997) and urban planning (Alfasi and Portugali 2004). It seems logical, therefore, to apply the principle of 'just-in-time' as part of 'responsiveness to consumer needs'. Such responsiveness would include capacity for extra seating on existing trains where demand fluctuates. Even in the early part of the twentieth century, this was common practice: 'Extra carriages, and plenty of them, must be added to the ordinary trains, and some of the trains must be run in two or more parts' (Golding 1918: 48).

To many of our respondents – children and adults – the issue of unresponsiveness among train operators was a major source of bewilderment. The following discussion took place in one of our focus groups (held in UK):

Jake (age 9):	They don't take any notice of how many people are using the trains, they just put the stuff there, the carriages and say 'you can use them' – people complain, but then they say 'well, you've got your carriages there'. They just put on as much as they think they will need and just leave them there.
Sam (age 6):	They're just not really thinking.
Julie (adult):	If a route is that busy at that time every Friday night – surely they must look at it and say 'ooh, we need another carriage on this one because it's absolutely packed out every time' ... there's never any kind of effort made to meet the needs of the people who are actually using it.

And in interviews others said:

I believe they should have sufficient spare capacity – but they obviously don't. Trains are like planes now aren't they, they go back, forth, back, forth, back, forth – so if there is a problem with the train, they have no backup most of the time. (Stuart – UK)

But if they paid attention at all to what's going on, given our experience, I mean we've seen that time after time – those trains at those times have been absolutely packed, then they could lay an extra carriage on. (Jeremy – UK)

Discourses to do with catching connecting trains, speed and reliability are clearly articulated within the context of time, place and space, as well as risk. The train is not simply a means of getting from one point to another. It is a place of intellectual activity and social interaction, and people expect and desire a comfortable space. These expectations key into our images of a train journey as uneventful in itself. After nearly two centuries of rail travel, we expect – at one level – to be cocooned in a fail-safe device. And yet – at another level – we are also well aware of the capacity of the train to shock us (Schivelbusch 1986; Kirby 1997; Harrington 1999a). This aspect of risk emerges in the discourse of crowded trains with no available seats:

There's a little train from Manchester to Blackpool North and it's the commuter train that we get at night when we go to [name]. And there are so many people standing, I find it a death trap. (Gayle)

Indeed, many of our respondents connected crowded trains less with discomfort and poor service, and more with perceived lack of safety:

That journey back from Manchester in November was an absolute nightmare.

I ended up in overheated mass crushes. Actually the crush was so bad when we had to change trains at Birmingham that people were physically being moved along in the crowd. You know, you were losing your feet, the crowd was so bad. (Janet – UK)

Rosie felt that her experience of the ways in which train operating companies react to overcrowding confirmed that this is a safety issue:

I often wonder really when they're like cramming people on and people are standing, like there must be some kind of limit to how many people they're allowed to have on a train. Because I do remember once, I think it was when we were going to Norwich, they said that some people would just have to leave the train, because they'd got too many people on it and things. But everyone just sat there, so they said the train wouldn't be leaving until some people like got off and got on to another train. So there must be a safety issue somewhere of how many people you can cram on.

Julie insisted that train operating companies have a moral responsibility for ensuring that all passengers are seated:

I don't know how often they invite people to move into these empty First Class carriages, even with the payment of a small supplement, I know they have that 'weekend first' supplement in some areas, but for when the train is full and there are lots of people standing, then they should have one in place all the time. There's just no excuse in my opinion for having empty carriages whilst you've got people standing – which of course is less safe and everything as well.

Several respondents referred to the design of rolling-stock as a potential source of danger, even though the external design has improved so that when an accident does happen there are generally fewer deaths (fire caused by burning fuel, as in the Ladbroke Grove rail crash of 1999, would be an exception). A major cause of this anxiety for some rail users is the system for stowing baggage:

I'm still quite aware ... that on some of the trains there's baggage all over the place. Some of them have it concentrated towards the door. I do think a lot more needs to be done about the design of trains and the safety level should be top priority really. (Rhian – UK)

When the 'Unthinkable' Happens

Rail crashes do, of course, occur. In terms of loss of life, the worst British crash to date during peacetime occurred in 1952 when three trains collided at Harrow in London. There were 112 deaths and more than 200 injuries. The greatest loss of life altogether, however, happened at Quintinshill in Scotland in 1915, when a passenger train collided with a wooden train carrying troops. With carriage doors locked, fire swept through the troop train and more than 200 people were killed. By even the most hard-hearted of measures, these were 'catastrophes' (Wolff 2002).

We have already noted (see Introduction and Chapter 1) that a constant theme of 'risk' runs through this book. Here we explore some of the different discourses which are embedded within the discourse of risk. It would appear, for example, that women and men think differently about safety and the risk of accidents. Other discourses emerge that relate to what is now a lucrative safety industry, itself dependent upon the presence and awareness of risks. First, however, a note concerning the historical time in which our research took place.

Some of our early interview data from the UK were gathered – coincidentally – during a period of deep instability for the railways in Britain. Severe flooding in 2000 caused major disruption on the tracks, as ballast was washed away in many places. But natural disasters were not the only problem. A spate of rail accidents – Southall (1997), Ladbroke Grove (1999), Hatfield (2000), Selby (2001) and Potters Bar (2002) – were still very much in people's minds. It has been argued that at least some of these accidents were directly attributable to privatization: 'Railways have long been by far the safest form of land transport, in part due to the absolute priority given to safe operation by generations of railway workers and managers. It has taken privatisation to call the fundamental safety of Britain's railways into question' (Murray 2002: 50).

Indeed, a spokesperson for the Italian railway service was said to have commented that in Britain 'they have had so many accidents recently that they have stopped reporting the data to the International Railway Union' (Willan 2002: 1). The accident at Hatfield in 2000 – although a less major accident in terms of loss of life – was a crash which became a crisis. A broken rail on a bend meant that track throughout the entire network, which had been regarded as completely safe just a week earlier: 'was suddenly found to be in such urgent and comprehensive need of repair as to require almost total shut-down … Railtrack can only have been acting on information about the state of the infrastructure which it already largely had in its possession, but had, pre-Hatfield, regarded as being safe to ignore' (Murray 2002: 116).

If the coming of the railways in the nineteenth century characterized a Victorian ideology promoting engineering achievement as synonymous with social progress, then the accident on the railway is 'as much a product of the industrial nineteenth century as the modern, sophisticated, steam-powered railway itself, and it embodies and symbolizes many of the age's apprehensions about progress, technological development and modernity as surely as the speeding express, the soaring viaduct and the bustling station express its positive belief in such concepts' (Harrington 1999a: 1). In other words, the accident epitomizes certain characteristics of technological, industrial, urbanized, mobile, mass-society existence. Like death itself, the accident is a great 'leveller'. It induces collective trauma and reminds us that we live alongside violence and terror:

> Although shipwrecks, mining disasters, accidents on building sites, in factories and on the roads were all far commoner occurrences than serious railway accidents, and in each case such accidents killed and injured more people every year than did mishaps on the railways, it was the violence, destruction, terror and slaughter of the railway accident which dominated the headlines, commanded public attention and pervaded the contemporary imagination. (Harrington 1999: 2)

In railway accidents death comes randomly, both across social boundaries and in microcosmic space. Individual opportunities to control and manage risks are few. One person may escape with minor bruising, whilst the person sitting next to them on the same seat is killed outright. This randomness and its effects on the communal trauma were exemplified by the BBC TV drama series *Casualty* when in September 2003 one episode focused on a rail crash. Subsequent episodes explored the accompanying communal trauma which gradually emerged among the emergency services and hospital staff.

Some accidents, argues Jonathan Wolff (2002), have more severe consequences than others, regardless of the number of deaths. This is because they have 'signal value': they illustrate a new type of danger and therefore increase the perceived likelihood of future accidents (Slovic et al. 2000: 151). Wolff suggests that people come to believe from these accidents that past statistics are no guide to future safety and that those who manage the system are not to be trusted. The way in which the media reports accidents, by focusing on individual tragedy, also contributes to our sense of risk:

> Tony Knox will be sick with terror when he boards a train this Thursday to take him to the spot just outside Paddington Station where exactly a year ago he hurtled into hell ... Some mornings Knox manages to get to his local station, Reading, and buy a ticket, but sits on the platform for three hours unable to force himself onto a train. But this week he is determined to face the fear so that he can join other passengers who were injured and the families of the 31 who were killed in the rail crash at Ladbroke Grove on 5 October last

year and pay his respects to those who lost their lives ... Knox, 41, was thrown out of his seat on the Great Western train in the crash. His smashed ribs and lacerations have healed, but even with weekly therapy sessions the nightmares do not stop and he cannot concentrate on everyday matters. He fears he will soon lose his job ... .First Great Western has refused to install stronger hammers than the ones that snapped when passengers tried to smash windows to get out of the burning train. Knox will be carrying a steel claw hammer in his bag when he travels on Thursday. (Walters 2000: unpaginated)

As one of our respondents was quick to point out:

They have to have a bad story for trains ... One guy from a Northern railway company rang the press and said 'all our trains have been running on time', and the press guy said 'no, not interested'. You can't win really. They want bad news. (Henry – UK)

Rail accidents, however, probably affect all regular rail users and not just those who are unfortunate enough to be on the relevant train. The potential for a 'near-miss' in influencing attitudes to risk is well-known (Wolff 2002). We tend to reflect that we could have been on that train, or do a mental audit of our family and friends: where they are; whether they intended to travel that day; maybe even telephone to check on their whereabouts.

Despite this general tendency in the discourse of risk, there may also be differences in the ways men and women analyse risk (Kraus et al. 2000). Many of the women we interviewed appeared to understand risk in an experiential or reflexive way:

You have to put it to the back of your mind when you are on the train ... I can understand people panicking about the reality when you have locked doors. (Rhian – UK)

It's dangerous, isn't it, sitting on the floor. That's how I always feel, if I do have to stand or sit on my bag, that – I just think 'if this train crashed now, I just wouldn't have a hope, you know. I'd just get completely thrown all over the place'. It's bad enough when a train crashes as it is. (Rosie – UK)

Men, on the other hand, seemed more likely to put their faith in the system, or to use statistics as a mental guide to measure risk:

I think there are risks with everything. Nothing can be 100% safe. And so I always feel far more comfortable travelling by train than any other form of transport. (Jim – UK)

I suppose it's having faith in the system at the end of the day, and faith in your colleagues as well. It just doesn't enter your mind, to be honest ... I don't have to think about it, because I think if we did have to, we wouldn't drive trains any more. We all accept that in life people do make mistakes and unfortunately some mistakes do have serious consequences. (Ben – UK)

Rationally I know that you're a lot less likely to be involved in an accident on a train than you are on any other form of transport. I mean there is one major crash every few years on the railways and of course it hits the headlines, but many people are killed on the roads every day, and that isn't reported to the same extent. (Stuart – UK)

Although rail travel has, for many years, been perceived as the safest form of land travel, we can catch a tantalizing glimpse here of gendered discourses in risk analysis. Wolfgang Schivelbusch (1986: 130) suggests that, if rail travel is experienced as a 'natural and safe process', then any sudden interruption of that functioning 'reawakened the memory of the forgotten danger and potential violence: the repressed material returned with a vengeance'. It is clear that some of our respondents perceive rail travel as something that should be 'natural and safe':

There is absolutely no excuse for a train to crash. There are excuses for aircraft to crash other than incompetence and yet it seems more dangerous to travel by train than anything else. (Kenneth – UK)

There are other discourses which are 'characterized by a fascination about extremely improbable circumstances with grave outcomes' (Lupton 1999: 12). The Health and Safety at Work Act (1974) and a whole series of transport accidents since then have had far-reaching consequences for the development of a multi-billion pound industry in 'safety' (Hall 1999):

[A] team from the [Railtrack's Safety and Standards] Directorate was turned loose on Railtrack itself early in 1999, before the accidents at Ladbroke Grove and Hatfield. The report the safety auditors compiled on their own employers' practices did not make comfortable reading – so much so that the audit was never released to the public and Railtrack itself did nothing about it. But it foretold almost everything that was to come to pass. (Murray 2002: 54)

This safety industry includes not just technological and medical research and development, but also whole branches of law, from university courses to legal practices. The railways are not immune from the influence of this industry, also trying to survive in a competitive capitalist market. On the railway, considerable amounts of money have to be spent now to achieve even a small increase in safety (Hall 1999).

Discourses of Money: Investment and Competition

Having identified some ways in which the discourses of risk apply to the journey – in picking up connecting trains, speed, reliability and safety – we now turn our attention to other discourses, this time in the wider field of money. In the context of a privatized railway system these discourses focus most often on investment and competition.

Our respondents were very clear about the need for investment – not just for maintenance of the railways but also for improvement. Many noted that current levels of rail provision – whilst not being enough to meet consumer demand – are at saturation point:

> I think the future of the railways, it's there, but it's got to be an investment, it's got to be a long-term investment. We've got to have new railways, like we have new roads ... Because certainly south of Rugby, Milton Keynes, down to London – and it's the same on all the routes going into the capital ... the railways basically down there have reached saturation point. You cannot run any more trains ... nothing is insurmountable these days, money talks at the end of the day. (Ben – UK)

Others, such as Stuart and Jim, were less sure about the need for, or wisdom of, completely new tracks:

> I think you should be able to run all trains on the same corridor, that sounds like a massive wastage if you are creating a completely independent set of tracks, I'm not sure that you'd ever be able to make it pay. I mean slow trains feed faster trains don't they? (Stuart – UK)

> I'm not convinced that completely new railways are necessarily a good idea because if you were to have a completely new railway line from London to the North West, and it was completely new, you would want to avoid towns and habitations and therefore there wouldn't be the intermediate stops on the journey...Very few people go from Penzance to Dundee. So you would lose the intermediate stops. (Jim – UK)

For the first couple of years following privatization, Railtrack's share prices (the most-sought-after form of private investment) rose to more than five times their value at the flotation: 'So proud of their achievement were Railtrack's senior managers that they insisted that the closing share price was posted anew each day in the company's signal boxes alongside such trivial things as traffic notices and health and safety information' (Strangleman 2002b: 2.5). Much of the initial investment, however, went on work that was largely cosmetic. 'Stations were easy:

improving them did not involve stopping the trains – and the improvements are immediately and obviously visible to the public' (Wolmar 2001: 211). Shareholders, of course, create an additional destination for 'investment' money. This aspect of privatization had evoked much anger and bitterness from the outset. Fears have not been allayed by subsequent events:

> Of course, money is bound to be an issue. But public funds are already pouring into the industry. Alas, too much of it is simply pouring out the other side ... Two Railtrack directors were each paid several hundred thousand pounds not to leave the company when it was placed in administration. The same two directors were given even bigger severance payments when they were ordered to resign by Network Rail just a few months later. A loyalty bonus and a leaving bonus all in one year is something new even in the annals of railway fat-cat excess. (Rix 2003: 1)

Discourses of money in relation to the railways are necessarily fragmented. This is because there is no easy solution to the problem that, in a first-past-the-post democracy, there can be no fundamental long-term agreement on social policy. Jim – railway worker, rail user and rail enthusiast – summed up the difficulties:

> People won't use public transport unless it is reliable, clean, and not too expensive. And to get that started needs a massive input of public funds. And that should probably come from higher taxes, that would be a sensible way of doing it. But if you put taxes up, that makes people vote against that particular government and get a government which doesn't have the same values for public transport. It's a very difficult political decision.

One aspect of the discourse of money is clear. The coming of the railways symbolized the passage of time and space from pre-industrial to industrial era. The privatization of the railways symbolizes the triumph of financial capitalism over industrial capitalism.

The Dogma of Competition

As we have already pointed out in Chapter 1, the move to privatize British Rail – as with other State policies concerning the railways – was a matter of political dogma: in this case, the mantra of the 'free market' as the elixir of capitalism. The new structure of the rail industry was predicated on the notion that unfettered market forces would stimulate healthy competition, both internally to the industry and externally with other forms of transport: '[t]he ideological obsession with competition resulted in a scheme that was flawed from the outset' (Wolmar 2001: 85). Ironically, even in the early days of the industry, competition for its own sake had been ruled out as uneconomic and wasteful: rail companies quickly learned to pool both assets and receipts where necessary (Jordan and Jordan 1991).

Undoubtedly, one barrier to limitless competition is the limited space available on the tracks: the obvious, but often unarticulated, truism is that trains must travel with sufficient distance between them to be able to stop safely. Track space became more limited in the second half of the twentieth century when many rails were lifted to save the cost of maintenance. Trains of widely varied capacity for power and speed compete for the same limited space, significantly lowering the efficiency of the system as a whole:

There's ... big growth on the trans-Pennine route, and the whole economics of it is based on trains that run fast and don't stop at intermediate stations. Where you have got a number of local stations, like between Manchester and here (Huddersfield), one train sort of bouncing along from one stop to another will have an effect on faster trains. It would mean that you can get fewer trains on that section of line. So although that particular route does very well for local stations ... trying to argue for more trains, say a half-hourly service, is quite difficult because of all the trans-Pennine expresses. And when you get to intercity routes it becomes even more difficult, wellnigh impossible, to argue for better local services, because there are so many fast intercity trains. (Tony – UK)

On the routes where space is at a premium, competition is made more complex – and more open to abuse or unfairness – by the fact that train operating companies also own stations:

At the moment [name of first train operator] dominate this track, they have the last say. If there is competition for the track, they always win and [name of second train operator] trains have to follow on behind, that seems to be the way it is set up ... [name of train operator] own ... [many of] the big stations, and they decide when trains leave those stations. Which means that if there are two trains standing at two platforms ... it is [name of first train operator] staff who decide which one leaves first, so they are going to decide in their own favour ... And sometimes it is very annoying for the [name of second train operator]. (Stuart – UK)

The major consequence of privatization is, of course, competition between train operating companies. Users of trains – whether workers or travellers – see at first hand the effects of such competition, which we discuss in more detail in Chapter 5. As Tim Strangleman (2002b: 1.1) suggests, privatization was based on a deliberately under-socialized account of the railway industry, and ignored the crucial role of a workforce which had shared a culture of camaraderie. There are serious potential consequences to such an omission, especially in an industry which, by its very nature, depends on such a culture of sharing important information about safety: 'the various organizations involved no longer cooperate readily with each other and the investigators in order to ascertain what happened [in a rail crash] ... [I]t is an accumulation of little mistakes that built up to cause a disaster' (Wolmar 2001: 157). Before privatization, track workers operated in gangs and knew their own stretches of track. Since privatization they have instructions not to talk to rival workers (*Financial Times* 22/2/2001, quoted in Strangleman 2002b: 2.26).

Competing with Other Forms of Transport

For most journeys, the railways compete for travellers with the private car. The love affair with the car, encouraged and supported by seductive advertising and political patronage, has been well documented (e.g. Davison 2004). British people use cars more than any other population in Europe (*Panorama* 2003).

> I think if we had a decent and competitively-priced train system, people would use it ... I think if you want people to use it, it's got to be at the same level as the cost of the journey in the car, or less really ... I think if people saw it as genuinely a better alternative, then people would use it. (Sandie – UK)

Despite the preference for other forms of transport, each day Waterloo Station sees more passengers than Heathrow Airport, and more people use the railway than at any time since 1947 (SRA 2003).The volume of rail use, however, cannot be divorced from the performance of the national economy as a whole: 'It is ... the growth in use which, however welcome, has led to deteriorating punctuality and reliability, exposing the inadequacy of the infrastructure and indeed of the organization of the industry' (Crompton 2003: x).

Freedom of movement is a strongly held value in liberal democracies. In 2003 John Kampfner, of the *New Statesman*, interviewed Richard Bowker, chairman of the Strategic Rail Authority:

> He identifies a succession of government errors: failure to think strategically in the 1970s; failure to invest in the 1980s; a botched privatization in the

1990s. Finally, in a desperate attempt to deal with gridlock on the roads, it tried to pile too many people on to trains that cannot cope ... I asked him about our obsession with travel, or 'hyper-mobility', in the jargon. If we can't cope, why not simply discourage people from moving about so much? 'With wealth comes the desire to travel,' Bowker says. 'We should see travel as a good thing, consequent on our position as a wealthy nation. But it has put a significant strain on our transportation system. There was a view back in the late 1990s that we had a real problem with congestion ... and you would be able to decant that off on to the railways. That is not the case. Both modes are heavily congested. The railways are no longer a fix for another mode's problems. We should embrace the freedom and the desire to travel but we need to make sure that our infrastructure can cope. It is no longer the case that the railways can simply mop up everyone else's congestion.' (Kampfner 2003: 1)

Henry also commented on the difficulties in attempting to shift travel to railways instead of roads:

Closing rural lines would only save a minute amount of money in the rail budget, but also trains could only ever take a small element of extra traffic that is currently being generated for motorways, it would only be a tiny amount. Even if railways doubled their capacity, it wouldn't even be noticed in any reduction of road traffic.

Many people have problems with the idea of train travel because (like other forms of social transport but unlike car travel and when walking) we lack independence and personal control over the train journey (see also Chapter 5 specifically in relation to the 'working' day):

On long journeys I would just rather go in a car because I'd find a car less hassling, particularly luggage-wise, and the freedom and independence, and not being under somebody else's decisions ... Ultimately [in a train] you're not in control. And that's what I don't like ... If you're in a car you think 'oh, we'll head that way' or something or 'we'll go off this way', whereas like when you're on a train you're stuck in their decisions about everything. You're just sat there, you can't do anything about anything, you've no freedom of choice about anything. (Rosie – UK)

There is something about the modern world and a car that is like a little bit of your home, you almost don't have to leave home to get somewhere. You have got something, your car, that is familiar to you, you've got your music with you, you've got your boot with all your things in ... You can drive directly to the place you want to go in the end, you don't have to get off a train and find transport to get you to the specific place you are going. There is also an element of control in the car, you're more in control in the car. (Kenneth – UK)

This sense of freedom, however, is in some ways an illusion. The freedom and control are real only in the initial decision to travel by car. These decisions are themselves often founded upon the nostalgic myth of a 'golden age' of motoring:

> The car is seen as the commonsense form of transport for a very large number of people, probably the majority of the population ... But I can't see that people enjoy it. It's fine when you're out somewhere in the wilds of Northumberland, on a road where you see hardly any other cars but driving round here is a nightmare! It's considerably slower than a corresponding journey by train; you don't have the opportunity to watch the view or read a book or engage in chat with fellow passengers. (Tony – UK)

> Eventually after years and years and years of traffic jams, when the initial euphoria of being a driver wears off, then it is very nice to be able to just get on to something that is going to bat along at 100 miles an hour plus, and get you where you're going. One can get some sort of sadistic satisfaction out of looking out of the window of the train and watching all the traffic snarled up on the M1 as you go through Watford Gap. (Colin – UK)

The people we interviewed spent considerable time in comparing rail travel with that of car and aircraft; there was little mention of coach travel. Several respondents clearly preferred air travel:

> If I am going somewhere I can fly, I would rather fly than use the train because it seems to me that air travel is far more reliable, even though ... there are far more things that could legitimately intervene to slow down an aeroplane and make it late. (Kenneth – UK)

More frequently, though, respondents referred in a negative way to air travel, although space and place are issues here for our methodology: our face-to-face interviews were all conducted south of Huddersfield. If we had interviewed people in Scotland, for example, responses might have been different:

> I mean if you're talking London/Glasgow, I don't think the car is a major competitor, it's the airlines, the cheap airlines really, and people have to make up their mind whether it's cost or whether it's time in getting there, or whether they want to go city centre to city centre ... By the time it's London to Inverness the plane is ahead I think, in terms of time and everything else. (Henry – UK)

Tony felt very strongly that, although air travel is perceived by many as the 'acme' of social transport, the reality is quite different:

> Unless you can spend a fortune going Business Class, it's a pretty unpleasant experience from beginning to end. You're stuck in anonymous departure lounges, reliability is awful – it makes rail seem absolutely ideal in terms of reliability! And then the actual plane itself is very cramped, you can't see much out the window.

Discourses of money key into other discourses to do with liberal capitalism. These discourses reflect concerns about freedom of movement, individualism and control. But they also reveal people's ambivalence regarding the direction of capitalism and its irrationalities.

Discourses of the Environment: Conservation, Social Policy and Politics

Environment and Social Policy

The truism is worth noting that railways affect communities. They do this in a number of ways, not least in that tracks, like major roads, set physical parameters for particular neighbourhoods (TEST 1991: 67). Unfortunately, far from encouraging the use of trains, this demarcation contributes to the alienation that many young people feel about rail travel. Julie – a parent with young children – believed firmly that:

> everything possible should be done to make it enjoyable and affordable for families to travel by train, so that children grow up realizing that the car is not the only way to get about – that going on trains and public transport is the way to go in the future, when our roads become totally clogged up and we're unable to get anywhere on them.

Henry agrees, but is sceptical about the possibility of persuading many people to give up their cars because British people now have such an individualist culture:

> I think the roads are just going to get too clogged up, but it will take an awful lot for the thinking of society to submit to the formality of times and trains and sitting opposite other people. We have put up quite big barriers ... a lot of people hate seeing other people, a lot of people just want to be in their own controlled space, they're really frightened of being with others and they will make any excuse to avoid it.

Whereas Tony notes that:

> involving communities in the railways is such an obvious thing to do but the railway industry has never been very good at doing it.

One community-based research project aiming to influence travel behaviour among young people found that:

> Young people experience safe environments for benign modes of transport such as walking and cycling (reinforced by parental discouragement and that of other adults, for the best of reasons). They often have a rare and transient relationship with trains and buses, frequently marked by unpleasant and unreliable quality of service. Not surprisingly, these are the very perceptions of danger and cost disadvantages which work to encourage long-term reliance on private transport. (Pilling et al. 1998: 1)

One of the reasons for this 'rare and transient relationship' with trains is the physical inaccessibility of stations to the wider communities. This was a major source of frustration among some of our respondents:

> I think if we hadn't ripped up the railway track in the sixties we would have an entirely different way of looking at our transport industry because we would have much more accessible public transport system, which should all have been maintained better. In the days when you could hop on a train very locally, albeit a slow train, you could get to the major station and get one there – but those days have gone. You have to drive to fairly major towns now to get on to the railway network. (Derek – UK)

Whilst Derek concentrated on the need to drive a car to get to the station, Colin emphasized more individual forms of transport, such as the motorbike:

> Thirty years ago you could take a motorbike on a train, put it in the guard's van, and pay a flat fare of three pounds anywhere in the country, as I did myself from Plymouth to Longport.

In the same focus group, Julie responded to Colin's point: as with motorbikes, so taking bicycles on a train journey is also a problem. In this case it is the changing design of local rolling-stock that is at fault:

> It's the same with Ipswich to Felixstowe train, they used to have the guard's van that you put all your bikes in. You can't put your bicycle on the Sprinter now. So they've actually gone backwards, even though, again, with the

environment and so on, cycling is supposed to be becoming more popular.

Julie's focus was on using trains for leisure purposes. Jasmine, on the other hand, tries to use her bicycle for commuting to work:

> The use of the bike enables me to make relatively efficient transfers from home to station, or station to work. It also cuts down on my fossil fuel consumption, and makes my commuting more sustainable. It also improves my own psychological well-being and improves cardiovascular fitness.

Cycling, as all these respondents point out, is growing in popularity, partly as a result of government policies (such as the National Cycle Way, cycle lanes in cities, and health promotion information). It is ironic therefore that many now-disused rail tracks have been converted into cycle tracks. In theory, this should improve the accessibility of the main railway lines. In practice, it does not solve the problems at the 'interface' of cycle and train:

> I think that lots of people would use their bicycles in conjunction with trains, if they weren't so completely haphazard about whether they will take bicycles and you end up with the ludicrous situation where they don't guarantee that even if you've gone somewhere with a bicycle, that you'll be able to come back. (Julie – UK)

The 'integration' of 'integrated transport' is at best haphazard and at worst can be a thoroughly unpleasant experience. Jasmine found that:

> Stations are not particularly easy to manoeuvre bikes around, storage space is often concealed and limited ... But the real incompatibility comes if you want to put a bike on the train. Space on the train is often limited, but worse than that is the attitude of the train managers ... I have had to pay for a light weight bike to ease carrying it at the station ... Even folded, it is treated by a minority of guards on the [name of first train operator] service as an intrusion into their service ... The [name of second train operator] (which, for me, is the slow, stopping service) allows bikes if they have room, and this seems to translate into more relaxed, practical, bike-friendly behaviour on the part of the guards.

Gillian also has personal experience of the frustrations in trying to do 'green politics':

> I took a cycle camping holiday in Cornwall. It involved taking the bikes on the car to Plymouth, leaving the car there, and transferring bikes and gear to

the train for Penzance, ready to cycle back to Plymouth in easy stages over the next week. At the ticket office in Plymouth we were told that only the individual train manager could tell us if we could put our bikes on the train. We had to lug them down the steps (laden down with camping gear) just on the off-chance that we could begin our trip. Although the week was, in the end, a success, that part of the journey was so frustrating that I would never attempt such a venture again.

Alongside this failing interface of green modes and rail, there is another failing interface between individual politics and social policies:

> Public transportation involves a degree of co-operation, people choosing not to travel by car, not to be independent, for the greater good. But it requires a degree of co-operation which can only be done by politicians, by government, by people working together. And private enterprise isn't geared to achieving that sort of consensus. (Stuart – UK)

For some of our respondents, questions of convenience, safety and service provision prevail in attitudes towards rail travel, but for others ecological politics are fundamental in influencing their decisions. Ecological politics include issues of conservation and pollution in addition to other forms of transport.

Conservation

Rail travel is perceived as being less environmentally damaging than other forms of transport in at least two ways. It is responsible for just one per cent of CO_2 emissions in Britain (SRA 2003), and it is proportionately more efficient than the car in its use of the world's resources:

> The private car is very wasteful, it's a big box to transport one person, and it is using proportionately a lot more fuel to transport one person than a train does. (Stuart – UK)

Some people are cynical about governments' real commitment to railways as being less environmentally damaging: 'All Western politicians are scared of car drivers, and don't give a stuff about nonsense like the Kyoto Accord, and if they thought that there were votes in it, they'd sell their grandmothers and shut down every inch of line they could get their sticky fingers on' (Marchant 2003: 135). Marchant's assertion is rather simplistic: there are plenty of 'votes in it' for social policies backed by ecological politics. The difficulty is rather that ecological politics do not accord with those of big corporations, whose size and economic power can increasingly dictate to government policy. Some of our respondents clearly felt that travel in Britain will become more difficult in the future; good 'risk management' is not only desirable but necessary:

> I do feel strongly about the environment, and how the huge number of cars on the road, as we all know, is wrecking the environment. And I believe in supporting the public transport system because I do believe that ultimately everybody will have to. Because it's already gridlock on the roads, and it's only going to get worse as time goes on. I quite firmly believe that efficient and cost-effective public transport that's well supported by everybody is the way to go towards improving our environment. That's why things that make it more difficult to use public transport and force you into your cars upsets me a lot, because it goes against the principles that I believe in. (Julie – UK)

Risk management in order to preserve freedom of movement in the future, however, is not the only discourse of rail in relation to the environment. Just as the verges of motorways are increasingly viewed as conservation spaces free from erosion by humans, in which threatened flora and fauna can be protected, so the side of the railway line is sometimes referred to as 'the biggest hedgerow left in the UK' (Sargent 1984, cited in TEST 1991: 182): a 'haven for wildlife', as one respondent pointed out. This hedgerow is ecologically valuable, but is also aesthetically valuable to those who use trains. As we note in Chapter 4, a large part of leisure activity on the train involves looking out of the windows. Network Rail has legal responsibility for line-side conditions, but conservation is clearly not at the top of its agenda:

> I have noticed that increasingly the side of the tracks is just one big rubbish dump and that is so sad because at one time they were quite beautiful and important to wildlife. I don't know if it's particularly bad through Chester – that line is quite disgusting, choc-a-block. (Rhian – UK)

In summary we can see ways in which the discourse of the train is interwoven with discourses of the environment and ecological politics. It emphasizes the connection between environmental degradation, individual lifestyle, social policies and liberal, first-past-the-post democracies. Indeed, there are those who argue from a discourse of risk that the long-established right to travel has become a freedom working against its own interests: '[i]t impacts the environment to an unprecedented extent, and this condition will worsen before any improvement takes place' (TEST 1991: 3)

Discourses of Politicians: Ab/using Nostalgia

Nostalgia (as we illustrate in Chapters 3 and 4) is a major strand in the general discourse of the railway. Here, we limit our discussion to ways in which nostalgia is used or abused in relation to personal or public politics of the rail industry. Politicians, argues Jack Simmons (1991a), have always been cynical about railways, either overtly or covertly. They have treated railways as a 'passing opportunity' in politics rather than as a long-term public service. There is a discrepancy between public statements from politicians such as John Reid: 'If we don't have a decent train system, we can't handle the other problems in creating an integrated transport policy. Train is the central element in solving all our transport problems' (Wolmar 2001: 112), and those made in private by MPs to their constituents:

I went to see my MP about another local matter and I also asked him 'Why don't you invest more in the railways?' He said – these were his exact words – 'railways are an outdated form of transport'. (Ben – UK)

Instances in which politicians use the discourse of nostalgia go back many years. As Prime Minister thirty years ago, for example, Edward Heath wanted to make a case for renewed industrial expansion. He warned that: 'the alternative to expansion is not ... an England of quiet market towns linked only by trains puffing slowly and peacefully through green meadows. The alternative is slums, dangerous roads, old factories, cramped schools, stunted lives' (Wiener 1981: 162, quoted in Payton 1997: 18).

Philip Payton (1997: 19) notes that by the early 1970s steam was already obsolete on British Railways: 'the celebration of railways as the cutting edge of modernity had been replaced long-since by a nostalgia which saw in the rural cross-country routes and branch lines a "timelessness" which was itself the epitome of England and Englishness'. Heath was thus using the discourse of nostalgia for political ends, rather than expressing a nostalgic view. As Henry comments:

trains are lauded as 'good' by politicians but not necessarily supported.

The discourse of nostalgia has also been exploited by subsequent politicians, especially in the debates around privatization. John Major, for example, noted that privatization would 'restore the pride and spirit, even the colour schemes, of the old pre-nationalisation companies' (Jack 2003: 19); John Stokes negatively compared the inefficiency of a nationalized service to the pre-nationalized companies: 'I remember the thrill of going to Paddington station en route to Oxford, and ... the chocolate and cream coaches, the glorious engines and ... the station master in top hat and tails' (Bagwell 1996: 133, quoted by Strangleman 2002b: 2.6).

The discourse of nostalgia is itself fragmented. Some argue that nostalgia is the great enemy of the railway cause (Jack 2003: 19), others that the designers of rolling-stock should capitalize on it:

> Rail should be playing up to its strengths a lot more than it does. I think some of the train design that you see at the moment, it's as though we feel ashamed of trains and we've got to make them look like something else, like planes. Some of the new ... trains seem to incorporate everything that is worst about a plane and a car, and don't use the sort of natural advantages of a railway carriage environment – being able to see out of the window, plenty of space – things that have been around for a long long time. (Tony – UK)

Thus, there are difficulties in attempting to colonize nostalgia, even for the railways themselves. This is because as a culture we are ambivalent about our own nostalgia: our fundamental love for railways coexists with a notion that trains are antiquated and 'uncool' (Martin 2003: 21).

Reflections

In this chapter we have explored a number of discourses relating to the railway. These are not the only ways in which trains are discussed, but they do enable us to locate railway travel within contemporary British culture. We have noted several times that perceptions and discourses appear discrete and fragmented. What connects all these discourses together, though, is that they are – in part – public discourses. In other words, they are 'conversations' about railways and trains which do not necessarily emerge out of, but do key into, discourses of government and social policy. In particular, they are all intermingled with the question and concept of risk: risk concerning travel itself; money, investment and the economy; railways and the environment.

Overall, we have begun to establish that risk debates are not just about the validity of technical data. At a more fundamental level, risk is about values and 'ways of seeing'. The people who have shared with us their own 'existential anxieties' illustrate more private, hidden, individualist discourses, and these discourses appear to fragment the discourses emerging through the mass media. Whether less 'authoritative' (see Introduction) discourses are 'biased' or 'accurate' becomes irrelevant because the concept of risk is now such a central aspect of human subjectivity (Lupton 1999). Train travel keys into a whole series of discourses of risk, which illustrates the degree to which the presence of risk (actual or perceived) is interwoven with the fabric of our culture. Its presence suggests deep anxiety about the ways in which we conduct life in the Western world: desire for uninterrupted freedom of movement; maximization of wealth and investment; protection of the planet; and a sense of history permeated through our nostalgic memories. Fundamentally, our analyses help to make visible the ideologies (defined as the 'mystification that serves class interest' – Barrett 1991: 157) which inform us of the relationship between what we do on or with trains, what we are obliged to do on or with trains, what we are discouraged from doing on or with trains, and what we are allowed, forbidden or obliged to say about railways, trains and train travel: 'It's not a problem of fantasy; it's a problem of verbalisation' (Barrett 1991: 131).

–3–

Signs and Signals
Finding the Train in Western Culture

Introduction

Continuing our theme from Chapter 2, our aim here is to further locate the train in Western culture, but this time in a symbolic sense: we are exploring the 'myth' of the train. Writing from the perspective of the railway historian, Michael Freeman points out:

> It is still true that, despite the vast array of writing on railway history and on transport history at large, the subject is too often examined in a way that disconnects it from the wider cultural milieu … [B]y situating the railway within the wider cultural frame of which it is indissolubly part we may come to a better understanding of its role and influence. (Freeman 1999b: 160–1)

As sociologists using multi-disciplinary approaches, we are attempting to locate the train within its contemporary 'cultural milieu'. The case-studies we use here – of music, poetry, books, film and art – are necessarily exemplary: an exhaustive list would take up more space than we could hope to achieve. Other explorations of the symbolic railways can be found in, for example, Richards and Mackenzie (1986), Simmons (1991b), Kirby (1997) and Goodman (2001). We identify the depth to which British cultural artefacts have been saturated with the 'myth' of the train, but in doing so we also find that such representations provide us with moral 'myths' about our own culture. We will thus seek the train in culture, but find our culture on the train. This culture is reinforced by the manner in which we 'weave narratives, stories and fantasies' around our everyday rituals and practices of daily life (Hall 1997: 3–4). The 'message' which emerges from these narratives creates a 'myth'. In other words, the way an object is thought/talked about has a particular cultural meaning – it is turned into a 'message', which embodies a specific historical context. When we receive the 'message' we apply it to our culture and it 'points out, it makes us understand something and imposes it on us'

(Barthes 1972, reported in Tallack 1995: 32). This is the meaning of the 'myth'.

What does this mean in practice for our textual analysis of trains and rail travel? The word 'train' (or 'railway', etc.) is initially a meaningless list of letters put together in our heads. In order to give it meaning we create an 'image', a two-dimensional picture of a three-dimensional object. This image or picture (including a word-picture) is known as the 'sign' or 'concept'. When we explore ways in which railways, trains and train travel are represented within cultural artefacts such as books, film, poetry, music and art, we ask ourselves the following questions: how is the image conceptualized? Why use that particular concept? Where is the link between the concept and the wider culture? What 'myth' is this message reflecting and imposing on the culture?

Myths both reflect and influence cultural ways of thinking. By absorbing such messages we understand how – in our culture – we are expected to:

- locate our identities (gender, class, ethnicity, age);
- locate ourselves in time (ways of looking at our history);
- locate ourselves to be (living among others);
- locate ourselves to do (ways of exercising power).

Each expectation is overlapped and interwoven with the others. The sum presents us with an ideological picture of the culture in which we are embedded.

Listening for the Train in Culture

As we noted in Chapter 2, freedom of movement is a cherished and heavily defended tenet of a liberal democracy. But transport is not simply the link between two or more localities. It is absolutely fundamental to most people's lives (TEST 1991). Partly because of that inalienable place in Western politics, history and culture, transport also has strong symbolic meanings in music (instrumental and vocal), visual art (pictures and film) and writing (books, poetry, humour). Indeed, images of railways and rail travel have been important in such cultural artefacts since the beginning:

As railways grew to be a normal, accepted part of life, familiar to most people, they came to provide a natural setting for imaginative works, in a train or at a station or on the line; but it was a setting different from any other, offering its own opportunities, imposing restrictions … For the railway is unconsciously self-revealing. It has become an institution. (Simmons 1991: 1)

Even before it was a 'normal, accepted part of life', railway technology had already become the source of many naturalized expressions within the English language itself (such as being 'on the right track', coming to the 'end of the line', and the 'long haul'). As far back as 1836 a Member of Parliament noted: 'our very language begins to be affected by it … Men [*sic*] talk of "getting up the steam", of "railway speed" and reckon distances by hours and minutes' (quoted in Francis 1967: 292). The use of railway terms in ordinary language was spurred on by the railway mania of the mid-1830s, when it became necessary for people to understand the technicalities for the purpose of investment. *Chambers Journal* published an article for the general reader, explaining terms such as 'getting up the steam' and 'going off the rails'. By the mid-nineteenth century the railways had come to 'enter freely into literary metaphor' (Simmons 1991b: 177).

As well as becoming part of our linguistic landscape, trains had an impact on our 'soundscape' (our cultural background of everyday sounds). Philip Pacey (2003) provides a list of hundreds of pieces of music – including such varied genres as jazz, light music, film music, classical pieces, rock and folk – which are inspired by railways. He quotes from Raymond Murray Schafer (1977): 'Of all the sounds of the industrial revolution, those of trains seem across time to have taken on the most sentimental associations' (Pacey 2003: 1–2). Michael Freeman (1999a), for example, refers to a piece of music published probably in the mid-nineteenth century, the score for which is 'annotated to indicate the various stages in the [rail] journey from Manchester to Liverpool; the tempo is continuously adjusted, according to assumed changes in speed. A crescendo is reached with the passing of the train through the Liverpool tunnel, echoing the striking combination of fear and fascination that such subterranean experiences brought to early railway travellers' (Freeman 1999a: 207).

In song, as well as instrumental music, the rhythmic sounds of the train can be brought into the service of the composer of songs. Take, for example, the song *The Six-Five Special* (released in 1957):

> Hear the whistle blowin' twelve to the bar
> See the lights a-glowin' bright as a star.
> Now the wheels a-slowin', can't be far.
> *Over the points, over the points, over the points, over the points* …
> The Six Five Special's steamin' down the line [italics added]

These two musical examples help, incidentally, to illustrate a historical difference between British and American cultures, which had an effect on both the development of the railway (Schivelbusch 1986) and the imagery of railways and trains incorporated into music. This applies perhaps most strongly to genres of folk music. In America, the railway is part of the pioneering tradition: 'The Americans positively revelled in their traditions: the railways were still part of the Wild West and every boxcar-hopping hobo had a tale composed of equal measures of grit and melancholy' (Whittaker 1995: 247–8). In Britain, however, it is the 'soul' of the industrial revolution – a history steeped in class-consciousness as well as money.

We find trains in music, therefore, but we also find music on trains. 'Music trains' (especially 'jazz trains') are a growing feature of both the British railway and British music cultures. The venture began in the early 1990s as an overt publicity tool for underused rail journeys:

> The main purpose … is to popularize the line, bring some sort of good news to the railway … And the idea was, there were trains running in the evening, no one was travelling on them, so why not do something different and get good publicity. So having live music with real ale was not terribly difficult to organize … it was the sort of thing that brings enormously positive publicity over the years. (Tony – UK)

As a promotional art form, music trains represent a contemporary movement beyond the 'iconographic' advertising (Leiss et al. 1986; see pp. 89–90) of the classic railway poster, in which the focal point shifts from the product to a setting which embeds the product in a symbolic context (O'Sullivan 1998: 292). With music trains, not only is the product (the train) the focal point, but people actually experience the product whilst consuming the art.

Railway Sounds and Poetry

The everyday sounds of the railways have been interwoven into the rhythms of poetry as well as music and song. Robert Louis Stevenson's classic poem, *From a Railway Carriage* (first published in 1885), for example, epitomizes the new truncating of time that the railways brought. The rhythm of the stanza captures the essence of fast-changing landscapes beyond the train windows:

> Faster than fairies, faster than witches,
> Bridges and houses, hedges and ditches;

And charging along like troops in a battle,
All through the meadows the horses and cattle.

The American poet, John Godfrey Saxe (1816–87) similarly brought the
rhythm of the train to bear on his poem *Rhyme of the Rail*. Interestingly,
unlike Stevenson's focus on the panoramic view of *From a Railway
Carriage*, his focus is inside the train:

Men of different 'stations'
In the eye of Fame
Here are very quickly
Coming to the same.
High and lowly people,
Birds of every feather,
On a common level
Traveling together.

Thus, whilst Stevenson emphasizes the pastoral rurality of England, Saxe
celebrates the communal and social levelling that rail travel encouraged.
Like the two poems above, the rhythm of the poem by Auden in the documentary film, *Night Mail* (Auden GPO Film Unit 1936), also follows the
rhythmic sound of the train:

Letters of thanks, letters from banks,
Letters of joy from the girl and the boy,
Receipted bills and invitations
To inspect new stock or visit relations,
And applications for situations
And timid lovers' declarations
And gossip, gossip from all the nations.

According to Ian Aitken (1998), *Night Mail* was one of the most critically acclaimed films to be produced within the British documentary film
movement of the 1930s. The film documents a trip undertaken by the
Royal Mail Travelling Post Office in 1936. It channels representations of
modern technology and institutional practice 'away from an account of
the industry and organization of postal delivery, and into an imagistic
study of the train as a powerful symbol of modernity, in its natural
element speeding freely into the countryside, away from the dark city
stations' (Aitken 1998: 19–20).

In more ways than one, the train is represented as the carrier of
community and relationship: first in the way the film depicts the work that
is done on the train, and secondly in the variety of relationships encapsu-

lated in the kinds of letters mentioned. Aitken argues that the myth here lies in the illusion that an anonymous centralized service embodies the human need to be remembered:

> They continue their dreams,
> And shall wake soon and long for letters,
> And none will hear the postman's knock
> Without a quickening of the heart,
> For who can bear to feel himself forgotten?

Nicholas Whittaker (1995: 162) suggests that '[l]ying in bed listening to the railways sing and chatter is one of the most comforting feelings I know. Unlike the screeching cars and roaring motorbikes that frighten us from sleep, passing trains fit in easily with the rhythms of nature.' There is, however, a cautionary note to add to this nostalgic memory. As with all the soundscape of trains and railways, the historical moment is paramount. The 'clackety-clack' and the 'de-rum-de-rum' rhythms – like the more dated 'whoo-woo' whistle sounds – are increasingly features of the nostalgic past, as bolted sections of railway track are replaced by continuous track. The traditional rhythm of the train becomes a 'white noise' (continuous, and only subconsciously registered, noises of everyday life). Even the soundscape of the railway is tied irrevocably to time.

Seeing and Hearing our Culture Through the Train

'Every aspect of the railway experience', argue Jeffrey Richards and John MacKenzie (1986: 357), 'can serve a symbolic purpose,' such as technological might, uncontrollable passion, or our journey to our final unavoidable destiny. In this section we begin to explore these symbolic purposes through analysis of art, films and fictional literature. There is a massive body of work 'reflecting and moulding popular attitudes to British railway travel' (Carter 2002: 47) and in the section on art we look at William Frith's *The Railway Station*, John Martin's *The Last Judgement* and promotional art from the 'golden age' of British railways. Taking a selection of the many possible films, we analyse *Brief Encounter*, *The Titfield Thunderbolt*, *Closely Observed Trains* and *Oh Mr Porter*. The main fictional literature we explore includes Charles Dickens's *Dombey and Son*; Edith Nesbit's *The Railway Children*; John Hadfield's *Love on a Branch Line* and the Rev. W. Awdry's *Thomas the Tank Engine and Friends* (in a single volume published under the name of Allcroft, who bought up the series).

'High' Art and 'Low' Art

Ian Marchant (2003: 3) notes that, in the Futurist Manifesto of 1909, Marinetti claimed that the railway was the living, breathing apotheosis of futurity and hence of aesthetic possibility. Marinetti would prefer to watch an engine enter a grand metropolitan station to viewing any number of Old Master paintings: 'for him the gargantuan breath of boilers, the gasping pistons and the screech of brakes were the authentic symphonic music of the time'. This reference to trains as art form was echoed by a number of our rail enthusiasts. Liam, for example, reflected:

> Growing up near the BR Western region Birmingham to London main line, I was attracted by the sound, speed, and (recognizing now for what I would not have been able to enunciate then) a deep appreciation of aesthetics: for me the old Great Western Railway ... epitomized graceful engineering, almost pure art.

Some argue that William Powell Frith's *The Railway Station* (1862) was perceived in mid-Victorian Britain as the 'picture of the age' (Leicestershire County Council 2003). Simmons (1991b), on the other hand, claims that no artist in the Victorian era really made enough of a reputation with their railway commissions to concentrate on them for a long period of time. On the contrary, he argues that as the people of Britain became more familiar with railways so there was a general decline in interest in artistic works of and growing indifference to the aesthetic qualities of trains. Never quite imitated (although George Earl's painting, in 1893, of King's Cross Station had some similarities) because 'nobody thought it worth while to depict a large crowd scene on a railway again' (Simmons 1991b: 145), *The Railway Station* is probably the most famous of all railway paintings: 'The first pen-and-ink sketch of it, drawn on the back of an envelope, still survives, and shows already much of the character of the finished work, nearly the whole of its "plot": the detectives arresting the criminal, the foreigner in argument with his cabman, the agitated family hurrying to the train' (Simmons 1991b: 128).

Those who work on the railways, according to Ralph Harrington (1999b), hold a unique place in the historical hierarchy of class. They were seen as artisans, but their particular expertise in handling the technology was revered, even by the middle classes. But this paradox could not be handled unambiguously in bourgeois art. Its significance is illustrated in the relative position of the train driver in the painting, which 'depicts passengers boarding a Great Western Railway train at Paddington ... And where is the driver? He is the most distant and indistinct figure of all, banished to the background, hardly visible on the footplate of his remote locomotive' (Harrington 1999b: 1).

Interestingly, in the earlier pen-and-ink sketch, the space and distance of the locomotive has not yet appeared (Simmons 1991b). But, in the final work, this location of the train driver symbolizes the ambiguity in which the identity of the driver was held. He is not to be fêted, because he is drawn from the working classes; but, at the same time, the middle classes are – consciously and uncomfortably – dependent on his expertise to keep them alive for their journey. Harrington notes:

> In a canvas filled with movement, he is still. He is at one with the placid power of his machine. Below him, on the platform, stands a stout figure, the significance of whom is interesting. *The Railway Station* was commissioned by the art dealer and financier Louis Victor Flatow. Flatow himself wanted to be in the picture: to be precise, he wished to be depicted as the engine driver. But the real engine driver, who modelled, with his machine, for Frith, would let no one but himself be depicted on the footplate of his locomotive ... Frith painted Flatow standing on the platform, looking up at the real driver on his footplate, the unchallenged master of a domain he was forever unable to enter. (Harrington 1999b: 3–4)

The classical painting, *The Last Judgement* (1853), by John Martin, illustrates the central event of the biblical Book of Revelation:

> On a throne in the heavens sits God in judgement, surrounded by the four and twenty elders. Below on the right the forces of evil, commanded by Satan, are defeated and tumble into a bottomless pit. To the left on Mount Zion are 'the good', already in 'the plains of heaven' and awaiting the call to appear before the throne. (Tate Gallery Online 2003)

Among the faces of the 'saved', Martin apparently included a high percentage of artists and poets, recognizable of course to their peers. The forces of evil, commanded by Satan, are being brought in by a train. On the sides of the carriages are painted the names of different countries. For Martin 'the steam locomotive was no less a source of satanic imagery then the fiery furnaces of the Black Country' (Freeman 1999a: 43). The train is depicted tumbling into Chaos; it is thus symbolized as a central player in the forces of evil. The painting is also 'a disturbing reminder to Victorian observers of the way railway accidents were commonplace in the first decades of operation' (Freeman 1999a: 227).

Alongside 'high' art, promotional art is an important genre and railway advertisements are an indispensable thread woven into the very existence of the railway phenomenon, whether in real life or in fiction. Edith Nesbit even includes them in a description of the station in *The Railway Children*. Whittaker comments:

> I've been here before, I thought, when I pitched up at Dawlish on my first Western railrover in 1968. Actually, until then, I'd never been further west than Bristol, but I recognized Dawlish instantly. I'd seen it a thousand times on holiday postcards, jigsaws, toffee-tin lids and on the covers of old annuals bought at jumble sales. The picture of a Great Western Castle at the head of a holiday train skirting the sea wall, puffing cutesy cottonwool smoke over the heads of the holidaymakers, is one of the enduring icons from the Golden Age ... The image of the trains skirting the sea is filed away in the folk memory, part of our collective watercolour dreams of old-fashioned Britain. (Whittaker 1995: 214–16)

During this 'golden age' of railways an entire sub-industry also grew up around this promotional art of railway advertising: 'That is a credit to the public relations departments of the Big Four who created the image of prestige streamlined expresses that still lives with us seven decades later. The elegant posters commissioned by the railway companies survive on many living room walls today to perpetuate this romantic image' (Wolmar 2001: 29). Ian Jack (2003: 19–20) notes with some irony that the idea of 'golden age' always 'arrives after the age itself has been waved off from the platform and vanished into the distance, leaving nothing behind but a hum in the rails'. Nevertheless, Gayle acknowledges the truth of Christian Wolmar's assertion – she does have on the wall behind her desk at work a very large and colourful railway poster of St Michael's Mount in Cornwall!

A broad definition of promotional art is that it 'crosses the line between advertising, packaging, and design, and is applicable, as well, to activities beyond the immediately commercial. It can even be used in a way which takes us beyond the domain of competitive exchange altogether' (Wernick 1991: 181–2). Promotional practice is therefore generated exactly on the boundary of art and advertising, implying a dissolution of the boundary itself. In their book of railway posters (1923–47) chosen from a collection of more than 6,000 held at York Railway Museum, Beverley Cole and Richard Durack (1992: 14) point out that promotional art in the 1920s was castigated as the 'poor man's gallery'. During this time a new breed of artist was emerging after one railway company in particular had received complaints from travellers about overcrowding, poor quality of carriages and insufficient numbers of trains. In response, Southern Railway embarked on what one magazine called 'a definite scheme of propaganda designed to develop kinship of interests between public and railway' (Cole and Durack 1992: 10).

According to Tim O'Sullivan (1998: 292), this art can be identified as an iconographic phase of twentieth-century advertising: 'the focal point of the typical advert shifts from the product as an isolated entity to encompass a setting or situation, thereby embedding the product in a symbolic context which imparts additional meanings to it [of family, status, and social hierarchy]'. It is interesting to note, therefore, that out of 212 pieces of promotional art picked out by Cole and Durack, less than 25 per cent actually display a train. Some posters were used to promote seaside resorts, in order to attract the 'day-trippers' – usually working-class people – on to the trains. This was not generally a popular move with the resorts, where tourist attractions would close down on days when train-loads of day-trippers were expected. Railway companies began diversifying into other forms of transport and the hotel industry. These other interests are also promoted on posters: ships, for example, belonging to the railway companies, could be used to promote more exotic destinations, aimed at the growing middle classes.

Fictional Literature

The railway forms a backdrop to the family fortunes of shipping merchants *Dombey and Son* (first published 1846–8). Charles Dickens graphically illustrates the catastrophic introduction of railways – for some (usually working-class) neighbourhoods – to the landscape of London:

> The first shock of a great earthquake had, just at that period, rent the whole neighbourhood to its centre. Traces of its course were visible on every side. Houses were knocked down; streets broken through and stopped; deep pits and trenches dug in the ground; enormous heaps of earth and clay thrown up; buildings that were undermined and shaking, propped by great beams of wood ... Everywhere were bridges that led nowhere; thoroughfares that were wholly impassable ... carcasses of ragged tenements, and fragments of unfinished walls and arches. (Dickens 1966: 68)

Dickens thus reflects the contemporary public ambivalence towards the railways, but unlike some of his contemporaries, acknowledges through Dombey's character that the railway 'has let the light of day in on these things: not made or caused them' (Simmons 1991b: 198). Not only does he conceptualize trains as the 'great land serpent', quite literally carving out tracks and changing landscape across the length and breadth of pastoral Britain: he also uses it to represent entrepreneurial thinking, and the emergence of the new technological working class.

In the story, the estranged wife of Mr Dombey runs away to France with Mr Carker. As their whereabouts in France is revealed and Mr Carker flees back to England with an enraged and humiliated Mr Dombey in pursuit, so the train is used to signify the threat and danger of the chase and the growing weight of moral censure:

> A trembling of the ground, and quick vibration in his ears; a distant shriek; a dull light advancing, quickly changed to two red eyes, and a fierce fire, dropping glowing coals; an irresistible bearing on of a great roaring and dilating mass; a high wind, and a rattle – another come and gone, and he holding to a gate, as if to save himself! (Dickens 1966: 821)

As Carker's pursuer catches up with him, Dickens uses the train as a means to administer the final blow to Carker's misdemeanour:

> He heard a shout – another – saw the face change from its vindictive passion to a faint sickness and terror – felt the earth tremble – knew in a moment that the rush was come – uttered a shriek – looked round – saw the red eyes, bleared and dim in the daylight, close upon him – was beaten down, caught up, and whirled away upon a jagged mill, that spun him round and round, and struck him limb from limb, and licked his stream of life up with its fiery heat, and cast his mutilated fragments in the air. (Dickens 1966: 823)

Despite the emphasis laid on it as a 'canonical' example of railway writing, *Dombey and Son* actually contains only four solid railway passages. 'In the standard modern edition these passages occupy no more than eight, of 833, pages' (Carter 2000: 119). But Dickens detested what he saw as the corruption involved in railway promotion and often felt the railways were 'sweeping away the relics of a past he loved' (Simmons 1991b: 197). Interestingly, nearly twenty years after writing *Dombey and Son*, Dickens himself would be involved in a train crash, which soured his views of rail travel still further (Harrington 1994: 18).

The classic children's book *The Railway Children* was first published in 1906. Edith Nesbit begins her story by defining 'railway children' by what they are not: 'They were not railway children to begin with. I don't suppose they had ever thought about railways … They were just ordinary suburban children, and they lived with their Father and Mother in an ordinary red-brick-fronted villa' (Nesbit 1995: 1). The iconic myth embedded in Nesbit's work is not, however, an uncomplicated nostalgic view of rural life. Elements of such idyllic existence are there, and they are interlaced with pictures of 'noble poverty' and 'false pride' – typical middle-class views of the early twentieth century. But, more subliminally, railways are also associated with poverty, lack of education and 'untamed' children.

Having been forced by circumstances to move from comfortable middle-class suburbia to a rural cottage in Yorkshire where the railway runs past the end of the garden, the children's 'railway experience' begins in earnest when they see the train emerge from the tunnel for the first time: it 'rushed out of the tunnel with a shriek and a snort ... like a great dragon tearing by' (Nesbit 1995: 23). Initially, therefore, the train – like the sudden change in the family fortunes – is conceptualized as dangerous and threatening.

Once the children have become accustomed to the presence of the railway, however, it quickly takes on a central role in their life experiences: 'Here in the deep silence of the sleeping country the only things that went by were the trains. They seemed to be all that was left to link the children to the old life that had once been theirs' (Nesbit 1995: 35). Embodied in the 'old gentleman' whose waving hand the children notice before the rest of his personage, the 'Green Dragon' – the business train to London – becomes a symbolic link to their mysteriously absent father. By midway through the story, no longer is the train just an exciting and absorbing link to a past life. It has evolved into something living, vulnerable.

Eventually poverty withdraws to the background as a fortuitous income becomes available. The children revert to receiving an education from their mother, instead of 'running wild and free'. Nesbit again defines their experience as 'not railway children': 'I wonder if the Railway misses us ... we never go to see it now ... we loved it so when we hadn't anyone to play with' (1995: 205). When their beloved 'Green Dragon' passes by one morning, and all the passengers wave ecstatically, knowing prior to the children that their father is on his way home to them: 'it almost seemed as though the train itself was alive, and was at last responding to the love that they had given it so freely and for so long' (1995: 207). The train becomes the real – rather than just symbolic – link to the father-love and comfortable home that is the underlying myth of the story. Other writers have similarly seen trains and railway tracks as a tangible link with home and family: 'Though I could hardly have been more traumatized just then, the trains kept me sane, cocooned in safety, tied securely to home by those ribbons of steel. Inch by inch they would pull me safely home ... all the way to the Tube station at Belsize Park' (Whittaker 1995: 165).

In John Hadfield's book, *Love on a Branch Line* (first published 1959), Jasper Pye – a young civil servant who struggles with being labelled a 'bore' – is given the task of tackling the Department of Output Statistics: a long-forgotten branch of and embarrassment to the Civil Service, buried deep in East Anglia. He finds an unreal nostalgic world of cricket, village fêtes, peacocks, sublimated women and alcoholic stupor. The railway is conceptualized in the manner of the 'heritage chuffers' of the early twenty-first century.

Carter (2000: 133) argues that *Love on a Branch Line* is 'whimsical railway neo-pastoral with the modern impulse attenuated to vanishing point'. He confers on it the title of England's Railway Novel, in opposition to the perceived 'canonical' writings of Dickens on the subject. In his view, the train epitomizes England – pure nostalgia, dwindling away to a nothingness. As English sociologists, however, we – Gayle and Gillian – read from it an account of upper-middle-class and minor-aristocratic decadence. The small branch line train – donated to the wheelchair-using aristocrat as compensation for his accident – figures as another part of the nostalgic 'golden age' of aesthetic enjoyment of life; the dream of the pleasure principle:

> There was something curiously poignant about the desolate air of the deserted platform – the paint peeling off the wooden railings, the timetables yellowing with age. Docks and thistles sprouted between the sleepers; cobwebs festooned the hanging lamps. I sat down on the sun-blistered bench which stood against the platform railings, below the bleak sans-serif letters which still proclaimed the name ARCADY. As the sun beat down on me, and I watched, far up in the sky, the convolutions of some almost indistinguishable but incredibly fast-moving aircraft, the contrast between the vapour trail of the jet-plane and this decaying relic of the 'permanent way' was so emphatic as to seem unreal. (Hadfield 1973: 106)

This is not describing the 'real' railway, but the 'railway of our dreams' (Marchant 2003). Neither is the story a simple nostalgic view of rail travel; Hadfield locates that nostalgia itself within the story. Written in the 1950s, it therefore reads as something of a prophecy for the twenty-first century, though only for that nostalgic railway of our dreams. The real railway experience (of the 1950s) surfaces just once: 'The woman opposite me in the train put down her needlework and leaned forward with a hesitant gesture of inquiry. "I see you are looking at the cricket scores," she said. "Forgive my intruding, but could you tell me how Leicestershire are getting on?"' (Hadfield 1973: 21). The picture emerging from this passage reads half a century later as another layer of nostalgia (along with needlework, middle-class diffidence and 'polite conversation' about cricket). For Hadfield – and, perhaps, for Carter – this apparently sums up social interaction on the trains of England. We continue our discussion of such social interaction on the real train of the twenty-first century in Chapters 4, 5 and 6.

The classic children's stories encapsulated in *Thomas the Tank Engine* were first created by a clergyman, the Reverend Wilbert Awdry, as a way of entertaining his young son, who was recovering from scarlet fever. Although the first of the Railway Series of books – *The Three Railway Engines* – appeared in 1945, the character of Thomas did not emerge until 1946. The series is of importance here because the cultural myths embedded in them continue to appeal to parents – not only in the Western world – struggling to inculcate moral understanding in their children:

> The highlight of any day out on a preserved line for the tinies is Thomas the Tank Engine ... If you follow one of those brown heritage signs with a little chuffer-puffer on it, round about Christmas-time, you will come upon a preserved railway with a train pulled by a steam engine which has a badly-drawn picture of Thomas the Tank Engine's face stuck on the front ... The preserved railway movement has mixed feelings about it ... because it's not authentic, in a world where authenticity is king ... Awdry would not have been pleased to see the brute facts of railway engineering and operation played with in this fast and loose way. Awdry was a buff, and the son of a buff, and he fought battles with the books' illustrators in order to preserve their factual integrity. (Marchant 2003: 244)

It is interesting, therefore, that – as a rail enthusiast – Awdry should engender his engines as masculine. Although engines at that time were given masculine names, those working in the industry – as well as earlier writers – normally referred to them, like ships, as 'she'. Even more interestingly, the coaches are feminine; their location in the stories reflects dominant mid-twentieth-century masculinist attitudes to women. They are towed, pulled and 'looked after'; they sometimes grumble or fuss over small things, and are constantly anxious and 'twittering' to one another. They cry and sob when things go wrong but, Awdry notes, also 'ran happily behind Thomas' (Allcroft 2000: 30). True to the demands placed upon women in the 1950s, the gendered coaches pick up the emotional and unpaid labour of servicing capitalism (Hochschild 1983). Annie and Clarabel (Thomas's coaches): 'don't mind what Thomas says to them because they know he is trying to please the Fat Controller, and they know, too, that if Thomas is cross, he is not cross with them. He is cross with the engines on the main line who have made him late' (Allcroft 2000: 26).

Awdry's engines inhabit an élitist middle-class world, in which they must spend time being apprenticed to their craft, learning to be 'really useful engines'. Trucks, on the other hand, represent Awdry's perception of the working class: 'Now trucks are silly and noisy. They talk a lot and don't attend to what they are doing. They don't listen to their engine, and when he stops, they bump into each other screaming' (Allcroft 2000: 17). Part of the élitism lay in distance between the classes; thus, working with the trucks was despised by most of the engines and sometimes used by the Fat Controller as a punishment for being subversive: '"Wake up, Gordon," said the Fat Controller sternly, "and listen to me. You will pull no more coaches till you are a Really Useful Engine." So Gordon had to spend his time pulling trucks' (Allcroft 2000: 77).

It is acknowledged that many of the stories in the Railway Series are based on actual events. The story of Toby the Tram Engine first appeared in 1952, a time when thousands of potential workers were migrating from the West Indies to Britain. The Fat Controller met Toby whilst on holiday, where he did not have enough work, and bought him. Toby is a different shape, a different colour (brown) and people fail to understand the way he operates.

Toby's story is one of marginalization and assimilation. He encountered prejudice but, after proving his usefulness, was partly painted blue, the same colour as Thomas. Thus, he was only partially drawn into the culture of Thomas and his friends: his coach Henrietta, on the other hand, was painted brown all over, 'like Annie and Clarabel'. Henrietta was thus totally subsumed – rendered invisible – within the dominant feminine culture. The myth of racial harmony is completed when Thomas, Annie, Clarabel, Toby and Henrietta work together with a special train on Christmas Day. Toby resurfaced later, in 1957, as another marginalized character, this time disabled or old; his parts were worn, he was slow and he was being sent to the Works ('hospital'), meeting a whole new generation of prejudice on the way.

Ian Marchant notes a dark side to the Awdry books: 'the Cambridgeshire Society of Imaginary Psychology point out that Thomas and Co. are "subject to stress caused by lack of control, the threat of unemployment and workaholism". Their case is devastating, unanswerable, and highlights the exploitation of the sentient locomotives by the Fat Controller' (Marchant 2003: 247). More uncomfortably, perhaps, *Thomas the Tank Engine* stories have deeply moral messages: 'be deferent to your elders and betters'; 'impetuousness is a sign of untamed childhood'; 'judge not, lest you yourself be judged'; 'be management material' and so on. Currently appealing to a new generation that may never even have seen a steam engine, the stories are increasingly linked by time and nostalgia to traditional middle-class values of delayed gratification, élitism and communitarianism.

Films

Lynne Kirby (1997) suggests that the cinema's interest in the train is because, in it, cinema finds a useful metaphor. The spectator is transported into fiction, fantasy and dream: 'the cinema developed images, myths and perceptions of the train as much as the train informed cinema's own ways of conceiving of itself' (Kirby 1997: 2). It is generally accepted that the world's first railway film – *Arrival of a Train at La Ciotat* – was released in July 1895 (Simmons 1991b). Less than one minute long and filmed by the Lumière brothers, it created a stir when first shown to the public in Paris: 'audiences who had never before experienced the motion picture leapt back from their seats lest they be mown down by what appeared to them such a startlingly realistic impression' (Huntley 1993: 6).

In truth, this short film had less to do with the phenomenon of trains, and more to do with the opportunity to reveal something of the potential that the railway offered to the cinecamera in the future: 'shooting a moving train, the fastest vehicle in the world in 1895, gave filmmakers an opportunity to show off film's powers of registration' (Kirby 1997: 19–20). Film-making was developing so quickly, however, that, just seven years later, *Uncle Josh at the Moving Picture Show* (1902) was released, argues Kirby, as a parody of the Lumière spectator responding to the train. 'The capacity of the railway to induce shock is, in part, the key to its historical place in cinema. What mattered most in early train films was the shock effect in and of itself, the thrill of instability of a new subject which was cut loose from its anchorage in traditional culture and thus potentially open to anything' (Kirby 1997: 8).

By 1900 the young film industry was already able to see the potential for titillation in the railway system. Two almost identical one-minute films were made in Britain, which were just three scenes long. The first scene was a train entering into a tunnel and the last scene showed a train coming out of the tunnel – different trains, same 'story'. The middle scene is one of a 'stolen' kiss. No one seems to know which film was a copy of the other (Huntley 1993). It is also unclear whether the films were shot for amusement, for use in 'peeping-Tom' machines, or to report or comment on what was a common crime on Victorian railways (Stevenson 2002). In a similar American film of 1903 – *What Happened in the Tunnel* – the tunnel itself:

> plays a key role in articulating the transgression. As a space of the ultimate suspension of temporal and spatial markers, of time and space lost to pure speed and motion, the essence of the train journey itself, the tunnel multiplies

this effect with darkness, the suspension of vision ... Based on an old joke from the late nineteenth century, the film satirizes the popular image of the vulnerability of women on trains when a middle-class white man tries to kiss a white woman just as the train enters a tunnel. The screen goes black, and in the next shot, when the train emerges from the tunnel, the man finds himself kissing the white woman's African American maid, who was seated next to her. The man is repulsed and ashamed, while the two women laugh hysterically at the switch they have effected. (Kirby 1997: 98)

As Kirby points out, the film resists the authority of the male gaze by allowing women the last laugh, albeit through a racist prism. The resistance functions at the expense of the African American woman, who is depicted with the sexuality denied by the white woman.

Britain was still engaged in a world conflict when David Lean and Noel Coward created what many would see as Britain's best ever romantic film, starring Celia Johnson and Trevor Howard. More than half a century later, our love for *Brief Encounter* (1945) is apparently still as strong (Richards and MacKenzie 1986):

Carnforth Station, *Brief Encounter's* historic steam train setting, is being restored to its former glory. Few films seem so trapped in a barely remembered past, but far from consigning this one to cinematic history, each passing year merely heightens its appeal. For what began as a simple love story has since become a national metaphor for an idea of England that has almost completely disappeared ... The station that [enthusiasts] ... plan to recreate should commemorate the days when railways were the emotive conduits of our daily lives. (Cook 2001: 1)

It seems that even the original station clock has been restored (Kent 1999) – a fitting symbol of the myths embedded in this nostalgic metaphor of England past.

The aesthetic culture of the middle classes of the time is epitomized in the location of the film:

Carnforth is ... famous as the location for one of the smokiest and best of railway films, Brief Encounter. It's hard to believe, looking round here today, that it was ever possible to shoot the film in such a location, never mind making it convincing ... It makes me wonder if any romance could be filmed at Milton Keynes Central or Birmingham New Street. Highly unlikely, and such a pity. (Whittaker 1995: 90)

Whittaker's reflections had already been tested when he wrote his comments. A remake of *Brief Encounter* in 1975 'was a disaster from every point of view, from the casting ... to the choice of a new location, on the electrified Southern Region at Winchester. What possible atmosphere was supposed to be created, in sight and sound, by the occasional comings and goings of multiple-unit electric trains, at a plasticised and sunlit station, is impossible to understand' (Huntley 1993: 15).

In the original black and white film the stations and trains provide both a backdrop and a carrier of myth. Each Thursday the numbed, over-protected housewife and mother (Celia Johnson) escapes by branch line train to 'change my library book, do the shopping, and go to the pictures'. After a (not so) chance meeting, Howard and Johnson share tea in the refreshment room (described as the 'most ordinary place in the world') and listen in on a conversation between the staff about 'leaving my husband', thus ushering in new ways of thinking for the audience. Anything might happen between departure and arrival; like many train films, *Brief Encounter* stages a 'recurrent scenario of coupling, uncoupling, and perversion with respect to the romantic, heterosexual couple' (Kirby 1997: 9). Each subsequent Thursday the train carries with it the promise of excitement, unpredictability, risk, and the possibility of a changing self-identity, to the railway station – 'an enclosed location where friends and strangers could meet, mingle, interact, and separate' (Richards and MacKenzie 1986: 358).

As the love affair develops in this film, the train is used to signify danger and threat – sometimes even by its absence in the film: when Trevor Howard decides to go to his friend's flat, hoping that Celia Johnson will accompany him, the invisible express train passes through the station and whistles – a piercing scream. It is made more threatening by its visual absence: 'We quickly realize how difficult it is to imagine a train film without the characteristic sound of a whistle blowing or the clickety-clack of the wheels on the track' (Kirby 1997: 248).

The train locates us within the theme of time, refracted through our understanding of railways in history and the way they took authority over global time: 'regulation of time by the railways was not simply a mechanism to ensure efficiency; it was a way of expressing power' (Kirby 1997: 52) – times of arrival and departure, for example, which exercise power over the lives of the couple. The portrayal of the train is also embedded in the timeless tragedy of illegitimized sexual attraction; it offers a space and a place for reflection, for reliving the romance, for the pain of parting. The myth (symbolic message) of the final tragic parting of the couple symbolizes a triumph for 'duty' over 'desire', 'community' over 'individualism'. Celia Johnson returns to her boring but safe life with her husband and children: if 'feminized men, masculinized women, and excess of any sort were to be contained and narrativized, then the sex roles had to be sorted out according to the code of Respectable Woman, who began to assert a legitimating, reformist influence over film' (Kirby 1997: 73). A curious sociologist might wonder how the trains could have been portrayed in the rest of her mundane life!

The attempts to save the Talyllyn railway formed the basis for the script for Ealing Studio's film *The Titfield Thunderbolt* (1952), where a group of villagers attempt to stop their branch line from being closed by offering to run the service themselves. During the public inquiry it appears that the group has lost its chance; this elicits an outburst from the local squire against the dead hand of Whitehall: 'Don't you realise you are condemning our village to death? Open it up to buses and lorries and what's it going to be like in five years' time? Our lanes will be concrete roads, our houses will have numbers instead of names, there will be traffic lights and zebra crossings ... [the railway] means everything to our village.' Thus, argues Tim Strangleman (2002a), Titfield prefigures many of the battles fought out in different parts of the country over the next thirty years against the Beeching axe.

The hero of *The Titfield Thunderbolt* – mirrored in the hero of *Love on a Branch Line* seven years later – is a rich alcoholic, who 'bankrolls a threatened branch line's rescue by an entire village simply so that he can drink all day in the buffet car (exempt from 1950s restrictive licensing laws) as the train trundles up and down the branch' (Carter 2000: 133). Throughout this classic film runs an overt theme of competition for passengers and profit between railway and bus. Some writers view the film as 'pungent social comedy, another clarion call from Ealing on behalf of the little guy who does things for himself' (Marchant 2003: 111). We would suggest, however, that this 'little guy who does things for himself' can only do so in the context of the community: 'Unlike reactionary appeals to community which consistently assert the subordination of individual aims and values to the collective, most radical theorists assert that community itself consists in the respect for and fulfilment of individual aims and capacities. The neat distinction between individualism and community thus generates a dialectic in which each is a condition for the other' (Young 1990: 307).

The film opens with a scene in which would-be passengers for the train only leave their homes when the engine's whistle is heard, rather than waiting on the platform for the train to arrive. Thus, the stage is set in which the train is already serving the community, rather than the community 'using' the train. The underpinning iconic myths, however, are of tradition, community, religion and tolerance (indeed, exploitation) of alcoholism. There is also a clear myth of class running throughout the film. The supporters of the train are led by essentially middle-class establishment figures, whilst the supporters of the bus – in competition with the train – are portrayed as working-class unfair 'cheats'. Thus, the train carries with it the myth of the middle-class 'upright' alliance of Church, State and feudal tradition.

In the award-winning tragicomic Czechoslovakian film, *Closely Observed Trains* (first released in 1966), the train is used in a complex fashion, to represent both the sensuality and sexuality of life, and the place of the State. Most overtly it is used by a group of soldiers for sexual relations with local nurses: 'railway fiction's suggestion that train-travelling women might hire out their bodies was rooted in some historical evidence' (Carter 2002: 52). The young apprentice guard at this small rural railway station – who sees his job as a way of avoiding work and adulthood – learns about the details of sex by spying on the groups on the stationary train. Later he is seduced by his girlfriend, who also works on the trains, but he takes fright and fails the 'test of manhood'. Humiliated by his failure to 'be a man', he then also fails in his attempt to commit suicide. More covertly the train takes up the symbolism of the young teenager's failed life.

The film is embedded in the context of the Second World War, German occupation and Czech resistance. Standing in for his supervisor, who is otherwise engaged in sexual exploits with a woman, the young man drops a grenade on a passing armaments train. But his more recent successful attempt to achieve sexual 'manhood' leads also to success in death as he falls upon the train just before the grenade explodes. The train thus symbolizes both manhood and death of innocence. Czechoslovakians of the 1960s would also have read into the text a message of the need for self-sacrifice in the fight against State Communism, represented by the train – a powerful carrier of perversion of both body and mind: 'The sense in which the train is … an emblem of History is powerfully evoked in the narrative symbolism of the tracks. Taking control of the huge icon of modernity is taking control of history, of one's destiny, and engineering it along the railways of the collective future toward a new end' (Kirby 1997: 189).

Commenting on the American iconic film *The Iron Horse*, Lynne Kirby notes that 'Constructing one nation is achieved … by wiping out, or at least suppressing, difference – geographical, social, religious, ethnic, racial, political, economic, and sexual. The agent of this dissolution is the railway, its aura of Manifest Destiny' (Kirby 1997: 205). *Closely Observed Trains,* on the other hand, debunks this myth of one nation forged together by the train. Other films also use the train to symbolize the power of the State, but the nature of trains is such that the same symbol can be used to communicate different myths, as we shall see.

Even though the comedy film *Oh Mr Porter* (1937) was made well into the twentieth century, people are still depicted as being afraid of the 'new technology' of the train. But the fear has progressed beyond – and become more complex than – the naïve, innocent fear of the turn of the century that caused people to duck behind their seats when the first film of a train was shown. Now we recognize the fear in the derision directed at the technology. This is much in the style of the derisive humour depicting the 'bossy wife' in an age of women's subservience. More significantly, perhaps, the railway symbolizes the power of the English State. In a rural backwater Will Hay uses the train to 'save the day' against the gunrunners of Irish nationalism. At one level the film is a myth of the triumph of law and order (English) over the resistance movement of rebels (Eire). More significantly, however, the triumph can only happen by breaking all the rules of the railway, such as smashing through level crossing gates, implying that English rule must be smashed if the railway (as progress) can be used to achieve social justice and peace.

A number of other films are not specifically about trains, but use them (or railway lines) incidentally, in order to portray a particular myth about the place of the State. *Life is Beautiful* (1998), for example, is the story of a family caught up in a concentration camp in the Second World War. The railway plays a small part in the film, but is deeply symbolic. As in the film *Schindler's List* (1993), the railway line ends at the buffers inside the concentration camp, depicting, both literally and symbolically, the 'end of the line'. One moral message lies in the irrationality at the heart of rational modernity (Weber 1947) – the scale and efficiency of extermination could only be carried out in the context of mass transport such as railways. Trains can be as powerful a means of death as any other weapon of mass destruction. But a more radical reading of the State is also possible in some films. If the railway (train or tracks) symbolizes a national identity and the power of the State, then such films show that the State is limited in its power. The end of the tracks in concentration camps, for example, symbolizes the point at which the State has 'done its worst' – but social interaction, and the individual's struggle for some control of life, goes on even to the moment of death.

From the Train in Theatre to Theatre on the Train

David Hare's play *The Permanent Way* is an analysis of the debates and consequences of railway privatization. Hare claims to faithfully record comments and debates that took place in the late 1980s and early 1990s. Michael Billington (2003: 1–2) notes: 'The show begins brilliantly with William Dudley's transport poster of an idyllic rural England acquiring kinetic life as a train roars down a track: a reminder of the romance of the railways before we get to the grim reality … a high-speed train racing towards us tilts and buckles as it goes off the rails.' Startling impressions created by film-makers were thus not limited to a hundred years ago – the capacity for trains to shock continues into the twenty-first century.

The Theatre of the Wheel, on the other hand, is the brainchild of Henry Lewis. It is a comparatively recent development in exploring the connections between rail travel and culture. *Brief Encounters on the … Line* is musical theatre that can be adapted for different localities and designed to be performed on trains (see Fig. 6). Its novelty – and sociological interest – lies in its dual purpose of entertainment and promotional advertising. As such, it is further evidence of the blurring of the boundary between art and advertising – which, for railways, began with promotional posters (Wernick 1991). The Theatre of the Wheel is an extension of the music and jazz trains described earlier:

> the actors are the passengers … it's a commuter train but people have often paid for that special carriage, to be in that carriage, and so they are ready for a show … In Yorkshire I was terribly worried about the noise of the train because the engines were underneath the floorboards, but what saved it really was the fact that everybody dressed up and the women wore long dresses so it acted as a sort of sound deadener to the noise underneath the thing … and

Figure 6 Theatre of the Wheel. Copyright: Henry Lewis. By permission.

we perform towards the centre of the train. The stage management is at one end, in the vestibule and they control the sound and everything, and that is where the actors change, it's just changing a hat or something, to suggest different characters, rather than doing a whole costume change. You'd have sort of dark trousers and a white top and then have different hats or a boa or something like that. (Henry – UK)

Henry is very clear about the role of the Theatre of the Wheel; it is an appeal to 'community pride' and railway nostalgia:

I want to remind people – this is a lofty ideal and probably people will take no notice of it – but I would like to remind people that they have a station, and they have a travel choice. If we get a lot of publicity, if we go to one of these towns like Falmouth, we're saying 'hey, you've got a station … it's not a down market thing, it makes Falmouth a railway town and that is something to be proud of once again'.

Analysing Myths

Textual analysis – methods of 'reading' cultural artefacts – is itself a culturally based practice. This means that a number of different readings are possible and equally valid. Our analyses here are informed by, and emerge from, our life experiences as white, Western, mid-life, intellectual women who happen to love trains. Having briefly explored some of the plethora of cultural artefacts connected with rail travel, we are now in a position to reflect on the myths about Western culture. We can see that they are generated in a number of ways; in other words, there are different ways in which the artefacts locate their viewers, readers or listeners. Sometimes there is an overtly political purpose – as in David Hare's play *The Permanent Way*, or the American film *The Iron Horse*, or documentary films produced in collaboration with governments. At other times the railway and train are themselves used symbolically; literature and art of the nineteenth century, for example, often presented the train as a threat, as dangerous, even as subversive (Bell 1998).

The most enduring feature of railways in cultural artefacts, however, is that the paraphernalia – tracks, stations, signals, trains – represent 'new' spaces, times, risks and possibilities, and have a seemingly infinite capacity to shock and destabilize previously held ideas and philosophies: 'The repetition and sameness of train space, in which all spaces are interchangeable and only temporarily occupied by different people, is … an excuse to upset expectations and the moral codes on which they are based' (Kirby 1997: 92).

Even considering the small number of artefacts we have analysed for this chapter, there is still a wide range of myths on which we can choose to focus. In order to make some connections with the following chapters, we have elected to explore issues of identity: sexuality and gender; status and class; national identity and the State, and nostalgia for the traditions of pastoral communities. As we noted above, these issues enable us to locate our identities; locate ourselves in time; locate ourselves to be, and locate ourselves to do.

Sexuality and Gender

Sexuality is the earliest and most basic form of symbolism in cultural artefacts. We see it being portrayed particularly in the silent films of the early twentieth century. The frequent depiction of a woman tied to a railway track suggests trains are masculinist, powerful, destructive and violent. The act symbolizes rape. Kirby (1997: 69) argues, for example, that the early film *The Photographer's Mishap* emasculates a stills photographer as 'the victim of a metaphorical rape: run down by the train like the woman tied to the tracks'. Equally basic and crude is the symbolism of trains entering tunnels: 'films like Alfred Hitchcock's *North by Northwest* (1959), in which a train entering a tunnel is meant to signify and parody sexual intercourse, epitomize this popular notion' (Kirby 1997: 77).

The film *Brief Encounter* holds a fragile balance between sexuality and romance. This perhaps explains some of its continuing place in people's nostalgic affections. The train helped to mobilize and recode sexual identity at a radical break in history when populations sought to create a different kind of society following the Second World War. The train thus provided a 'dynamic stage of romantic and sexual encounters. It is as if the very fact of accelerated motion and speed pulled the carpet from beneath the feet of traditional modes of social interaction in public space' (Kirby 1997: 76).

The sexual symbolism of trains is refracted, but not perfectly mirrored, in their genderedness. Lynne Kirby argues that, even though the train is an example of the cult of speed and masculine power, there is also often an affective relation to the machine that introduces a complexity into the gendering of the train: 'While the very image of the locomotive being driven by the engineer undoubtedly suggests a phallic reading – the train as an object under the control of a man – the locomotive was often endowed with feminine properties. This presents a paradox for gender definition' (Kirby 1997: 175) – and, indeed, presents writers of fiction like the Rev. W. Awdry with a dilemma, as we noted earlier.

It is worthy of note that 'there were never any trains named after Jane Austen or George Eliot or the Brontes; the only woman worthy of railway attention was Boadicea, no doubt because she was half naked and drove a wild chariot' (Whittaker 1995: 63). Whittaker, of course, is actually referring to engines here, not trains. But genderedness is not just about names of engines; it is revealed in discourse – the ways in which people have discussed trains. Marchant (2003: 65) asserts that 'Trains are masculine; the engines are never referred to as "she".' Marchant's analysis is somewhat simplistic and he is also factually incorrect; the history of gendered engines is more complex.

Writing in 1905, for example, Nesbit uses the station porter to identify trains, like ships, as 'she'; the 1937 film *Oh Mr Porter* begins with a 'christening' ceremony for the railway engine in the style of launching a ship, always a 'she'. In *The Titfield Thunderbolt* we find a passing reference by one railway buff to another to the train as 'she'. Many songs and poems, such as *Night Mail*, also refer to engines as female. The issue became more complicated over time, especially in reinforcing traditional gender roles in children: both the *Thomas the Tank Engine* and *Ivor the Engine* children's series depict engines as male – and, in the former, the coaches are all female. During this period from the 1940s to the 1970s, gendered identity in Western culture became less fixed and stable for other reasons: it was perceived by many to be 'in crisis'. Also, there was a perception that the wombs of women were needed to replenish a population decimated by war.

Marchant (2003: 65) notes that rail enthusiasts are 'almost exclusively masculine too. From the 1930s until into the 1960s, this is what boys did.' But the reality is again more complex. We – Gayle and Gillian – would call ourselves rail enthusiasts, for example, and we have certainly met many other such women since our research work on trains has become known. And before the 1930s, in 1918, Harry Golding wrote in *The Wonder Book of Railways for Boys **and Girls*** (emphasis added): 'Nearly all boys and girls, and most grown-ups, cherish an affection for a moving train' (Golding 1918: 91). But at the same time we cannot ignore the historical reasons why railways have always courted women in various ways: 'their interest in women went beyond seeing them as passengers, as ticket-buying riders of the rails. Women served a much larger function: they stood as symbols of cultural legitimacy and guarantors of respectability' (Kirby 1997: 85).

Status and Class

In nineteenth-century railway literature and art there are numerous representations of class. As we have already noted, in *The Railway Station*

Frith separates the engine driver from all other classes milling together on the platform; in *Dombey and Son*, Dickens uses the railway in different places to represent both the destruction of working-class ways of life and moral outrage of élitist authority. Class and élitism, as we have seen, is used more overtly in Awdry's Railway Series of *Thomas the Tank Engine*; the (young, middle-class) engines are encouraged to keep their distance from (working-class) trucks. Working with the trucks was a punishment. In Nesbit's *The Railway Children* the train is portrayed as synonymous with working classes: dirt, untamed children and lack of discipline. Those who work on the railways are also seen as working-class – different – to be pitied and 'helped' by their charitable 'betters'.

In John Hadfield's *Love on a Branch Line* class is portrayed in a more subtle and subversive way. The obsolete, whimsical train trundling up and down the branch line, going nowhere, represents the (redundant) aristocracy, symbolized in village fêtes, cricket and decadent alcoholic stupor. The main railway, although relatively classless in itself, is still colonized by traditional middle classes, who remain closeted in a world of cricket, embroidery and boring personalities. From Britain of 2004, Hadfield's branch line seems socially polluting; the sense of redundant, visionless upper middle (conservative) classes and aristocracy is represented by the whole railway system. This vision reaches its political zenith in Hare's *The Permanent Way*:

> [T]he big question is whether the railways can be seen as a metaphor for modern Britain: a land where nothing works. It is a point Hare has made repeatedly in accompanying interviews and that is vividly expressed in the play's prologue by anguished travellers: 'We're all doing our best but it isn't working,' says someone, apparently speaking of the country as a whole. (Billington 2003: 2)

The railway in Hare's play thus symbolizes the bankruptcy of ideas of 'society' and 'government for the people, by the people'. It raises disturbing questions about the genuineness of representative government.

The State and National Identity

Railways have played a key role in wars and colonialism of the nineteenth and twentieth centuries. It has been said that imperialism itself was a function of the railways (Kirby 1997: 5). Film-makers have used trains in hundreds of documentary, fiction and 'docudrama' films depicting different aspects of war. *Boer War*, for example, shows a temporary military railway in South Africa; *Children's Coronation* (1953) shows how the railway industry has been used to mythologize the collaboration between State and royalist sympathies (Huntley 1993: 28). Films like *A Beautiful Life, Schindler's List, Dr Zhivago, Closely Observed Trains* and *Oh Mr Porter* all use the train or the railway to represent the State. It sometimes symbolizes the unassailable power of the State, at other times a tool of subversion.

As a form of behaviour defined and regulated by the State, crime forms a major source of myth generated by the train. It is no coincidence, argue Richards and MacKenzie (1986), that one of the earliest feature films to tell a full story is *The Great Train Robbery* (1903). Railways very quickly came to provide a natural setting for imaginative works, offering unique opportunities and restrictions (Simmons 1991a). Writers of crime fiction, for example, face a common difficulty: they must find a way of disposing of the murdered body. Carter (2002: 47) notes that 'Parliament's requirement that railways should be common carriers, accepting any traffic which might offer', was a gift to writers. Corpse-laden trunks could be hoisted on to luggage vans of passenger trains, deposited in left-luggage offices or left in cloakrooms.

Over the last 150 years, the design of trains has undergone many changes, including (in Britain) the demise of the compartment. This phenomenon had not only offered some relative privacy, but also became a place of potential danger, as we shall see in Chapter 6. The opportunities for crime afforded by the design and use of trains have been used by writers of fiction and makers of film for many years, and 'classics' abound, such as *Murder on the Orient Express*; *The Thirty-nine Steps*; the dramatization of the 'other' Great Train Robbery in 1963 (originally given the misleading title of *Gentlemen Prefer Cash*); *Under Siege 2*; *Mission Impossible*; and various James Bond books (and films).

Tradition and Community

The nostalgia for timeless pastoralism and rurality is a major feature of most British myths of trains (perhaps less so in many American ones): there is thus an 'identity relationship between railways and place, not least with regard to the cultural construction of rural Englishness' (Payton 1997: 17). But the place and timelessness of pastoral tradition cannot be divorced from the importance of time; *From a Railway Carriage, Night Mail* and *The Titfield Thunderbolt*, for example, all emphasize the continuity, or desire for continuity, of a pastoral way of life. If continuity is a key feature of the construction of rural Englishness, as Payton argues, then so too is the ideal of 'community'. Nostalgia for the communitarian myth, which – for Britain – usually includes a branch line railway, takes many forms. From the 'high art' of Powell Frith and Martin to the community of railway engines in *Thomas the Tank Engine and Friends*, runs a theme of the 'established' and the 'outsider' – for 'community' always defines who does and who does not belong (Elias and Scotson 1994).

The myths of the train, transmitted through aesthetic culture, tell us who we are, where we have come from, how to live with each other and how to reclaim our identity in the future. They also tell us that we can find ourselves on the 'wrong side of the tracks' because the ideal of the community:

> privileges unity over difference, immediacy over mediation, sympathy over recognition of the limits of one's understanding of others from their point of view. Community is an understandable dream, expressing a desire for selves that are transparent to one another, relationships of mutual identification, social closeness and comfort. The dream is understandable, but politically problematic ... because those motivated by it will tend to suppress differences among themselves or implicitly to exclude from their political groups persons with whom they do not identify. (Young 1990: 300)

Reflections

Lynne Kirby (1997: 251) notes the irony that the nostalgic value of the train is seen as 'a symbol of the historical, the traditional, the "good old days" ... when everybody knew their place'. We forget that it was precisely the train that did so much to throw social place into crisis and to create a rupture with the past on an unprecedented scale. Our limited selection of myths for discussion in this chapter – sexuality and gender, status and class, the State and national identity and tradition and community – all have a function. They all help to locate the train within space and time. In the following chapters we begin to explore the space and time of the railway journey. At some junctures, this means looking at the train; at others, looking into (the space of) the train; at yet others, looking out of (the place of) the train.

–4–

All Aboard the 'Play Station'
Leisure and the Train

Introduction

[What do I like about trains?] Loads of things! In no particular order: the sheer magnitude of the machinery: the way hundreds of tonnes of metal can safely travel at over 100 mph – its womb-like environment: the feeling of a safe haven, a place of comfort, providing tranquillity in motion between where I was and where I will be – the microcosm: thrown into close quarters with strangers for a time, people of different backgrounds share one space, even though they would not normally do so. The train is a place where stories are shared, or at least overheard. Especially over long journeys, the train provides insight into the lifestyles and livelihoods of my fellow travellers ... the landscape: the train is the only method of travel where you can truly experience and enjoy the landscape without distraction or concerns for safety – in conjunction with the above point, the train accesses parts of the landscape that can be accessed no other way. (Eddie – Canada/UK)

Having considered the social, political and cultural significance of the train and train travel, we now move on to explore the relationship between the train and leisure and work. In Chapter 5 we consider the experience of both railway workers and passengers who use the train to travel to work and/or as a space in which to undertake productive labour. First, though, in this chapter we think about the train as a space and source of leisure, as well as a vehicle that gives access to leisure, highlighting the fact that the train is more than a vehicle that gets us from A to B.

Much has been written on the practices and process of 'doing' leisure. Leisure studies is an academic discipline in its own right as well as leisure being of interest to sociologists, historians, sport psychologists and social geographers, amongst others. The growth of leisure studies has led to the problematization of the phenomenon known as 'tourism' (Rojek and Urry 1997). For some people (e.g. Hall and Page 1999; Page 1999), 'tourism' necessitates not only undertaking journeys but also staying away; for others, there is a question over whether it is possible to make a distinction between 'tourist' and 'visitor' (e.g. Masberg 1998). Stephen Williams (1998: 3) notes that the word 'tourism' has a number of meanings and interpretations:

> dictionaries commonly explain a 'tourist' as a person undertaking a tour or circular trip that is usually made for business, pleasure or education, at the end of which one returns to the starting point, normally the home. 'Tourism' is habitually viewed as a composite concept involving not just the temporary movement of people to destinations that are removed from their normal place of residence but, in addition, the organisation and conduct of their activities and of the facilities and services that are necessary for meeting their needs.

Whatever definition of a tourist or traveller is used, transport is clearly a vital element in any discussion of tourism: 'Transport provides the essential link between tourism origin and destination areas and facilitates the movement of holidaymakers, business travellers, people visiting friends and relatives and those undertaking educational and health tourism. Transport is also a key element of the "tourist experience" ... and some commentators view it as an integral part of the tourism industry' (Page 1999: 1). Yet we would argue that we need to look beyond the tourist to fully understand the relationship between the train, train travel and leisure and work. In this chapter we begin this analysis.

Railway Stations as Objects of Leisure

Some of our respondents spoke of their interest in railway stations, demonstrating a similar fascination to the one Frith had when he painted *The Railway Station* (see Chapter 3). However, it seems that some of the activity and splendour captured by Frith is now lost:

> a little bit of looking around, but there's not much focus at St Pancras really. The buffet isn't really there any more – no, some stations are more interesting than others. I'm trying to think of one that is! Possibly a country station is more interesting now – a country station that was grand once, and has some long-distance trains coming in, is probably the most interesting. Or a little café that's not part of a chain where they do homemade food, that can be delightful. (Henry – UK)

The philosopher Ludwig Wittgenstein (cited by Bauman 1992: 226) argued that '[t]he only place where real philosophical problems could be tackled and resolved is the railway station'. And, despite some historical changes, railway stations still give good access to 'people watching', an activity that Gillian and Tony particularly enjoy:

> [talking about Birmingham station] but also the people, the milling around of people, people going and people coming. There was a philosopher once who said if you want to study humankind you should go and stand on a railway station. And I think that is very true because it is such an exciting place to be. I think it's this connection between the people and the technology of the train … I love to watch a train coming into a station, and the way the humanity pours out of the train. I love to see that. (Gillian)

> And stations are excellent places to people-watch, especially somewhere like Crewe, which is the centre of the railway universe! (Tony – UK)

'The Train's the Thing'

Ian Marchant (2003: 191) describes his fascination for all things railway – the track, the track workers, the buildings, the abandoned and wrecked carriages. Our data suggest that, like Marchant, many rail enthusiasts have varied interests and concerns, even though the traditional stereotype of the 'rail fan' is a boy or man whose focus is on the engines themselves. Rail enthusiasts were keen to tell us of their long association with trains and of the reasons for their initial interest. As we noted in the Introduction – but particularly relevant here in our discussion of the train as an object of leisure – for some, initial interest was stimulated by the size, speed and power of the train:

> The rolling stock, be it locomotives or otherwise, was often very grand and handsome and just a little bit frightening. So the appeal seems to be at a rather subconscious and hard to describe level. My childhood memories of these magnificent creatures always seem to include sunny warm days. (Damien – Canada)

Interestingly, when Jayne refers to size and power, it is in reference to safety and this has resonances for us with our discussion of safety in Chapter 2. Unlike some of our other women respondents, Jayne focuses on the train as safe rather than dangerous, but her narrative – like that of other women – connects to the experiential:

> I like the large physical proportions of a train (over that of a car for instance). I like the speed and the power that trains exhibit, but they are like gentle giants in that these attributes are controlled and safety is paramount. Train

crashes while horrific when they happen are very rare unlike road traffic accidents. I appreciate the use of traditional materials such as steel and timber on the older types of rolling stock which has meant that they have remained in service long after their intended retirement.

For others, family connections are relevant. Shared family leisure activities and family history connect the private and the public spheres in interesting ways. An interest in model railways in the home led some to an interest in the real thing in the public sphere, or work activity outside the home stimulated a leisure interest. For example:

[there] was a growing interest in model railways and that was largely due to my brother because he had a really splendid interest in model railways ... his enthusiasm spilled off on me I guess. (Joseph – UK)

I've been interested in trains ever since I can remember. I received a model train set from my grandmother when I was four and played with it constantly (I still have it). It helped a lot too that my parents took me on vacations to Europe and we used trains to travel everywhere! (Justin – Canada)

My family tree includes railwayers, railway executives, a railfan and severe cases of wanderlust. I think all of these add up to my passion for trains. (Nick – USA)

I've been interested in trains since I was a child, mainly due to my father's interest and of course because his father was a professional railwayman all his life. Before he died in 1968 my grandfather often used to invite me to the signalbox where he worked on a Saturday afternoon, and I can still remember my first ride with a driver ... when I was about seven years old. (Philip – UK)

Sometimes, however, respondents seemed to fight against these family connections:

I am not interested in trains, but have been brought up with them because my father, grandfather, great grandfather have all worked on the Railways, as well as my mother and sister. So I guess it is kind of in my blood. (Karen – UK)

Train-spotting, of course, is a historical 'activity' that has changed over time. As Nicholas Whittaker (1995) notes, the technology now available to the rail enthusiast makes for a very different experience for some long-term train-spotters:

[I have been interested in trains for] fifty-four years so far. [I] started as a child aged five in the steam era. Most of my contemporaries were also interested in trains ... Many, such as I, retain the interest into adulthood though it changes slightly as we grow older. For instance, I did not own a camera when I was a child and thus could not take photographs. Now I use both a 35 mm camera (using many cassettes of slide film per annum) and an expensive digital camera. As a child I kept most of my records in notebooks and in the few specially published books that were available then – now all my records are computerised. In those distant days only a few books on British Railways were available – now there are numerous books for many countries. As I child I stayed within a radius of about ten miles from home – today I go all over Europe and the USA. (Barry – UK)

Common in the literature is the view that train-spotting is a male activity: 'Trainspotting in its heyday between the mid 1950s and the late '60s was definitely a hobby suited to the outdoor, adventurous type of youth, someone full of boundless energy and not afraid to travel, sometimes hundreds of miles, with a night or nights away from the comforts of home' (Harvey 2004: 1). Richards and MacKenzie (1986: 13) observe that '[t]hey stand, men and boys of all ages, come rain, come shine, oblivious of the seasons, clad in the regulation uniform of their breed – the anorak – with Thermos flask of coffee, spam sandwiches, bulging notebooks'. Also:

Trainspotting has always been a democracy, embracing all men, from right scruffs to Right Honourables. No names, no pack drill. Unlike the golf club or the Chamber of Trade, no one cares about your income, your profession, or who you know. What you know about trains is what counts. It's one of the few areas where you'll see professors comparing notes with latch-key kids. (Whittaker 1995: 42)

Our data (and our observations) largely support these perceptions. Yet this is not to say that women have no love of, or fascination for, trains:

I love to stand next to an open door, feel the wind blow, listen to the noise the train makes, and meet people. Working railfan trips as a car host is fun. I think what got me really going was our trip to Ecuador in 1985 where I got to ride on the roof of box cars and watch the country unfold before my eyes. (Marian – USA)

I'll tell you that I've always loved trains. Um when I was little we used to go to Scotland lots, from London, on steam strains in summer because my mother's family lived on a farm in the Highlands, and my mother and I would go up quite early on the train. I just remember leather belts on windows and black spots on faces from the steam and so on. And being on a sleeper was very exciting … And then I went to school on trains, on the underground, and I suppose I just felt very comfortable for twenty or thirty minutes twice a day. (Grace – UK)

Our research also leads us to challenge lay and academic discourse that supports traditional gendered stereotypes and represents a prejudiced view of rail-fans. An extreme example of lay discourse here can be found embedded in 'other' stories: 'He didn't seem like a nutter or a train-spotter' (*That's Life* magazine (2004): 'true life story'). The following example of academic writing is equally prejudiced:

As far as we can tell, no work has yet been done on the psychology of the train-spotter. But a number of possible motivations suggest themselves. The sexual connotation of trains is well known, particularly trains entering tunnels. Is this obsessive watching of trains sliding in and out of stations to be construed, in the child, as a substitute for sex and, in the adult, as a desire to prolong childhood indefinitely and avoid coming to terms with mature sexuality? This gives us the concept of the train spotter as voyeur, permanent observer rather than regular participant.

But perhaps a more likely interpretation is to be found in the aspect of the hobby known as 'copping', the keeping of lists of trains seen. Is this a desire to provide order and system in a disordered universe, to give life an encompassable finite purpose? That would account for its appeal to males of all ages, and equally explain the absence of females, whose finite universe has traditionally been provided by the home, housework, and the shopping. (Richards and MacKenzie 1986: 13–14)

As Whittaker (1995: 288) suggests, now that individuals are socialized to consider leisure as a product and a product that must be paid for, they are unwilling to believe that fun can be had simply and cheaply without a catch. For the rail fan, the catch is that of being laughed at. Consider Richards and MacKenzie (1986: 14) once again: 'Perhaps we should draw a veil over further speculation and simply describe train-spotting as one of those lovable British eccentricities, like garden gnomes, toy soldiers, strong tea and talking about the weather.' It is ironic, therefore, that an American enthusiast, Ron, should feel it necessary to point out to us:

You may not be aware that the general opinion of railfans in the US is significantly lower than what I understand it to be in the UK. I understand that 'train-spotting' is an accepted hobby there, whereas here only 'nuts' are interested in trains.

Thus, rail enthusiasts almost everywhere risk a challenge to their identity, as the 'stigma' of train-spotting, which is not necessarily visible to the viewer (although again the stereotype is of a greasy-haired, anorak wearer), has a 'known-about-ness' (Goffman 1963b) that marks the individual. Views such as those of Richards and MacKenzie are not only patronizing but inaccurate.

Lights, Camera, Action

For some rail enthusiasts, taking photographs of trains is an important part of the leisure experience:

> I live beside a busy railway line and can take very good pictures from within a few metres of my house. (Owen – New Zealand)

> I do photograph trains. Actually I must have hundreds of pictures of Amtrak trains, but only when I ride them. Every trip I take, I photograph it coming in and leaving. (Amy – USA)

> All my slides (about 8000 at the last count) are sorted by country, number, class etc. and the details are recorded on my computer. I sell around 100 slides per year to various railway publications and book authors. I also 'lease' slides to a company that retains them for seven years and sells copies to the public. I get an annual lease fee, a percentage of sales and all sold are credited to me by name. (Barry – UK)

> I shoot slides and get them scanned onto a CD. From there, I build web pages and treat that like showing off a photo album. (Julian – Canada)

Some like to do this alone but, again, the stereotype of the train-spotter – as an isolated loner unable to make friends – is a false one. Whittaker (1995: 124) notes: 'In common with most hobbies, train-spotting has an underlying social function, offering all kinds of people a ready-made excuse to talk to each other.' Some of our data confirm this:

> Typically, I will photograph NZ trains up to three to six times per year, usually in conjunction with organised 'train excursions', so with lots of other people. I am involved with a voluntary rail excursion running group ... and serve from time to time as voluntary 'passenger' support person (known as a 'carriage steward'). (Greg – New Zealand)

> If I had to give you some sort of average figure I would say that I spend between forty and fifty days per year photographing on my own, and about

thirty days per year as part of an organized group, invariably overseas. This is usually part of the railway club to which I belong. (Barry – UK)

These accounts also demonstrate the time commitment that enthusiasts put into their hobby and the use to which photographs are put. For others, train-spotting is a more occasional hobby:

I seldom go out on railway photo 'missions'. I take my camera if I am partic- ipating in a special rail event, usually video camera or 35 mm colour print film. Occasionally, also, I will drive somewhere specifically to see a rare working of a steam loco or to get a particularly scenic railway shot – but usually I don't go far out of my way for these ... Sometimes several months will pass between events. (Edwin – New Zealand)

Even if the activity is infrequent, however, the results are clearly still very precious:

Oh, boy. Should I say what I'd like to do or what I get to do? I try to find one to three days a month to get trackside with my camera. I tend to plan day trips rather than shoot locally. Time has allowed me to complete a three-day rail safari through New England last month and I am leaving in a week for a five- day quickie to Chicago ... My slide collection is my most valued material possession and I consider it an archive that will one day be more valuable than it ever will be during my lifetime. I occasionally seek to be published in rail journals and I do plan to publish some of my work myself in book form. (Nick – USA)

Just as train-spotting itself has changed, new technology brings new opportunities for leisure. Joseph's (UK) account demonstrates clearly that, for some enthusiasts, 'It's the train that's the thing':

there's a very interesting thing in the back of this magazine [producing advert for computer programme for 'virtual railway'] – this is a picture of the Mallard, very beautiful engine, one of the fastest, but then I read that [advert] and that just horrifies me that my grandchildren could play trains without playing trains! ... I suppose it is because it isn't 'real' and I think model rail- ways are real.

Trains, Nostalgia and Romance

Indulging in nostalgia about trains and train-spotting is itself a leisure activity for many. In his discussion of nostalgia, Tim Strangleman (1999: 729) argues that '[t]he railway industry is perhaps one of the most fruitful for exploring notions of nostalgia because of its place within the nation's psyche'. Nostalgic activity can take place in the private sphere: for example, creating or operating a model railway, or reading a book about trains. Whittaker (1995) suggests that this is particularly the preserve of the train-spotter grown old, the individual with disposable income who hopes to relive the past through the pages of a book (or a model railway). Similarly, Colin Divall (2003: 261) argues that a visit to a transport museum which enables us to view the vehicles of our childhood can rekindle pleasurable memories and connect us to the past: 'although people often feel distanced from history when it is presented in anything like the largely impersonal, abstract and unfamiliar explanations of much academic thought, they respond much more positively to a past perceived in personal terms, as relevant to their own lives'.

Our own visit to the Railway Museum in York whilst writing this book (where, of course, we watched the people as much as we looked at the trains) leads us to endorse this. We are not suggesting here that only adults enjoy such experiences. We observed girls and boys having fun at the museum and, of course, the leisure industry is aimed at children too, as one book we found at the York Railway Museum library demonstrates:

I-SPY with David Bellamy ON A TRAIN JOURNEY

Everyone loves going on trains. They take you to places you've never been to before, and show you lots of exciting things on the way. I-SPY on a Train Journey tells you some of the things you will see – trains and track, signals and sidings, fast, modern trains, old slow ones and even old fast ones too. Anything in fact you might see on your journey.

Like all I-Spy books, *I-SPY ON A TRAIN JOURNEY* has activities with scores, the grading of which has a particular 'status' significance and irony here:

When your scores total 1,250 points you may award yourself the rank of TRAIN TRAVELLER *Second Class*. When they reach a complete total of 1,500 points you are entitled to the rank of TRAIN TRAVELLER *First Class*.
(1984: 2, emphasis added)

Maybe, then, the junior train watcher of today will become the nostalgic adult of the future. It is clear that, for some of our (adult) respondents, railways represent an important link with the past. For some, it is the 'railway experience' that is significant; for others, it is the train itself which enables the passenger to connect private and public historical time:

I look out for the unusual, like spot a steam train or something, going in the opposite direction. Something like that draws a lot of interest, even if you're not actually travelling on it. (Colin – UK)

I like the association with the British culture and the classic, older steam trains have – the station architecture, the reference to the sophistication of train travel, an enjoyment of superior quality (service and materials) combined with the romance of rail travel and how this in turn has been captured in many memorable films. I take pleasure in a train's presence and majesty epitomised in its considered understanding and understated proportions (which I feel the newer trains have not incorporated into their design as they employ less subtle exterior and interior aesthetics). (Jayne – UK)

We maintain that this nostalgia is not rooted in the snobbery that Whittaker (1995: 189) worries about: 'I hated this Orient Express snobbery, a reconstructed past with a suitable class system. The whole thing was a pose. It had nothing to do with the love of trains at all, but was more concerned with a hankering after the old upstairs–downstairs era.' Rather, we suggest it is part of the way in which we connect with our cultural and national roots in order to identify who we are, even though, as Whittaker points out, the 'nostalgia' is also a 'product', packaged for our consumption (see Fig. 7).

Figure 7 Train watching, Canada-style. Copyright: Mike Jager. By permission.

Sights for Sore Eyes

Looking out of the carriage window focuses on the outside of the train space; on the passing 'spectacle' (Green 1990; Letherby and Reynolds 2003). Much of the romanticism (Campbell 1987, cited in Featherstone 1995: 24) of train travel is connected not so much to the train itself as to that passing spectacle. Sightseeing has a long history. John Urry (1990: 4), for example, reflecting on the growth of tourism between 1600 and 1800, argues that '[t]here was a ... visualisation of the travel experience, or the development of the "gaze", aided and assisted by the growth of guidebooks which promoted new ways of seeing'. These new 'ways of seeing' are unpacked further by Siegfried Kracauer (cited by Rojek and Urry 1997: 6), who comments that '[m]ore and more travel is becoming the incomparable occasion to be somewhere other than the very place one habitually is. It fulfils its decisive function as spatial transformation, as a temporary change of location ... Travel has been reduced to a pure experience of space.'

Chris Rojek and John Urry (1997) argue that the tourist uses sights along the journey to give shape to their passion for travelling. Those sights can be of an extraordinarily short duration, as short as a few seconds of clock time. For some people, though, the sights are not just about a passion for travel; they help to keep the traveller connected to the process of travel:

> While aeroplanes ... have their own set of rituals ... and these rituals are also exciting, there is something about not being able to see anything much out of the window that can engender a certain 'unreality' to the travel experience – you can't see the process by which you leave point A and arrive at point B. With a train you aren't alienated from the process of travelling to the same extent because you can see the full landscape. (Viv – New Zealand)

There is, however, little doubt that some sights do form 'signifiers' of images of times past:

> the train system was established from the 1840s and so it went through particular countryside. The bus systems rely on motorways and so it's quite a different concept. (Jeremy – UK)

> Since railways were built years ago, they tend to travel through areas of the country not seen from modern freeways. (Martyn – Canada)

Urry (1990: 9) is concerned with the 'packaging' of tourist sites, rather than unexpected sights. He suggests that the gaze of the tourist 'will

involve an obvious intrusion into people's lives, which would be generally unacceptable, so the people being observed, and local tourist entrepreneurs, gradually come to construct backstages in a continued and
artificial manner'. But this does not apply to all the spaces outside the
train on an average journey. Those spaces are rarely designed with
tourists in mind – indeed, the sense of historical time (or even illusion of
timelessness) is part of the attraction – but they do undergo a cultural
(rather than material) transformation into a form of ritual and spectacle
(Green 1990) to rail travellers (see Fig. 8). It is interesting, though, that
the 'tourist gaze' has adjusted to twenty-first-century speed. This
comment from the nineteenth century makes us smile:

> Although railways are comparatively of recent date we are so accustomed
> to them that it is difficult to realize the condition of the country before their
> introduction. How different are the present day ideas to speed in travelling
> to those entertained in the good old times. The celebrated historian,
> Niebuhr, who was in England in 1798, thus describes the rapid travelling of
> that period: – 'Four horses drawing a coach with six persons inside, four on
> the roof, a sort of conductor besides the coachman, and overladen with

Figure 8 Heart of Wales Line train: cultural transformation of spectacle.
Previously published in *Rail* Issue 436, May/June 2002 – 'Heart of Wales Line'.
Copyright: John Hunt/*RAIL*. By permission.

luggage, have to get over seven English miles in the hour; and as the coach goes on without ever stopping except at the principal stages, it is not surprising that you can traverse the whole extent of the country in so few days. But for any length of time this rapid motion is quite unnatural. You can only get a very piece-meal view of the country from the windows, and with the tremendous speed at which you go can keep no object long in sight; you are unable also to stop at any place.' Near the same time the late Lord Campbell, travelling for the first time by coach from Scotland to London, was seriously advised to stay a day at York, as the rapidity of motion (eight miles an hour) had caused several through-going passengers to die of apoplexy. (Pike 1884: 3)

As we noted in our Introduction, we each have an emotional attachment to the scenery we view on familiar train trips: Gillian through the Fens and Gayle along the Devon coastline. We are not the only ones:

I think I would look out – I think it's more that I would look out for that first part of the journey because it's a part of the journey I would know. I would look out of the window and see those landmarks. I don't think I would particularly say to myself before the journey, 'I will look out for those landmarks'..(Joseph – UK)

I think the nicest railways are the single tracks. I went away to school camp one year down to Kingsbridge in Devon and there was a single track line there which was fascinating. There is another one in North Wales that's just about still hanging on and operates just on an up and down line business, Llangollen and Corwen. (Theo – UK)

Of course, these affectionate, nostalgic feelings can be harnessed by those concerned to maximize their profits as they were in the mid-nineteenth century (see Chapter 1). The following is taken from the *Windowgazer Guide Edinburgh/Glasgow–Penzance* Virgin Trains:

THE ATMOSPHERIC RAILWAY
One of Brunel's few failures, the atmospheric system was installed between Exeter and Newton Abbot in 1845–7. An ingeniously simple (and clean) arrangement of vacuum tube, rod and piston, pumping stations and natural air pressure 'sucked' the carriages along. High costs caused angry stakeholders to pull out, and locomotives took over in 1848.
DEVON COASTLINE
The steep sandstone cliffs, coupled with breaches in the sea defences, have made this one of the most troublesome sections of railway in Britain to maintain. In the early years, passengers occasionally had to detrain, clamber over the rocks and get on to another train waiting on the other side of a

breach. A long-gone signal box at the southern end of Parson's Tunnel had movable screens to protect the windows, and waves still sometimes give passing trains a sea bath. Before the Second World War, the GWR began to buy land to create an inland route between Dawlish Warren and Newton Abbot, tunnelling under Haldon Down. The war put paid to the plans and the land was sold off.

The train operating companies clearly exploit the romantic feelings we have surrounding the interface of train and scenery. There is thus a tension between the nostalgic railway of our dreams and the railway of consumerism and quality.

In addition to this exploitation of our romantic sensibilities, there are further ironies: for example, the fact that some heritage sights are visited by many more 'tourists' than the original working station or railway. Marchant (2003: 260) laments: 'One of the pretensions of the preserved lines is that they capture the atmosphere of a real country railway ... But like any heritage project, these pretensions are undermined by the sheer weight of visitors ... If the line had had this many passengers when it was open, it would never have closed.'

Perhaps even more ironic, given the points made above – and despite their concern to sell the scenery outside the train – some train operating companies make it almost impossible to indulge in the tourist 'gaze':

> I like looking out for parts of the journey. I certainly dislike the new [name of train operating company] trains because the seats, some of the seats are slap up against the window pillars so you can't see out. So not much thought has gone into that. I like to be able to look out, to look at the scenery or the railway bits and pieces at each side of the track. (Joseph – UK)

In this sense, the experiences of some passengers have changed little since Great Western Railway forced their poorest travellers into window-less boxes (see Chapter 1).

Of course, there are other things that we see when travelling on a train that are not (yet) marketed as 'sights to be seen'. A front garden, for example, is a private creation intended for public viewing, a representation of the identity of the gardener or home-owner, and likely to be viewed as important to their image (Stoneham and Jones 1997; Bhatti and Church 2001). Conversely, a back garden is usually more private: a space and place where games are played, entertainment takes place, washing is hung out, rubbish is sometimes kept and, on occasion, sunbathing takes place. Thus, the back garden is a place for family and friends, not strangers. Perhaps this is why, despite the increased media attention to private gardens, Charlie Dimmock's (a presenter of a UK garden make-over programme, *Ground Force*) activity feels a little like 'spying':

> Charlie Dimmock can't help smiling whenever she garden-gazes out of a train window. Coasting through Surrey towards London Waterloo from her Hampshire home, she chuckles inside as she gets a bird's-eye view of rows of back gardens with a few recognisable touches ... 'I love sitting on the train and looking at the gardens seeing how people have done them differently,' she says ...
> I can see where they've been watching *Ground Force*, with the pale blue trellis, bits of decking and stuff like that. It always makes me smile when I recognize that. (Gooch 2004: 19)

And, of course, Charlie is not the only one who does this:

> You also get a completely different experience of things than travelling by road, where you see the acceptable side of things. So on the train you'll pass houses with the backs quite close to the railway lines, or rubbish tips with all manner of things there. (Aidan – UK)

> You [can] peer at people's backyards which are much more interesting than the 'front' they put on for passing traffic! (Edwin – New Zealand)

However, some of our respondents reflect on the possible cultural dimension to such 'snooping'; Henry suggests, for example, that Americans may be less keen to engage in it:

> One of the reasons that Americans won't use their trains is that they all go round the backs of all the cities, which are very third-world [*sic*] and grim ... Fascinating – but the Americans don't want to see it!

Gazing on the Horrific

Some sightseeing can be conceptualized as 'visual scavenging' – the possibility of seeing something unusual. This is not always a pleasurable experience:

> At one point the train slowed down and the driver came on the PA system. He introduced himself and then said 'Please do not – I repeat, do not – look out of the windows on the left hand side of the train.' Well, of course, everyone craned their necks to have a look, and it was a body lying beside the tracks. After we'd gone past and the train was speeding up, the driver came on again and said 'I just wanted to spare you that.' It was quite bizarre really. (Gillian)

Yet for some there is a fascination with the horror of the rail accident: an arguably voyeuristic attitude to the 'unthinkable'. When we asked our self-defined rail fans whether crash photography was a popular activity, some said they would not travel to do this but – if the opportunity presented itself – they would take photographs. Most, however, distanced themselves from the human distress:

> I wouldn't take time off work myself to do it, but if I came across a train wreck, subway or tram wreck, I'd take a pic if it was interesting in some way, though not if there were any gory bits. (George – Canada)

> I can see the attraction although it is hard to describe. I would not go so far as to take off work or travel a very great distance to see a wreck and in terms of photographing one it would largely depend on what kind of train had crashed. If it is a train that I wouldn't want to photograph running then I would be less likely to photograph it in an accident ... To see heavy 130–lbs yard rail twisted like spaghetti ... all these things are in themselves awesome. I could never photograph human suffering or blood or anything like that. In fact I couldn't look at it. Likewise I wouldn't photograph any accident survivors if the train were a passenger train. That would be to intrude on someone's privacy. Besides, the train's the thing. (Damien – Canada)

Others admitted to a fascination akin to 'ambulance chasing':

> Yes, there are railfans who are wreck chasers, and I have done it, and will probably do it again in the future. Why do I do it? Why do people on our high-ways cause large traffic jams in order to 'rubber-neck' the results of an acci-dent in the opposite lanes? Why do people congregate at the scene of a shooting that resulted in death? I guess this is a reaction to the morbid side of our human nature in wanting to see for ourselves, first hand, what the outcome is or was. (Archie – Canada)

So, as Urry (1990) argues, there is a tourist gaze which seeks out the unusual or the darker side of sightseeing. And, although our data suggest that this is normatively male and structured by voyeurism (Craik 1997), there may be reasons other than fascination for this type of activity. Some of our respondents insisted that photographic expeditions of this type do not take place very often and that, when they do, the main motivation is profit. Interestingly, Eddie and Barry have a very different perception of the market value of such photographs:

> I have absolutely no interest in railway crashes, though it would be interest-ing to be on a minor one someday, just to say 'guess what happened to me,

and I still love trains!' If one happened nearby, I might go photograph it in order to sell my photos to the press. But that's about it. (Eddie – UK)

There is little point in rushing to the scene of a rail crash, for instance, with a view to taking a lot of pictures for sale. The press and media are known to monitor the emergency services radios and will be there long before any amateur. (Barry – UK)

Others were keen to stress that they would only travel to such an accident as a public service:

I would travel to a train accident *only* if there was a constructive way to use the photos in an Operation Lifesaver display, or if I could actually be of service on the scene ... As far as what I would photograph, it would be the car at the crossing or the pedestrian or other feature of the accident that could be used to educate others as the dangers associated with highway rail grade crossing safety or trespassing along the railway rights of way. Anything to keep the incidents down and to encourage others to use the rails for freight or passenger service whenever possible. Do I get paid by the railway for doing this? No. (Miles – USA)

The Train as a Place of Leisure

Having examined the train as an object of leisure in its own right and as a vehicle which is part of, or from which one can indulge in, the 'spectacle', we now move on to consider 'leisure' time within the train space. Thus, we explore when and how the place of the train is reconstructed into a place of leisure.

Game Space

In addition to the revenue made from ticket sales, train companies can profit from the leisure time and space that train travel affords us. It is interesting that on long aeroplane journeys access to food and to the in-flight movie is usually free, whereas on the train food and entertainment are often for purchase. For example, on Great Western Trains:

NOW AVAILABLE TO RENT ON BOARD
Rent a DVD player and film for just £5.99
To order, simply ask a 'Just Press Play' representative on board this train.
Payment is by credit or debit card only. A £150 deposit is payable, this will be returned at the end of the rental. Players and films will be collected 15 minutes prior to arrival at your destination station. Equipment must not be removed

from the train. Terms and conditions available on request (Just Press Play: undated).

In the shops (or, as they are often now known, retail outlets) on many trains it is possible to buy books, CDs and games. Yet again we could argue that the motive here is to exploit the time that we have available for profit, not only through the selling of goods but through the marketing of a public place as a private space where one can engage in personal, private activity. Certainly, there is a blurring of the public/private boundaries here (Edwards 1993).

Space and design are issues for leisure travellers. Some train operating companies cater particularly for the leisure activities of children, providing table tops with draughtboards or snakes and ladders boards and (sometimes free of charge) the games to play on them. Others realize and market the potential for the adult use of 'executive toys' in trains, complete with power points. As Gillian overheard from a mobile phone user in a 'quiet coach', 'I'm on a brand-new [name of train operating company] – it's wicked! It's got its own radio – that'll save my batteries, won't it.'

Those who engage in leisure activities on the train tend to behave more passively within whatever space is available than those who work on the train (as we shall see in Chapter 5). In other words, most leisure activities undertaken on trains tend to be those which can be achieved within a limited spatial area because of the design of the constructed space:

> [If you can't get a seat with a table] you can pull out the little table in front of you ... and you can put your stuff on there. There's usually enough room, and also sometimes there's a net there as well, and if you're not using something at the moment you can put it in there. So if your table starts to get too crammed, you can get the thing you're not using and put it down, and put the thing you want to use on the table. (Jake, aged nine – UK)

With a particular type of space in mind, several respondents spoke of engaging in specific leisure activities, some of which they keep exclusively for train journeys (see Fig. 9):

> We only play our Travel Connect4 on trains – it's become a kind of tradition that we get it out for train journeys. Also [my son] hardly ever looks at comics except on a train. (Julie – UK)

> Well I only ever play Scrabble on holiday, but we do particularly use Scrabble when we are travelling – so I guess we play more Scrabble when we're travelling than at any other time. (Sandie – UK)

Figure 9 'Child's play' on the railways. Copyright: line drawing by David Bill (Billy). By permission.

I'll read a novel or just stare out of the window, which I do find very pleasurable, particularly at certain points in the journey. I'll sometimes do a bit of my own writing – I don't do that very often. I'd like to do it more, that's very pleasurable. (Rhian – UK)

Well, I like it better than most transports. For one thing, you don't need – all the people are there with you, one person doesn't need to be driving, like in a car ... I just like to play one game or something, and take my Gameboy. If I can complete a level, then that's enough for me and I turn it off. (Jake, aged nine – UK)

It's like you have lots of fun playing games. And it's like really good. When we go with our Dad, he's got this mobile phone that he takes with him, and we can play games on it, and that's really fun. I like playing with my Mum and Dad, and I can't play with them when I'm on a car journey cos my Mum's got to look for the right way. (Sam, aged six – UK)

Interestingly, leisure was sometimes described as a way of filling time:

On the way to Cornwall we usually play two games of Scrabble. Each game takes about an hour so that's two hours of the journey gone. (Jeremy – UK)

Although a place of leisure itself, the train, particularly when moving, provides an opportunity to incorporate the outside space as part of the leisure activity:

> And we play I-spy on the train because you can often 'spy' something out of the window that's gone before anyone can guess it. It puts a whole new angle on the game of I-spy! (Julie – UK)

'I-spy' is, of course, a game with a long history and one that can be played with or without the available instruction (*I-SPY ON A TRAIN JOURNEY*) or guide book (*Windowgazer Guide,* Virgin Trains see p. 117).

Activity and Inactivity

Leisure activity on the train can be part of the rail enthusiasts' wider interest in trains themselves:

> When I travel on a train, I usually have an itinerary that I've made up from sources in my possession. Sometimes, I will use this as a place to record times, events, etc, so I can write a trip report for one of several railway organizations to which I belong … I tend to act as a typical railfan would in that I watch the operation of the train much more than the average person would taking into consideration my extreme interest in things and actions railway. (Archie – Canada)

> When I ride a train, I try to meet the staff and get to know them. That way they'll get to know you and tell you what is going on. I always take my camera and video so as to record anything of interest. As I normally travel on steam excursions there are photo stops. This is where you can meet some of the other passengers. (Ashley – New Zealand)

> I like to keep track of the performance of the train. Is it running to schedule? Is it (weight vs. speed) gaining or losing time and is this due to operating conditions or locomotive performance?… I might glance at a newspaper or magazine but never read anything so intensely that it interrupts my interest in the train's performance. (Edwin – New Zealand)

And, for some, simply the excitement of being on the train surpasses any desire to be inactive:

> My favourite activity (or is it inactivity?) is just sitting and looking out of the window at the passing scene. I find a total fascination with what is going past, whether this is on a short or long journey. I don't like to read because I might

miss something outside. Even on a night journey I still like to watch the lights going by, sometimes imagining what exists there and what people are doing. There is also the fascination of all the rolling stock one sees, branch tracks curving away, bridges and rivers to be crossed, industries with a guessing game as to what they manufacture. In summary, train travel is a very busy time for me. (Grant – New Zealand)

But leisure time is not only about activity; it is sometimes about rest and freedom from responsibility:

there have been many … times I think when I have got on a train and thought 'oh, I've got so many hours now just to rest' – particularly in India … So it was a real space just to be able to sit and relax and think 'I don't have to do anything now because this train is going to take me to the destination' so I can just sit and relax, just have some space and sleep and things like that. (Sandie – UK)

I think you kind of have time when you're on a train. You have time to kind of reflect on both the journey – which is generally a pleasurable experience because you're going somewhere you want to go or you have to go – but also you have time to – it's quite helpful looking out of the window and seeing the world go by, because it reminds you of what your relationship with that world is and it raises questions I think as you're travelling, that's what I find. It's different from driving because when you're driving you have to focus a bit more on the road in front of you because you're responsible for safety … So it feels okay, so you can travel with somebody else and that leaves your head free to do what you want to do. (Grace – UK)

I like the fact that you can sleep, read, listen to music, daydream or look at the scenery without any responsibility. (Jasper – UK)

Like Jasper, several respondents referred to the pleasure of sleeping on a train journey. Simon Williams (2003), drawing on Taylor (1993), suggests that sleep has become a leisure pursuit in recent times, and Chris Shaw (2004: 46) goes as far as to suggest that 'if we were honest enough, more than a few of us would put it down as a favourite pastime on … CVs'. Since the Middle Ages, sleep has become a privatized activity but there are still some public spaces where sleep is acceptable, the train being one of these (see Chapter 6 for a more complex consideration of this issue). For some respondents, sleep was not a possibility but an inevitability:

When I am commuting I usually try to go to sleep or I spend the time thinking whilst looking out the window at the scenery … My preference is to sit where it is quiet and almost invariably in the warmest carriage ... If I am travelling by myself on a longer journey I will choose a uni-directional seat ... Sometimes I take reading material with me but I usually find I cannot help but to fall asleep after about forty minutes with the movement of the train (especially if the interior is heated). (Jayne – UK)

Sometimes, of course, the journey is far too exciting for sleep:

[travelling through Kenya at night-time] we did try and settle down for the night but of course it's a new experience so one has very little sleep really ... it's far better to turn yourself around so that you can observe what's going on outside when you arrive at the stations, or you reach places that have got electric lights. (Aidan – UK)

Making Friends on Trains

Spending time with friends is an important leisure activity for many. Sometimes our friendships may be transitory, as Gordon's account demonstrates:

I am usually seen up the front talking to the Driver (some of them are good mates of mine). On the Units in Wellington, the Driver's compartment is to the right side of the Passenger compartment so the front seat is next to the driver! (Gordon – New Zealand)

In one of our many conversations with others (following an 'and what area do you work on?' type of question), we were told of the pleasure and freedom of talking to a fellow passenger you will never see again, a stranger regarding whom you have no responsibilities, an interesting person you might otherwise not have met. Rhian's and Jasper's experiences are relevant here:

I got involved once in a conversation with a fairly elderly woman who had just come back from a day where she had been acting as an examiner for young dancers, and I got talking to her about ballet and she had been involved as a dancer herself many years ago then she taught ballet and she had been in quite famous ballet companies. We had a really interesting discussion about women's bodies and dance ... Another very interesting conversation I had recently was when someone just started talking to me about their body piercing. That was fascinating she was just sort of launching ... into this display about her tattoos and various body pierced bits ... She got up in the middle of the carriage and she had these loose drawstring trousers on and she lifted up her trouser leg and had this Celtic tattoo. (Rhian – UK)

You can converse with people and will probably never meet them again. (Jasper – UK)

Stuart, Derek and Tony on the other hand – like Gayle – have 'train friends' (people whom they have friendly relationships with on the train but never meet anywhere else). Note also in Tony's account the references to the peculiarities of the British and to 'people watching': both themes that have arisen elsewhere in this chapter (and throughout the book):

There were only three carriages on the local train so if you sat in roughly the same place, you'd tend to see the same people every day. Well, you'd probably meet them on the station anyway, so you did get to know people … there were two or three gentlemen in particular, I think they were mainly lecturers or teachers who were at my sort of intellectual level, and we had plenty of conversations together. They could keep us going for a long time. And you were aware that there were other groups too – there were one or two women's groups, and there was one woman who was obviously very much the co-ordinator of it all because she had a loud voice and at the station you'd hear her greeting people and telling everyone the gossip, you know … it created a sort of family atmosphere on the train. (Stuart – UK)

Quite often on the platform, quite a lot of people are very British, like to get out their copies of *The Times*, *The Guardian*, *The Independent* or *The Telegraph*, and start reading … But we do talk yes, but quite a lot of people like to have a glance at their paper or listen to music, or they may close their eyes and relax and just enjoy the journey. Cos the journey in from Crewe [to Liverpool] is actually very pleasant – it's all through Cheshire countryside. It's not as though you're doing a lot of urban travelling – you're very shortly out of Crewe and into the countryside … The surroundings are generally pleasant, so you pass the time of day with people and talk. The topics are very wide-ranging – cars, the economy, politics, have you seen this article in *The Times* – but a lot of these people you'll have been – in my case, I've been travelling with them for six or seven years. You just pass the time of day with them really … work comes into it, yes, and all the home life stuff – not in any depth, but certainly people on the Crewe section know the name of my wife and what she does for a job, roughly where I live, what sort of car I drive – just sort of very mundane conversation really. (Derek – UK)

If I'm travelling by myself and there is no one to talk to, I will generally have a sort of nice two-seater. If there's a group of us – sometimes there's up to seven or eight of us – we will try and get two tables that are next to each other. But nobody minds if you close your eyes, nobody minds if you read your paper – it's quite relaxed. It's far more relaxed, and much more sociable, than if you're stuck on the motorway, because you'd be in the car, on your own, with just you and the radio. It's an altogether more gregarious activity going on the train. I find trains quite fascinating, a good place to people-watch. (Tony – UK)

Arguably, in a society where the 'celebrity represents success and achievement within the social world' (Marshall 1997: x), 'celebrity spotting' is perhaps the ultimate in 'people watching'. Charlie Dimmock's experience is again relevant here:

[celebrity] has made her instantly recognisable wherever she goes – but not by everybody, she reveals, as she recalls a chance meeting with an old school friend as she boarded a train ... 'We hadn't seen each other for 20 years and she still looked exactly the same. She came over and said "Hello Charlie how are you?", I said "I'm fine how are you?" and so it went on, and then she asked what I was up to now. I thought, oh gawd, I can't blow my own trumpet, so I just said "Bits and Bobs, doing one or two things", and she just nodded.
    ... It was half-term and children were standing on their seats trying to look over at me, but I thought I can't tell her what I'm doing now, it's too late, it'll seem like false modesty. Then the guard came and said "Oh, hi Charlie" as he clipped our tickets. She said, "You know a lot of people don't you?" So I mumbled something about using the train a lot. Then lots more people said hello, and eventually one lad came over and asked for an autograph ... My friend looked at me strangely, but didn't say a word. Then later I got a letter from her saying "You could have told me!"' (*e-motion* 3: 19–20)

Gayle, a fairly regular commuter from London to Stoke-on-Trent (on the Manchester Pullman), is happy to admit how much she enjoys spotting the occasional *Coronation Street* (British television soap opera set in Manchester) actor. And when on the train on or around the West Midlands, she sometimes wonders if the person behind her talking to their neighbour is really from *The Archers* (British radio soap opera set in the Midlands). Various train operating companies encourage this type of pursuit. Their on-board magazines include interviews with well-known public figures (usually from the television, film and music industries) who, amongst other things, sometimes travel by train. Thus, the train operating companies themselves achieve a kind of celebrity status, once (and still, to a lesser extent) achieved by the naming of the train after a famous person.
    Even the most sociable of us, however, do not want to 'make friends' on every train journey:

Occasionally I have got into conversations with people, that's been quite pleasurable as well. I try, I'm quite anti-social on trains, I don't particularly like to get in conversations with people on trains because I think my life is such that it's quite nice to have a period when I'm not talking. (Rhian – UK)

Some people are strange – you look diagonally across or you glance at them from time to time. I mean, a woman you would understand that they might want to avoid the gaze but even some men, you get the impression that they are actually avoiding you studiously, they do not want to relate to you, they do not want a conversation … But other times you say something and they respond and you get talking. Sometimes they talk too much and you think … 'This is getting boring and I would rather be working.' But you take a chance. (Stuart – UK)

There are two different kinds of companions on trains, those you want to avoid and those you want to be with – and I've got a great story about a moment on Marylebone station, when I played hide-and-seek with somebody who was doing some work for [name of organization] and I didn't find them very interesting or entertaining, and I just kept moving round this pillar, on the grounds that if I moved very slowly he wouldn't see that I was there. And I knew he was coming to Leamington, and I had to make sure that he didn't see me, and that I didn't get in the same carriage as him. Because if we had been in the same carriage we would have had to talk *all* the way from Marylebone to Leamington, and I didn't want to do that. So it just depends who you are with, doesn't it? Which is why, unless you're with somebody you want to be with, it's better to be on your own in a train, watching what's going by and making your own relationship with it, you know? (Grace – UK)

Compared with most of the data we have collected, Kenneth's view is perhaps the most extreme:

you wouldn't want to sit next to a talker because you want to get on with what you are doing and not interact with mad people. (Kenneth – UK)

The Train as a Place Giving Access to Leisure

The most common-sense view of the relationship between the train and leisure is of the train as a vehicle that gives access to leisure. Certainly, in Britain since the mid-1800s, the train has served this purpose for both upper and lower classes:

There is a very large class of English folk who, not liking foreign habits or the cost of foreign travel, enjoy our magnificent seaside resorts … so long as they are kept fairly clear of the 'tripper', who brings in his train the donkeys, the brass bands, the organs, the Punch and Judy, and other nuisances …

Middle-aged people will recollect the scare produced at Brighton by the invasion of thousands who wanted their 'sniff of the briny', and enjoyed their eight hours of the seaside very heartily and happily. Dignified Brighton, residential Brighton shut itself up on 'trippers' days', but it was not to be dislodged. (Bernard H. Becker *Holiday Haunts* 1884 cited by Delgado 1977: 42–3)

In the grim lives that many children in Victorian and Edwardian Britain were compelled to lead, there was at least one day in the year that was remembered with pleasure – the annual outing. Sunday schools, charities or any society concerned with the welfare of children set aside a day in the summer to give children an outing in the country or by the sea. Possibly it was the only holiday the children had. The preparations were made and the outing paid for in part or whole by charitably minded people who devoted their spare time organising such events. (Delgado 1977: 77)

The rivalry between private railway companies in the nineteenth century to attract holiday passengers (Swinglehurst 1974) was replaced in the mid-twentieth century by competition between the (then) nationalized railways and road and air travel. Of course, it was not just the cost that was at issue here for, as Graeme Davison (2004: x) notes: 'If car worship had a heyday it was in the decades after World War II. Contemporary poets and novelists reached for the high-flown metaphors of love or religious ecstasy to describe the mystic union between car and driver.' And, with reference to the aeroplane, Alan Delgado (1977: 157) suggests: 'The aeroplane, like some magic carpet, conveyed the holidaymaker to sunshine and freedom away from the enclosed island in which he spends most of his [*sic*] days.' Perhaps this explains why, for some people, aeroplanes are associated with access to leisure, whereas trains are associated with commuting and access to work. Maybe it also explains why some of the contemporary train operating companies are keen to make the trains seem more like aeroplanes. Ironically, with falling air prices and many more routes and services, the aeroplane is increasingly becoming a commuter choice for some.

As Rosie notes, many people choose different types of transport for different types of journeys:

Getting in-between cities, that is good. Because that's the only thing that is hassling about having a car, is trying to negotiate new cities that you don't know, trying to find parking spaces. Whereas, particularly if you're going somewhere for the day ... I wouldn't dream of going by car. I think the difference is that, I'd rather go on trains on day trips and things, but on long journeys I would just rather go in the car.

This is not to say that people use the train to access leisure facilities and not for going on holiday any more. In our respondent group we have examples of people who use local, national and international trains for many of their leisure activities. Within the UK, Tony, for example, speaks of a local train service; Rosie (above) limits her journeys by train to day-trips, and Gayle – well, Gayle uses trains for everything:

> [talking about the use of a local line] it'll be a mixture of shopping trips, using the train to get to work, college maybe – all sorts of different social purposes – I think it's quite interesting the pattern of use of this line here, you get some of the trains coming in. The ones we see around eleven o'clock in the morning – they tend to be as busy as the train that gets in at quarter to nine, the commuter train. That line is quite a busy service, but the eleven o'clock one is quite as busy, especially in the school holidays. (Tony – UK)

> I use the train a lot for leisure (as well as for work). Basically, if I want to go anywhere in Britain, I go on the train. (Gayle)

Others travel by train even further afield:

> The other [thing I like about trains] is the distances one can travel by train. [name of partner] and I have both travelled from Rugby to Vienna by train, while [name of friends] and I have done a return trip from Ostende to Copenhagan in a single journey (fifteen hours overnight) … And of course, travelling at 300 kph (186 mph) on land is a thrill which can only be enjoyed on a daily basis by train travel. (Philip – UK)

> We travelled from Mombasa to Nairobi … and back again. (Aidan – UK)

> We went from ultramodern downtown Beijing to sooty old industrial cities to tiny little primitive farming villages in Inner Mongolia, with no plumbing, where a family invited a group of Westerners into their home just because they saw us passing. (Ron – USA)

And whilst the train provides us with the opportunity for such adventure, as we highlighted earlier, it simultaneously provides us with a space for reflection and relaxation:

> [talking about travelling through India] I think there are times when you are travelling and you're just feeling so bombarded by another culture you're in, that the train provides personal space so you can escape back to your own culture. So I have always taken a Walkman when I'm travelling and take a selection of tapes, usually ones that I've picked because they're my favourite tapes, or I have made compilations of songs and things that have meaning

about home. So at times when I've had to get on the train – like when I felt so vulnerable on that journey, you just put your Walkman on and it takes you back home. You can shut your eyes and you can be back in your own home if you wanted to be, sort of thing. So it is that sort of space just to remember who you are, sometimes when all around you is so different and you've just had enough of it for a while. (Sandie – UK)

Reflections

In this chapter we have looked at the relationship between leisure and the train. We began the chapter with a quote from Eddie which highlighted some of the ways in which people can enjoy trains. Leisure on or around the train can be undertaken for its intrinsic value and/or to fill train time. For leisure, we can act entirely outside the train or within the space inside the train, or can transcend the enclosed train space and engage with the places and spaces outside the train. This challenges the traditional and prevailing definition of the tourist and tourism. Our critique, however, is not limited to leisure and the train but is relevant also to an analysis of the relationship between work and the train. Although we have consigned issues of work and leisure to two separate chapters they are not completely discrete. Those who engage in leisure activities on the train may also at different points of the journey undertake productive labour. And one person's work activity (which may possibly reflect their own position in the consumer/quality drive of contemporary society) may impinge on another's enjoyment of nostalgia and romance:

[explaining why travel very rarely on trains] I did used to like train journeys. There is something about them, I don't know what it is. You're on your own yet you're not on your own, and you're in a carriage and yet you can see so much outside that you don't feel confined. But trains were nice in those days, they were clean, and had a nice comfortable seat, a good table, the food was good – it's not like today. They all just get their laptops out today don't they? We went on this day trip to Manchester from here and they all got their laptops out – it's the way of life now isn't it? (Jessica – UK)

–5–

Working on the Line
Working Patterns and the Train

Introduction

> I probably spend say half the time going down [to work in London], on the laptop and half reading. I might be reading the Ecologist or something like that, so it is probably about half and half because the battery on my laptop won't last the whole journey anyway, so I have to ration it ... On the Birmingham line there are newer trains that have got plug-in points ... What I try to do is put in the normal working hours in the day, seven and a half to eight hours, particularly if I have chosen to travel later in the day. I feel that I am travelling in working time and I should be using it. If I start at six-thirty in the morning or I travel the night before, then that is not normal working time so I might be less inclined to do work.
>
> Stuart – UK

Continuing our consideration of the relationship between the train and leisure and work, in this chapter we consider the experience of both railway workers and railway passengers. We explore the historically specific experience of those who work for the rail companies today and the experience of individuals who use the train to travel to work and/or as a space in which to undertake productive labour. Stuart (above) (a rail passenger) highlights a number of issues – for example, in relation to new technologies and to the 'working day' – of relevance to both railway workers and railway passengers. As Miriam Glucksmann (2000: 18–19) notes:

> Recognition that 'work' is not synonymous with paid employment, and does not take place only in a structurally distinct 'economy' in industrial societies, but may be undertaken within a variety of socio-economic relations and take a variety of forms, raises questions that go to the very heart of the concept of 'work'. Work may be embedded in non-work activities, and the identical activity may constitute 'work' in some situations but not others.

Glucksmann's point that work can be paid or unpaid, and can take place in the public or the private sphere, is relevant to our sense of personal identity and often has implications for our social contacts. Time is significant to any consideration of work, not least because, for people in regular employment, the day is usually organized around work, and a person in full-time employment is likely to spend more hours of a (waking) day working than doing anything else (Adam 1995). Space is also relevant in that workers are subjected to specific architectural and managerial constructions of organizational space, but some workers are more able than others to exert control over their working environment (Halford 2004).

Here, we consider the significance of these issues for those who, in various ways, work on the railways. Yet, as previously noted, the issues considered are not totally discrete from those we explored in Chapter 4. Ian Dey (1989: 466) suggests that 'work-time itself is contrasted with time spent on activities defined as 'not work', work as leisure time or play time ... [W]ork time ... implies a period during which work is undertaken primarily for payment.' Like Glucksmann (2000) above, however, we would argue that this raises a problem in terms of defining work. Some occupations, or tasks within an occupation, are perceived – and sometimes experienced – as more like leisure than work (e.g. artists, actors, writers, tour guides or gardeners). Furthermore, discussions concerning work may take place during leisure activities (e.g. during a game of golf, or during an evening social event) and leisure sometimes takes place during the working day (e.g. 'popping out', surfing the net, playing computer games or doing the crossword). Some of these complexities are relevant to both railway workers and passengers on a train, who all may engage in 'non-work' in work time or work in 'non-work' time. Thus, the train is a further example of a place and space where work and leisure activities overlap.

Railway Workers' Experiences

Nostalgia and Romance

As Tim Strangleman (2004) notes, before the privatization of the railways in Britain many of the senior managers in British Railways had worked their way up though the ranks. This was a time when 'being a railwayman' was associated with a sense of pride; enthusiasm for the railways was a significant motivation for individuals who pursued a railway career. Those of our respondents who themselves had some experience of the railways at this time spoke of working up through the ranks on a variety of jobs:

During the war … the government took over the railways, and they were nationalized. I was working for the London North Eastern Railway, like my dad was, from the 1930s. He had been in Sheffield in engineering, and it was a terrible time. They all closed down, the steelworks. Eventually a friend offered him a job but said he would have to start right at the beginning again, start at the bottom. And he did, he started at the bottom on the railways and worked his way up to be a locomotive superintendent, where there were big depots … it meant that about every six months we moved house because you had to for promotion. (Jessica – UK)

I started on the railways at the age of fifteen. I started as a cleaner cos obviously you worked your way up to being a driver … in them days when I started it was steam locos and you worked your way. Basically what you were doing then was waiting for dead men's shoes, basically, all the time … You started as a cleaner, a fireman, and then what we call a pass fireman, you became a regular driver. It actually took me twenty-five years to become a regular driver – it took me eight years to pass out to be a driver but then, as I say, I was then a pass fireman, so then I was waiting for that period from eight years to twenty-five years to become a registered driver. (Ben – UK)

[when I worked for BR I was a] signalman, guard, technical officer – various things really! Mainly on the operating side … I certainly decided to hop from one job to another. I've always been interested in the operational side of railways … I suppose my most enjoyable job was a guard. Quite a lot of variety and travel, freight and passenger. Probably enjoyed them both in different ways … But then, yes, you could be collecting tickets on one day and working the freight train Settle to Carlisle the following day. There was a lot of variety, which was nice. I enjoyed that. (Tony – UK)

However, affection for the job by traditional railway workers was considered by some – during Beeching and beyond – to be a disadvantage and even the cause of the unstable state of the industry. With nationalization came modernization and rationalization, all of which had huge implications for the workforce in terms of the number of people employed and the status associated with traditional railway occupations (Strangleman 2004). In addition, the 'pro-car' and 'anti-railway' agenda of the Conservative Party in the 1980s led to even less State support for the railways (Strangleman 2004). As Strangleman (2004) notes, all of this has also had an impact on the wider community:

in the numerous autobiographies of railway workers who lived through the period, the emphasis is on the stability and continuity that the railway represented to the whole community. The rural railway stations and branch lines were the links between the traditional communities and the modern world.

Strangleman is suggesting here that railways represented all that was British (see Chapter 3) and that the breaking up of British Railways threatened the British identity and way of life. Grace (UK) agrees:

> Whereas here it feels like you can't, and I think that's what I'm most cross about, because what the breaking up of British Rail has meant is that there's no cohesion, there's no – and actually that lack of cohesion is partly a mirror image of what's going on in society as a whole, in a sense. I'm very cross about the loss of that to a variety of differently-oriented companies, who have no relationship to each other and actually don't give a damn about contacts and connections and so on, and in some senses even Railtrack itself, which appears to have no real commitment to safety or security. So it feels like decisions made by the government, under Thatcher and subsequently under Blair, have undermined an important system of communication. It started under Beeching, I suppose, with all sorts of branch lines being closed so that people in rural areas couldn't get to anywhere else.

New systems bring with them new ways of working, and long-term railway workers have a sense of nostalgia for the past. Compare Peter Parker's account with that of Ben's:

> The driver grieved over past glories. Once an engine-driver was what most boys wanted to be; now nobody bothered to stop and have a word with him about the journey, good or bad. Once the King of the Road, rising from cleaner, through fireman, to the throne on the footplate; now he was in unglamorous exile. Once he was inseparable from his locomotive, his castle and his home, cherishing it and its reputation for meeting the timetable, frying breakfast on the shovel; now he and it were computer-programmed through the depot. Once sure of his place, superior, knowing the shedmaster; now he was adrift in the impersonal professional world of area managers and operating managers ... Gradually the driver's grip on things was in truth slipping. It was as if esteem was lost with the loss of steam, self-esteem and other people's. (Parker 1991: 258–9)

> There used to be [camaraderie], yes, but certainly since privatization that has gone ... [name of train operating company] drivers are what we call millennium drivers, they're straight off the street, you might say, in their early twenties, and they've gone driving and within twelve months they are a driver. They're given these nice smart uniforms and they look down at us

as if we're something they've scraped off the bottom of their shoe, to be honest … But in our days we used to work on all sorts of trains. But within us own company, yes, there is a camaraderie, and certainly there was before the split up. And certainly more in steam days than what there is now because in the steam days you used to know all the station staff, you used to know all the shunters, you used to know all the signalmen. Whereas now we don't know anybody. The signalmen are so remote, signal boxes are far and few between nowadays so all we know of a signalman is a voice on the end of a telephone, we don't know who they are, they don't know us. (Ben – UK)

Since privatization, then, the railway labour market is fragmented; within most sections of the railway workforce the pay is low and there is little long-term job security (Strangleman 2004). In addition, railway workers have been given a new corporate image. Many personnel have job titles that make them sound more important than before – for example, guards have been replaced by train managers, buffet staff by retail service managers and (our personal 'favourite') ticket collectors by revenue protection officers – and uniforms are bright with shiny buttons. It is possible to argue therefore that the railway worker has been 'McDonaldized': George Ritzer (1993), citing McDonald's as a paradigm case, argues that rationalization – where more and more emphasis is placed on efficiency, predictability, calculability, replacement of human by non-human technology and control of uncertainty – is occurring throughout America and, increasingly, other societies. Employers typically use techniques of socialization and control to ensure the employees have little or no autonomy, and that their attitudes and demeanour, as well as their movements, are subject to managerial control.

Some of us who travel on the railways, rather than work on them, are aware of these issues:

It is very nice when they have human announcers, but they are computerized a lot now, which is a bit sad. It's taking away the human element, and that is part of the fun of trains, having real characters, but it is labour-intensive and they have tried to get rid of everybody they can. (Henry – UK)

They can't feel proud about what they do … we lived very close to … one of the major stations in North West London, and one of the members of our church congregation had been the station master, and part of his responsibility as he saw it was to make the station garden look wonderful … And you kind of feel when people worked for the railway in the past it was significant, it mattered. If you go back to when we were children, the man who ran the station had a really serious role didn't he? ... He saw himself as a significant player in the local community. Whereas now, if you work for [name of train operator] trains, you're not, you're absolutely not, even if you're a train driver. For which you needed an incredible amount of training and whatever, it's very sad. I just think we've lost [something]. (Grace – UK)

For me one of the big problems at the moment is the deterioration of conditions for people who work on the railways. It must be horrendous at the moment for staff who work for [name of train operating company]. (Gayle)

I have never had an encounter with railway staff that's been anything other than courteous. I think that, in the main, the frontline staff have a hell of a job to do and they have always been helpful, particularly at Crewe – there is one woman who works there in Passenger Relations who has been superb ... made sure I have got a taxi and everything. (Rhian – UK)

Like others represented here, we too feel some sense of loss in relation to the British railway system. But, as two individuals who still love trains and (usually) train travel, we feel saddened by the fact that a significant minority of the current and retired railway workers we know actively decide not to use their free passes for railway travel (for an example, see Chapter 2). So we feel pleased by the fact that Jim uses at least one of his passes each year to travel to London, specifically to buy himself a new Liberty tie. Karen's connections, on the other hand, make us quite envious:

I have the luxury of phoning my sister or brother in law (both railway operators) to find out the whereabouts of the train, if it's on time, running late or cancelled. I often phone or text them when on the train to find out why the train has stopped or is running late.

Locating the Contemporary Railway Worker

For the contemporary railway worker there are still pleasures to be had through work, in terms of personal and political satisfaction (see Fig. 10):

If you've ever driven a train there can be an immense thrill of power and legitimate high speed. Feeling a diesel loco turning out 2,580 horsepower while hauling a 400–ton train at ninety mph is something which is never forgotten. As a railway operator, there is the challenge of keeping the system running in all weathers, something which still gives me a buzz – and a cause to work

Figure 10 Bob the train driver. Copyright: Robert Hart. By permission.

unsocial hours for a privilege. I couldn't do my job as well as I do without being interested in it to a degree which allows me to draw on a personal knowledge and wealth of experience gained over many, many years. (Philip – UK)

My first 'proper' job was a Technical Officer for InterCity, British Railways; partly because my work colleagues would voluntarily furnish me with information and partly because I became genuinely interested in the advantages trains had over other forms of public transport … I had begun to realize that even if a pollution-free fuel was invented this would still not solve the problem of congestion on the roads and that travelling by car was not the future of sustainable transport design. (Elaine – UK)

Whilst recognizing the problems caused by organizational change, perhaps we need to be careful not to overemphasize the loss that the British railway worker has experienced. As Strangleman (2004) notes, railway workers are by no means the only workforce to have suffered from a loss of their occupational identity and are not the only workforce thought to have engaged in 'real' British labour. We could end this section by arguing that the organizational change in the railways clearly demonstrates how the romantic railway of our dreams has been replaced by the railway of consumerism and quality, but it is important to think further than our nostalgia for the steam-train driver (see Fig. 11).

Figure 11 Jon the 'trolley man'. Copyright: Gillian Reynolds. By permission.

Just a brief glance at two editions of the South West Trains' customer magazine, *e-motion*, demonstrates that there are many different types of railway worker:

IMPROVING YOUR RAILWAY
As reported in the last issue of e-motion, Network Rail is currently carrying out major weekend track improvement work between London Waterloo and Wimbledon. This work is vital to all engineers to renew most of the sets of points in the area.(*e-motion* 3: 4).

PUTTING PEOPLE FIRST
Beverley Shears ... Human Resources Director South West Trains, reveals how putting employees at centre stage is bringing real benefits to passengers ...
We are responsible for the recruitment, training and development of more than 5,000 employees at South West Trains. We have to ensure that the right people are in the right place at the right time in order to deliver the service that our 300,000 passengers expect daily. As the largest and busiest commuter train operating company in the UK, it's a huge and complex operation – and quite a logistical challenge ...
    We are changing the culture of South West Trains so that it is more employee-centred and customer-focused. We are aiming to exceed the expectations of passengers by not only providing a high-quality, reliable train service but also a committed, motivated and well-trained workforce. (*e-motion* 3: 11)

HIGHER STANDARDS AND CLEANER TRAINS
WE HAVE TAKEN FURTHER steps to improve passengers' travelling experience by introducing a new intensive training course for employees who keep our carriages clean.
The new Train Presentation Centre of Excellence at Fratton steps up the level of training given to employees with a week-long course that combines classroom-based learning and practical, on-train assessments.
Keeping the South West Trains fleet clean is a massive job. Each train is thoroughly cleaned every night, as well as at regular intervals throughout the day whenever possible. South West Trains employs around 300 train presentation staff who clean more than 1,000 carriages a day. (*e-motion* 4: 4)

LOST AND FOUND
In our regular series looking behind the scenes of South West Trains we talk to Trevor Creasey ... Lost Property and Central Despatch Assistant, about the weird and wonderful world of the lost property department at London Waterloo. (*e-motion* 4: 11)

The 'world of the lost property department' may be 'weird and wonderful', but other departments may seem more confusing. As one of our respondents noted:

> I ... worked for BR when I was about seventeen – Equal Opportunities didn't exist for British Railways and my Dad got me a job as he did my mum and sister before me. I worked in a department where I never quite understood the connection between what I did and trains, but I'm sure there must have been some link. (Karen – UK)

Clearly, many of these occupations are relevant to the railway of consumerism and quality, but we have previously noted (e.g. see Introduction) that the discourses of romance and nostalgia and of consumerism and quality sometimes clash. Many of the same people who enjoy the stories and sights of railways past also want – even demand – a competitive, efficient railway service.

Rail Travellers

Part of our own shared work history is the three years we spent in the early 1990s sharing an office whilst working towards our respective doctorates. During this time we both taught part-time alongside our PhD studies. Amongst other tasks, we were each given some seminar work teaching sociology to Business Studies students. In our search for articles to tempt these students to develop a 'sociological imagination' (an understanding of the relationship between biography, history and the social structure – Mills 1970), we sought out articles that were theoretically 'lightweight', interesting and relevant to this particular group of students. For the week when unemployment was the topic we found two articles – one in the *New Statesman* (Hogarth and Daniel 1987) and one in *New Statesman and Society* (Manning 1989) – both on long-distance commuters.

In sum, the basic argument of both of these articles was that, to avoid unemployment, increasing numbers of workers, from professional/managerial to unskilled manual groups, were not 'getting on their bikes', as the Conservative MP Norman Tebbit had reportedly urged them to do, but taking what Manning (1989) called the 'Tebbit Express': that is, living and working away from home in the week and travelling home at weekends. Hogarth and Daniel (1987) argued that this kind of commuting had long been the pattern of certain occupational groups like commercial travellers and some types of construction workers who follow contracts on building sites. It is also characteristic of some upwardly mobile single young people in the provinces before they become established in their own households. Hogarth and Daniel (1987: 11) argued, however, that the distinguishing characteristic of the new pattern of commuting was that it had spread to mainstream occupations; to 'people in the prime of life with families', who adopt this pattern as a permanent way of life – working in the South of England and returning to family life in the North, where it is cheaper for families to live.

Since the mid-1990s, Gayle has been a 'full-time' commuter and Gillian an occasional one, although Gillian has rarely stayed away during the week and until recently neither has Gayle: both travelling daily from Stoke-on-Trent to various destinations in the West Midlands, especially Coventry (in fact, with general reference to trains and railways, Coventry has become as relevant to us as Dawlish and the Fens – see Introduction and Chapter 1). As to our occupation and our gender, neither Hogarth and Daniel (1987) nor Manning (1989) mentioned academics; women, noted Hogarth and Daniel (1987), were only present in the occasional instance when they were the main (usually sole) breadwinner. But from our (admittedly more recent) experience we know that many women and some academics (obviously we include female academics here) use the train to travel to and from work. We do acknowledge, however, as Linda McDowell (1999: 129) points out, that: '[i]n general women travel shorter distances as a consequence of their childcare responsibilities ... although these relationships are affected by social class, credentials and salary levels and by ethnicity'. The fact that through the latter part of the 1990s neither of us had the care of young children made it easier for us to commute.

Our personal and research experience also leads us to challenge the rather sad and weary – and, in different ways, sexist – picture that Whittaker (1995) and Horne (undated) paint of the commuter (not least in the Midlands):

I hated fighting for a seat on the 7.18 from New Street with a load of Brummie businessmen. They thought they were early birds, but to me they looked more like Christmas turkeys. I could laugh at them but the laughter had a nervous edge to it. (Whittaker 1995: 136)

I am sitting on the floor of New Street Station, leaning against a white-tiled pillar, doodling into a sketch book ... A train has emptied ... Together this group represents a social scientist's wet dream, a near-full demographic spectrum of working people in the Midlands: both sexes, most races; some in jeans, some still in overalls, a few in mini-skirts and the rest in suit-and-tie or suit-and-heels. They have come from the Coventry train ... It is Friday night but they don't seem pleased. Most of them still have a bus to wait for, a taxi to hail, or another train to catch. (Horne, undated)

We demonstrated in Chapter 4 that the train is not just a vehicle for getting from A to B, but an object of – and space and place of – leisure. For some, as we have seen here, it is also a space and place in which to prepare for work and undertake work activities.

Transition Space: Preparing for Work and Home

As we noted in Chapter 4, the train can be a place in which to relax. This applies to commuters as well as those engaging in journeys for leisure. Some of our respondents spoke specifically about train space as a physical and psychological space in which to prepare both for home and for work:

> The great thing about a train is that – particularly at the start, but also at the end of the day – I find it a very much more relaxing environment to travel in, because you're not doing the driving and you're not sitting in traffic ... Coming home at night, no matter how bad the day is, you know you haven't got to immediately get behind that wheel and drive all the way home – I tend to look forward to whatever is planned for the evening. The day at work has ended ... Home life begins with the journey home. I will think about things we are going to do in the evening, I generally think about things that are not at all to do with work ... I am very able to divorce myself from work really, and I think the train helps me to do that – it provides an almost natural break between work and home, the train does, whereas the car would be linked to work and to home. It's a very strange thing – it's like a continuum if you use the car between work and home – whereas the train is divorced more. The car – which is associated with home – is at Crewe. It never ever goes to Liverpool, which is where the work is. (Derek – UK)

> I do sometimes read, sometimes I sleep. When I was working in London it was really helpful because I was knackered by the time I got on a train, and I'd sleep all the way to Leamington, or Birmingham, depending on where I was living. It seemed good, something very soothing about the rhythm of the train I think. I'm not a great sleeper but I can sleep on trains if I need to, so that's good. And because I used to work twelve-hour days in London, I didn't use my journeys for working. Lots of my colleagues did lots. But I never did, I saw them [journeys] as time for reflection or sleep. (Grace – UK)

For some, though, the train offers neither the privacy nor the opportunity for release of tension that some people feel they need. Henry (UK) suggests some reasons for this:

> This man had two neighbours and he lives somewhere in Yorkshire, Leeds way, and he said 'I've got a neighbour on this side, a neighbour on that side, they both get into their cars at the same time, and they both drive to the same place of employment, they both work in the same office.' They want their space, they don't want to share it, and they do exactly the same journey to the same office, I think they both worked for the council somewhere. There's a terrific propensity to have your own lovely private space ... You know, a lot of arcade games are set up like motorways – I mean you wouldn't do it at that pace, you wouldn't race at the same pace as you see in those arcade games, but perhaps the driving is a form of relaxation and excitement and freedom in between work constraint and home constraint ... Whereas a train is quite passive, they have to sit there like this, but actually being in the car is a bit of freedom.

According to Graeme Davison (2004: ix), cars are 'homes away from home, little oases of privacy, where drivers sit alone with their thoughts ... ': they are also a powerful 'status symbol' (see Chapter 2). Although, as we suggest below, some people compete for private space and/or are keen to prove their status by where they sit on the train, we also have evidence (for example, see Chapter 4 and Chapter 6) that there are times when train travellers enjoy the companionship that train travel affords. What we are saying here is that we do not totally agree (see Chapter 6 for further discussion) with Whittaker (1995: 136) when he writes:

> Ideally we'd all like four seats and a table to ourselves, the space and privacy to take off our shoes, bite our nails, give up on the crossword without feeling publicly stupid. Nostalgia merchants go on about the Golden Age of rail travel, sharing compartments, talking to each other, enduring delays and cockups with real Blitz spirit. There may be a small element of truth in it, but it's mostly legend. We hated the smell of each other's lives really. What we were yearning for all that time was the freedom of the car age: the freedom to pick our noses, to flash the V-sign at people and make a quick escape.

The Office Now Boarding

For some the train is definitely a place where work takes place, not least because commuting has become a far more significant part of the working day for much of the population of Britain: 'The 60 minute commuter belt of the 1970s, which widened to 90 minutes in the 90s, has burst the two-hour barrier. This commuting time used to be dead time, however with the advent of mobile phones and laptops it means we can work on trains, phone friends, and even do our shopping' (Henley Centre 2003).

Shared Space
For those who wish to undertake work on the train it is necessary to seek out a space in which to construct an office (Letherby and Reynolds 2003). Constructing such a 'place' can be likened to contemporary 'real' office practices of open access and 'hot-desking'. In hot-desking (sometimes called location-independent working), 'workers do not have their own desks but are allocated work space according to their personal needs, keeping their personal belongings in lockers or filing cabinets' (Quinion 1996: unpaginated). It is thought that the name might derive from 'hot bunking', the name given to the sharing of sleeping space by sailors on watch in wartime (Quinion 1996), which is also relevant, of course, to those of our respondents who enjoy a nap whilst on the train (see Chapter 4).

When wanting to undertake work activities, our respondents found that sharing train space with others involved competition and issues of privacy. Kenneth, for example, outlines his own needs:

Kenneth: ... the ideal situation is where you have a whole table to yourself but that isn't always possible. But minimally you want the seat next to you free so you can put things on it because there is usually a big pile of papers that's worth spreading out ... There was a chap the other day ... and when [he] went to the bar or the buffet I moved over there and had to move some of his stuff over the table so I could spread my things out, so there was a bit of negotiation there.

Gayle: Did he say anything when he came back?

Kenneth: No, no he smiled, very friendly. I don't think he was deliberately commandeering the table for himself, he was just using the space available to him but I do think that people behave in a very territorial way in trains.

Whereas Kenneth requires as big a space as possible, Gayle, on the other hand, attempts to create a private working space. Her account highlights the fact that shared working space is not just about territorial quantity of space but also involves negotiating appropriate etiquette for private work in a public space:

Even though it's not as easy to work, I prefer the two-seater ones because they're a bit more private ... One [woman] was on a mobile phone continually for an hour. She was making call after call, and being called – it was constant. So the other woman said to her 'I think it's really inappropriate that you keep using your mobile phone on the train.' And the woman using the phone said 'some of us work, you know'. So she was working, she was doing her job. For me, mobile phones get in the way of me doing my job, whereas she had to use her mobile phone for her job. (Gayle)

The space in which the work takes place – the train carriage – may not initially conjure up images of public libraries, but, in terms of 'private' work being undertaken in a very 'public' space, several respondents noted the similarities and differences with this other, perhaps more obvious, public working space. For example:

He [she is relating a conversation with a colleague here] said 'going on a train is like being in a public library, and I really like these places that are public but people are doing things on their own'. That's really interesting, isn't it? You have this little space that's your own and it is similar to a library except that they don't have signs up saying 'no talking'. (Gayle)

If someone were to come and look over your shoulder in a library, you'd think they were abominably rude. But if I'm sitting over the table [on a train] from someone who is working, I'm really itching to look at what it is they're doing. So people are forcing that private work to become public. (Gillian)

As Jane Ribbens and Rosalind Edwards (1998: 8) point out, '"public" and "private" are tricky and ambiguous concepts, which cannot be identified by reference to physical locations of home, neighbourhood, workplace or government'. Like the library, the train is a public space but, unlike the library, there are obvious rules of interaction neither between passengers nor between passengers and staff:

It doesn't happen very often, but people do try to talk to me when I'm working. I've got this piece of work, and I've got to do it before I get into work. And I leave it for the train. And if someone tries to talk to me on the train, then that's difficult to cope with. (Gayle)

There are a number of times when I have travelled when there have been quite a few incidents that have been quite interesting that have distracted me from working. There seems to be quite a lot of hassle that people working as guards on the train have to put up with. That can be quite distracting because you are put in a position where you think 'do I get involved'? (Rhian – UK)

Of course, working on the train is not always a solitary activity; we ourselves have experience of working with others, including each other, on the train (see Fig. 12). As we talked excitedly about this book, we wondered if our fellow passengers were as interested in our conversation as we would have been. Working together on the 7.04 from Stoke-on-Trent one Monday morning we were sharply reminded of one persistent gender stereotype):

> *(SCENE: Gillian and Gayle sitting opposite each other at a table. Each is reading through some (different) notes. Gayle's large work diary is on the table. The train manager walks down the train and Gayle says 'tickets, Gillian'. As he clips the tickets the following exchange takes place.)*
>
> Train manager: Good morning, having a 'Girl's Day Out' are we?
> Gillian: No.
> Train manager: Oh, I'm sorry. I thought you were together.
> Gayle: We are, we are going to work together.

We feel sure that this exchange would not have taken place if we were two men. Just as we assume that doctors, solicitors and artists are male (and put 'lady' or 'woman' before such a noun if the job is undertaken by a woman), we 'naturally' assume that all commuters are male and that

Figure 12 Not a 'girls' day out': the authors at work. Copyright: Gillian Reynolds and Gayle Letherby. By permission.

women remain more 'appropriately' in the private sphere (e.g. McDowell 1999; Letherby 2003). In addition, as Linda McDowell (1999) notes, workplaces are constructed as gendered places; it seems that the train as a place of work is also 'masculinized'.

Hierarchical Space
It is possible to argue that the reason that the train manager did not recognize us as workers was because at some level we did not look the part. Derek's experience seems to support this:

> On a rare occasion [that I found myself standing] I would park myself in First Class – oh yes. I have no qualms about that! And generally speaking, train staff in that situation are very understanding. But it helps if you look the part – suit and tie. I am sure that plays a part in the decisions that staff take about whether to ask you to move on or not. (Derek – UK)

Neither of us wears suits and we were not obviously displaying any of the technology of the modern white-collar worker. If Whittaker's perception is anything to go by, these are the ways to identify a commuter:

> These businessmen had no time for chatting anyway, they were too preoccupied with findings ways to look important. Mobile phones and laptops are the currency now, but things used to be more modest. The snap of locks on a briefcase, the click of a Parker biro, some ticks and scribbles on a document, such simple gestures were enough to mark you out as a vital cog in British commerce. (Whittaker 1995: 137)

Not only does Whittaker's account exclude women; it also implies that the only people who commute hold senior positions in the workforce. Clearly, some parts of the commuter train are occupied by such persons:

> In the business area, in the area where I sit, there are lots and lots of other people doing exactly the same, nearly every businessman who has got his laptop will get it out. (Stuart – UK)

Additionally, the train operating companies are aware of the need to market their facilities to people or businesses, who (they feel) are more likely to be willing to pay for extra resources: 'In First Class there's plenty of space on the fixed table in front of each seat to catch up with work' (*Hotline* 2003). Sometimes our respondents are resentful about this:

> I'm not sure that company policy actually allows us to travel first class, unless you are above a certain grade. I'm sometimes jealous. I see lots of other

people travelling First Class and I think, you know, 'Are they a lot higher than me, or are their firms better off?' I mean our company hasn't been making a profit until fairly recently so I think they have cut everything to the bone, and those are the sort of things you don't get – First Class travel. I sort of agreed a budget with my project manager when I started this scheme, which was that I wouldn't spend more than a thousand pounds a month on expenses and in fact it's usually six or seven hundred pounds a month. Because a lot of the other applicants lived much nearer to London you see, so the cost of using them would be much less ... so I tried to make myself sound attractive and not too expensive. (Stuart – UK)

Clearly, working space on trains is hierarchically distributed. This concept of hierarchical space refers to the ways in which the design of buildings (especially administrative buildings) reflects the social relations being conducted by the organization within the architectural space. Interesting analogies are possible here with first or club class being comparable to the 'director's suite' – where one person is allocated a disproportionately large space – and standard class mirroring the cramped conditions of the most menial clerks. Those of us who do not travel first class but who attempt to work on the train sometimes find this frustrating:

that's one of the things that bugs me about [name of train company] is that they cater so much for those in First Class. 'They're so important, and they have to work, and we have to give them little signs to put on their desks – tables – that show they don't want to be disturbed, and we must give them email and internet facilities – this, that and the other.' But every person on the 7.04 train has got their laptop out or reads. (Gayle)

On the other hand Kenneth – incidentally, a much less frequent traveller – has a more pragmatic view:

I would never pay myself to travel First Class as it's a ridiculous waste of money but if someone else is paying, it seems no reason why not, and yes, I did have a First Class ticket on the grounds that I would be working on the train. But I can't say it obviously made much difference ... All I want is a table. (Kenneth – UK)

There are, of course, always more clerks than directors employed, and problems of space therefore impinge disproportionately at that level. Similarly on trains, when difficulties occur it is likely to be those in standard class who are most affected. Standard class, then, represents the antithesis of the director's suite and, like clerical workers, occupants of standard class are more likely to have their work disrupted by circum-stances beyond their control:

It's a work-shaped space. A bit like a Portakabin on wheels. (Gillian)

Despite this, large numbers of people are still travelling (by train) long distances between places of work and home; also, within employment, workers travel longer distances for a particular task. Many of the routes used by workers on trains are now outside the traditional commuter zones of the South-East. But similar problems emerge, such as overcrowding and stretched facilities. These impinge on tasks that have been planned, but then cannot be achieved:

the train was late and I then was rerouted to various places and it ended up that the only way I could get home was to get a different train to Rugby in which I had to stand for two hours, very, very cramped ... there was no way when you could barely find enough room to stand that you could possibly do any work. So any work I had planned to do at that point was totally out of the window. (Janet – UK)

Susan Halford (2004) argues that workers' constructions of organiza-tional space encompass issues of control and resistance and other experi-ences, memories and identities. Thus, she suggests that 'space and spatiality practices at work are constructed from a diverse range of embodied resources' and 'are intimately connected with identity' (6.1) which 'may appear to return us to familiar tensions between structural and cultural conceptualizations of work' (6.3). We suggest that all of this is also relevant to work that is undertaken by passengers on a train.

Productive Space
In *The Protestant Ethic and the Spirit of Capitalism*, Max Weber (1930: 155–8) argues that:

[T]hat side of English Puritanism which was derived from Calvinism gives the most consistent religious basis for the idea of the calling ... For the saints' everlasting rest is in the next world; on earth man must, to be certain of his state of grace, 'do the works of him who sent him, as long as it is yet day'. Not leisure and enjoyment, but only activity serves to increase the glory of God according to the definite manifestations of His will.

Waste of time is thus the first and in principle the deadliest of sins. The span of human life is infinitely short and precious to make sure of one's own election. Loss of time through sociability, idle talk, luxury, even more sleep than is necessary for health, is worthy of absolute moral condemnation ...

Thus, inactive contemplation is also valueless, or even directly reprehensible if it is at the expense of one's daily work.

The implication here is that it is important to work as much as possible. Time, then, is a valuable resource tied to work and economic exchange (Adam 1995) and, despite recent public debate on work/life balance, it seems that, for some, the train provides an opportunity to fit more work into the day. Also relevant here is that the 'growing flexibility of working hours and the progressive decentralization of the work site have led to greater uncertainty' (Tulloch and Lupton 2003: 62). This means that people work harder and longer because they worry about losing their jobs. Despite the fact that, for some, the train is a 'contested workplace', many people – even those who usually travel standard class – do seem to manage to achieve their productivity goals on the train and effectively extend their working day:

Gayle:	Well I'm in every day at nine o'clock and that means I leave the house at six.
Gillian:	But what's interesting there for me is that you say 'I'm in for nine o'clock', you don't say 'I get to work at nine o'clock.'
Gayle:	Oh no, because I start work on the train.
Gillian:	So actually your working day starts at?
Gayle:	7.04, assuming the train is on time of course!

Also, I am a morning person, so I work best in the morning. So even if I do catch an early train I might be inclined to work in the morning because it is my most productive time, knowing that going home on the train I shan't be up to work, I shall read or sleep or whatever. Because my job is in London, I am travelling because I happen to live in Cheshire. As far as I am concerned, I am commuting – and I should be putting in seven and a half hours when I get there. (Stuart – UK)

Furthermore, the train provides an opportunity for work which is not available when using other forms of transport:

Train is my choice of mode of travel because I can do lots of work and get up and walk around if I want. If you're driving you've got to stop and find a loo, whereas the train is just so convenient ... I can make phone calls, and go through a lot of my pieces for The Mail on Sunday and proof-read them to make sure they're ok. I do a lot of diary stuff and call my agent – although the reception is a bit dodgy coming out of Winchester; it's like going into a black hole! (Interview with Charlie Dimmock in *e-motion* 3: 19)

When I was travelling down to Stevenage by car I'd try and compensate for that. If I had gone down Monday morning, for example, in the car and not arrived till, say, eleven o'clock in the morning then I would probably work late-ish on Monday in the office to try and make up some of the time that I had spent travelling in the morning. I mean, I could argue that the firm should cover that travelling time because they couldn't provide work close to home but it's not the way I tend to feel. I tend to feel I should attempt to give my employer an honest day's work. (Stuart – UK)

The thing that distinguishes rail travel from driving is that you have the space and time to be able to work through it ... There's nothing else to concentrate on – it's such an obvious thing to say but it's important to say it. If you're a driver you've got to be focused on the driving itself. (Jeremy – UK)

I know people who travel to work, who don't really live that far away, that take forty-five minutes, and that's completely dead time if you're using a car. There's not much that you can do unless you're dictating into a Dictaphone or something. But I know people that travel to my place of work, who spend thirty-five to forty-five minutes in that car. Well in that time on the train I could have marked three essays or written a first draft of a few letters or ... (Gayle)

[talking about partner] I think he enjoys trains but I think he deals with them slightly differently, I think at the moment he sees them as a really good way of working. He came back from London yesterday and said he'd done five hours' reading – four hours' reading – which otherwise he wouldn't have done. (Grace – UK)

Respondents also spoke about the different tasks that they undertake on the train, providing, of course, the appropriate space is available. In order to use the space and time effectively, a certain amount of planning is necessary both prior to the journey and also on the train. So working on the train, just as working anywhere else, involves time management, organization and planning:

You have got long periods of time when you tend to be fairly uninterrupted so you can actually get into your work quite well. You need to get a long run at it so the longer journeys I do find them quite useful for working ... Access to a table, not just one of those pull-down ones, distinct lack of people partying or playing with electronic gadgetry, be it children's toys or phones, it doesn't have to be that there is no-one else sitting anywhere near you, but those kind of things. So there is enough space to arrange your papers and write. (Janet – UK)

I finish quite early on a Thursday afternoon and I take with me administration that I would have stayed and finished ... I'm quite careful where I sit so that as much as possible I'm not going to be bothered by noise, but also it's something to do with I've got myself into a system where I say that I'm going to have done so much work by a certain station [laughs] so actually that's quite a good incentive. (Rhian – UK)

It's always a fail-safe position to know that you've got that three quarters of an hour to look at something in the morning on the way in, it's a slot of time – you know you are going to be on the train for forty-five minutes minimum. So you do have that safety net if you need to read something like a report for a meeting – for a nine-thirty meeting which you haven't had chance to look at as fully as you'd like to. Or reading up on a case which is going to court today but you only got the papers for yesterday, which can happen quite often. Yes, it's just there as a fall-back position. I'm not over-keen on the idea of doing it first thing in the morning, but I know the option is there if I want to. (Derek – UK)

Of course, individuals have always undertaken productive labour away from the workplace. For many years, and increasingly, workers – especially those defined as professional – have been able to 'work from home', which is distinct, of course, from the highly feminized 'homeworking'. With reference to domestic labour, feminists have redefined the concept of work to dissolve the distinction between the private space of unpaid work and the public space of paid work (e.g. Witz 1993). We would suggest that, just as housework was historically ignored, so now is train work. There are some differences in that the work people do on the train may be more highly valued than housework; but, although the tasks may be highly valued, the space in which these take place may not. How many office diaries, for example, allow employees to record 'working on the train' as a legitimate activity? New technology, such as the mobile phone and the laptop computer, may make the office space on the train more credible; yet, as highlighted earlier (see Chapter 4), this may have a negative impact upon the tasks of other passengers (engaging in work or leisure).

Furthermore, 'work', as noted earlier, is a contested term and defined differently by different people. Rail passengers may feel the need to engage in productive labour that is not linked to their occupation at all. For example:

If I'm on my own, I will quite often spend five or ten minutes looking at a bit of my Bible, have a think about that, spend some time in prayer – cos it's an excellent environment for doing this, for me. Most of my prayer life is spent on trains. It's also a very good time as well to do organizing in your brain – the day, the things that are going to happen, of late on a Wednesday I've been particularly pre-occupied with my joke for the Alpha course, thinking 'how am I going to tell this one?' I just think it is an environment that gives me a time for reflection. (Derek – UK)

I was on a train a couple of years ago and sitting near to me was a young Jewish man reading the Torah. After a while he began his ritual for prayer – strapping the phylactery on his wrist, and putting the big beige shawl over his head and shoulders. As I watched in amazement, he stood up and used the end of the carriage like a 'wailing wall', it was mesmerizing. My own feelings were a mixture of admiration for his obvious sense of commitment to his faith, irritation at the way he made – in my view – a private activity so public, and mortification at his apparent lack of self-consciousness. (Gillian)

Dey (1989: 465) suggests that nowhere are the conventions which govern our perception and management of time more reified than in the world of work, where 'time is typically taken as an objective medium in terms of which economic activity can be organised and measured'. He adds that the 'discipline of work-time, in the form of the working year, the working week or the working day, has become a central but taken-for-granted characteristic of all industrial societies'. As we have highlighted above, our data challenge these conventions. The train is a place that provides a space for a variety of tasks:

For example the last train journey I took was for a conference ... but the time of year was at the beginning of June, which meant that we were in the middle of exam marking so I spent my time on the train marking Final papers, which tends to be mostly what I do on the train. Or if I am going to a Final exam board as an external examiner at other institutions I will be revising or familiarizing myself with what I've already said in terms of marking and what I am going to say at the meeting. So preparation for the meeting ... I may also do things like plan future work ... working out teaching schedules for the next session or working out staffing – the sort of administration that needs to be done a fair bit in advance because you have got limited resources and you are trying to work them through, or in some cases writing memos or letters that the secretaries will write on official notepaper later. [I engage in] work in both directions. Usually on the way there it's work for the exam board and because of your workload you tend to carry some work with you for on the way back. (Janet – UK)

Thus, the train provides a space for the management of workloads. Indeed, there are some tasks that frequent train users leave specifically for the train:

I'll do anything moveable away from the office I'll use that time. (Rhian – UK)

And on Sunday morning when I'm trying to do some work, I think 'what can I leave for the train?' There are lots of things that I leave, that I only ever do on the train now. (Gayle)

So, in our challenge to Dey (1989), we find Glucksmann's (2000: 160) analysis useful. Thus: '[a]ttempting ... quantification [of time spent on labour as a means for calculating "who does what for whom"] ... has definite limits and becomes highly problematic when work relations are embedded in disparate other social relationships or processes, as they so often are, or occur in different and incomparable economic "spaces".'

Reflections

In this chapter we have considered how respondents who work on the train – both as railway workers and as railway passengers – negotiate a productive workplace. Zygmunt Bauman (1998) suggests that those in the 'work world' live in time, and space matters little to them; but those in the 'workless' world live in space and, for them, space dominates time. In terms of our analysis, we would agree that those in the 'work world' do live in time and sometimes use the train to 'put in their hours' for a 'full' working day. In order to do this, individuals attempt to take control of the train space by constructing a workplace. Those who engage in leisure, on the other hand, can in some ways be compared to Bauman's 'workless' person as they are more likely to passively accept the limitations of the available space. However, we would also argue, for people who engage in both leisure and work, space dominates time. As we have noted in a previous publication (Letherby and Reynolds 2003), some people put down their work when they reach a particular point in the journey in order to engage with the space outside the window.

With reference to rail passengers, yet again our data lead us to challenge traditional definitions of tourist and tourism, not least because of the possible blurring of work and leisure activities (e.g. for some respondents the rail photography we referred to in Chapter 4 should be referred to as work rather than leisure). Historically, the labour of the railway worker has been associated with romance rather than drudgery. Yet, as with any other occupation, the railway worker's relationship with work – both in the past and to date – is multidimensional.

Before ending this chapter it is important to note some methodological limitations in empirical research. The railway passengers represented in this chapter are all what Grint (1991) describes as 'high-trust' workers, workers who have some degree of autonomy over the time and place of their tasks. We are also referring to a limited type of work – namely, portable work (a bricklayer, for example, could not do their bricklaying on a train!). What we did not explore with respondents was whether or not working on the train enabled them to have more leisure time at home or merely extended their working day. We appreciate that there is a gender issue here. Women are still more likely to bear the brunt of the 'double-shift' of labour (Hochschild 1983; Witz 1993; McDowell 1999). What is clear is that, for at least some of our respondents, work begins when you leave home and not when you arrive at work. When does it end?

–6–

Standing Room Only
Personal Politics and the Train

Introduction

In this, our final substantive chapter, we are concerned with issues of personal politics and the train. Feminists were the first to argue that what happened in the private sphere and what happened between individuals was as important as what happened in the public sphere. For feminists, then, the personal and the private are political and of theoretical significance (e.g. see David 2003; Letherby 2003).

As we have noted in previous chapters, there is a blurring of public and private around and within the train. Here, we consider some of the tension this creates for individuals, both individually and in terms of their relationships with others. We focus mainly on the relationships between railway workers and railway passengers and amongst passengers; we have not, in our research, significantly explored relationships among railway workers, except in the context of their work identity (Strangleman 1999; see Chapter 5). We consider 'good' and 'bad' behaviour, emotions and emotional experience and the relevance of signifiers of identity such as class, gender, ethnicity and disability. As such we are concerned with:

> the normal and the abnormal, the expectable and the unexpected, the ordinary and the bizarre, domesticated and wild – the familiar and the strange, 'us' and the strangers ... [and the relevance of the fact that the] difference which sets the self apart from the non-self, and 'us' apart from 'them', is no longer given by the pre-ordained shape of the world, nor by command from on high. It needs to be constructed, and reconstructed, and constructed once more, and reconstructed again, on both sides at the same time, neither of the sides boasting more durability, or just 'givenness' than the other. Today's strangers are by-products, but also the means of production, in the incessant, because never conclusive, process of identity building. (Bauman 1997: 25)

With all this in mind, we draw on many of the themes and issues addressed elsewhere in the book and suggest that all social life does indeed occur on the train.

'Good' and 'Bad' Behaviour

'Travelling' Manners

Norbert Elias (1978: 3 and 5) suggests that:

> The concept of 'civilization' refers to a wide range of facts: to the level of knowledge, to the type of manners, to the development of scientific knowledge, to religious ideas and customs. It can refer to the type of dwelling or the manner in which men and women live together, to the form of judicial punishment, or to the way in which food is prepared.
>
> ... Western society seeks to describe what constitutes its special character and what it is proud of: the level of its technology, the nature of its manners, the development of its scientific knowledge or view of the world, and much more.

'Civilization' describes a process, or at least the result of a process. The way in which we define civilization is historically specific, and – to some extent – there is a common-sense view of what is, and what is not, appropriate behaviour at this present historical time:

> Manners on a train are manners like anywhere. These days they are hard to find. People will trash on the train like any place else. There are slobs wherever you go these days. That does not mean you can't find nice people that will help you with your luggage, make good conversation, or help you in other ways. (Amy – USA)

> Good manners should be to be considerate, enjoy, listen and ask questions if you aren't sure about anything ... Be patient, the diner only seats so many and they will do their best to accommodate you ... the snack bars are closed at certain times to give the attendant a break. Be considerate of your fellow passengers when preparing for a train ride and keep your cologne to the minimum. Bad manners would be to be loud, some people 'want to be heard and think they are experts on everything'. Leaving your seating area messy. No consideration for the persons seated around you. Those riding with children should be considerate of other passengers and above all – don't let small children have 'the run of the car'. If people are talking don't interfere with their conversation. Above all remember, you are only paying for one seat (in most cases). (Pat – USA)

Pat raises an issue of space here. The fact that men often seem to feel that they can occupy more of the available space than women on a train (for example, by spreading their legs far apart) is because men are 'presence in space and women are insignificant' (McDowell 1999: 41, drawing on Bourdieu). Women are therefore less likely to use their bodies than their 'things' (such as bags) to appropriate more personal space.

When asked what they disliked about trains, most respondents said it was individuals who did not adhere to these, and other, common-sense 'rules'. This applied to both railway watchers and railway travellers:

> if you go to stations, say in Kent, where the stations had too much land and now they have sold off that land around the station so the houses are built almost up to the station, you will find that a lot of the houses, normally semi-detached, nearest the station, are for sale and they've got windows broken because there is so much yobbishness around stations. (Henry – UK)

> Just general rules for politeness in public spaces, really, e.g. not making excessive noise, although also letting everyone get a fair shot at the view if standing on an observation platform on the outside of the train, if there is one, not standing in front of people at photo stops. (Viv – New Zealand)

> when travellers are ignorant of the needs of their fellows, and proceed to shout into their mobile phones or foul up the toilet – when the on-board crew show no love for their work or they run out of supplies before the intended destination – basically, the train is not the problem – it is only unpleasant when the people on board are unpleasant. (Eddie – Canada)

On the whole, therefore, what (rail user) respondents disliked the most on trains tended to be the other passengers.

The idea that our behaviour in public places needs to be managed (Goffman 1963), that we need to be socialized into more publicly acceptable behaviour, is not new. Examples of such socialization can be traced back to the Middle Ages and the development of 'courtly' or 'civilized' manners. Norbert Elias (1978) draws on manuals of etiquette of the time. In studying such manuals, he makes the point that, if 'etiquette' demands, for example, that men should turn their backs to other people when urinating in public, it was because the actual behaviour justified the demands.

Over the centuries, of course, conditions and cultures have changed. Writing about railway travel in the nineteenth century, Susan Barton (2002) argues that individuals travelling on the Victorian railway had to undertake considerable cultural negotiation to learn how to behave towards other travellers. She suggests that learning how to cope with the management of space in railway carriages was part of an evolving culture of modernity in the mid-nineteenth century. At that time, behaviour in the first and second and third classes differed significantly and perhaps set the tone for some of the norms and values about train travel etiquette today:

> In the first and second-class carriages quiet amongst the passengers prevailed, unlike in the third class where reading was not a common pastime and chatter, jollity or argumentativeness continued. Only the privileged classes at this time underwent the experience of no longer speaking to each other and being increasingly embarrassed by their companions. In the lower class of carriage the noise could be heard in the more expensive parts of the train. 'Merry conversation and laughter range all the way into the boredom of my isolation cell' remarked P. D. Fischer, travelling in the genteel but to his mind, dull, first class. (Barton 2002: 8)

Thus, on British trains, at least, a set of manners and an unwritten but internalized code of behaviour evolved among travellers perhaps more familiar with rail journeys: expected conversation was polite and perfunctory and the creation of personal space was negotiated, not least by placing personal belongings on adjacent seats. In the Victorian era, then, rules of conduct on trains were enforced by the scrutiny and potential disapproval of other passengers and what counted as 'appropriate' behaviour evolved over time and was learned experientially by rail passengers (Barton 2002):

> I think one always thinks one own age is worse in these things, like than any other age. I read somewhere that Victorian travellers would get apoplectic about other passengers' behaviours. I suspect it has drifted down a bit. (Henry – UK)

Some respondents certainly felt strongly about current levels of 'anti-social behaviour' on trains. Rhian (UK), for example – referring to trains in Britain – applauded the management technique of introducing Quiet Coaches where mobile phones, radios, CD players and other sources of noise are discouraged (if rarely stringently monitored):

> I think I'm very hard-line on this, not very liberal, but I think that it would be quite a good idea to introduce, actually, just one carriage where you can use mobile phones. A bit like smoking, I think, I know, I accept that smoking is anti-social and I don't like sitting in a carriage full of smoke but I think mobile phones are as equally anti-social and should get the same treatment.
> ... I was in the buffet at Stoke station when this guy in front of me was waiting in the queue to get a cup of tea and he was talking on the mobile phone at he same time as he was trying to order food ... he carried on talking on the phone and everything else he did in the transaction was purely through

gestures, paying, taking the money back. No please or thank you and it struck me as really interesting in terms of cutting across all kinds of accepted practice about politeness and courtesy, the person behind the counter just did not exist basically. So yes mobile phones are a nuisance.

Sometimes, however, what might be considered 'bad behaviour' in another setting occurs, we would suggest, because the space of the train is conceptualized as neither totally public nor totally private. Such blurring can lead to a sense of confusion about what is appropriate behaviour:

Well I was bored, you know, and the woman next to me was writing a letter and I couldn't help but look over her shoulder to see what she was writing, then I read: 'I'll stop writing now because this nosy cow sitting next to me is reading everything that I write.' (Tina – UK)

Bodily Excess and Body 'Modification'

The structure of society demands and generates a specific standard of behavioural and emotional control (Elias 1978). With specific reference to bodily control, Victoria Pitts cites Mikhail Bakhtin (1981) as arguing that 'the grotesque body is the eating and drinking body, the body of open orifices, the coarse body which yawns, hiccups, nose blows, flatulates, spits, hawks' (Pitts 1998: 69). As Pitts (1998: 70) herself adds, the body of modernity has privatized and closed the orifices, and encouraged a pure, smooth, pristine surface: 'fiddling with the smoothness is a denaturalized act of subversion'. Yet, as we have highlighted above, there seems to have always been a need to remind people of just what is appropriate and inappropriate. For example:

Please do not spit in the carriages. It is offensive to other passengers and is stated by the medical profession to be source of serious disease – Notice in Victorian Railway Carriages. (Povey 1974: 61)

Shoes have enough to face without having to pick up all the spitting that goes unchecked in and around the transit system. If there isn't a bylaw about this, there should be, to be consistent with many other transit systems. If there is a bylaw, some extra enforcement is obviously necessary. In any case, the current situation detracts from the overall transit environment. (*Ottawa Transit Riders Association Newsletter* March 2002).

Despite stringent efforts to curb antisocial offences such as spitting, like providing railway workers with DNA kits to take swabs of saliva to aid prosecution (BBC 2004), it appears that there is some disagreement or confusion over just what bodily matter is acceptable and what is not, as the following entry on a discussion forum at a Canadian urban transport website demonstrates:

> Try as she might, Liza Hodskins can't forget the moment during a Red Line ride to Silver Spring when she was roused from her reading by a familiar yet unexpected sound. She turned to see the woman behind her flossing her teeth … In terms of sheer equipment, though, the flosser can't compare with an unidentified woman who has been spotted on the Orange and Red lines with her portable curling iron … It's no secret that people primp and shave and put on cosmetics in their automobiles during morning drive time, insulated behind glass and steel from one another in a way that gives them the illusion of privacy. But more and more, it seems, commuters are doing their grooming on public transportation, inches from strangers in packed trains and buses. It's a blurring of the line separating public and private space … There are women who paint their nails and those who strip them of paint with cotton balls soaked in pungent polish remover … And then there are the clippers, a class of men and women given away by the unmistakable ping in otherwise silent subway cars. Emilia Kelley … watched a woman finish clipping her fingernails only to move on to her toenails one summer morning on the Red Line. 'She slipped off her shoe, pulled up her foot and started clipping away.' (Layton 2002: AO1)

Again, we owe our dominant expectations to the past, not least to Emily Post, the arbiter of good manners whose 1922 book, *Etiquette*, set the parameters for 'polite' society. 'Grooming should be done in a restroom or at home' (Post, cited by Layton 2002: A01). 'Polite society', however, also often means that we are over-reserved and embarrassed to acknowledge the presence of imperfect human bodies in public spaces. One way of addressing this is through the discourse of humour (see Chapter 2). Andrew Holmes and Matthew Reeves attempt this in their 2003 book, *Pains on Trains: a Commuter's Guide to the 50 Most Irritating Travel Companions* (see Introduction).

Although none of our respondents spoke of the extreme 'body modification' processes mentioned by Layton above, some do use the train in order to prepare themselves physically for the day. For example, Karen said:

> I like the fact that you can do so much when travelling by train and it is the only form of transport that does not give me motion sickness, unlike planes, boats and cars. When I used to commute to Euston from Bletchley I would get up, wash and dress and be out of the house in about fifteen minutes and on the train I would preen myself ready for the day. I would meet my friends;

catch up with them briefly and then put my makeup on. I got quite skilled in putting on my mascara in rhythm with the motion and the train.

This is interesting in terms of the presentation of self (Goffman 1969) in public in that the train appears yet again as that transitional space and place (akin to a bathroom) between home and work. There are, however, some aspects of body management and some bodily functions that are more difficult than mascara to control on the train. Ian Marchant (2003: 164) notes candidly that:

> The train lavatory is too precious a resource to be treated with selfishness. It is to be prized by you, and passed on to your fellow passengers in a decent state. Because if you do a floater, you're going to be sitting next to the person who finds it for the next three hours. If you make a mess, everyone will have to look at it. Or sit in it. If you 'let one go' it's gonna be coming right back atcha down the corridor … These are amongst the world's most public loos.

Women in particular may find the train to be just one of the public spaces that take no account of the need to manage aspects of their reproduction bodies such as menstruation, pregnancy and menopause (Shilling 1993: 38). Just as trains and some passengers are not sympathetic to the bodily functions and specific needs of women, neither are they to the bodily functions and specific needs of children. Parents are likely to find few facilities to assist them in the bodily care of their children:

> They should have baby-changing facilities and somewhere for when you're feeding babies. (Julie – UK)

Clearly then, amongst other things, the train space and those within it are intolerant of natural bodily functions:

> I call the 7.04 from Stoke 'The Farty Express'. You know quite a lot of people have a sleep on the early train and when we sleep we sometimes make noises: we snore and fart. Usually people are very indulgent and smile knowingly at each other when another passenger makes such a noise. Not always though, one of my friends was on the early train to Euston once and he woke himself up from a sleep with a very, very loud fart and he shrugged and smiled sheepishly at the people near him. They didn't smile back, looked disgusted and turned away. As if they never lose control of their bodies in such ways themselves. (Gayle)

So, although we suggested in Chapter 4 that the train is a public space where sleep is considered acceptable, the 'privatization' of sleep in modern Western society ensures that this bodily function (and the associated bodily noises and smells) is considered to be acceptable only if it does not impinge on others (see Fig. 13). When such representations of the 'grotesque' (Pitts 1998) occur, sleep is perceived as more appropriate for the 'backstage' (Goffman 1969), or 'behind the scenes of social life' (Williams 2003, drawing on Elias 1978).

Figure 13 'Anti-social' sleeping? Copyright: line drawing by David Bill (Billy). By permission.

'Train-watching' Manners

Just as there are norms surrounding the behaviour of railway passengers, there are norms surrounding the activities of train fans. Again, it appears that most of this is common sense. What is interesting here, though, is the fact that 'thinking of others' (a matter of consideration) appears to be rated as highly as 'observing the rules and not breaking the law' (a legal requirement with possible serious sanctions attached):

> The main thing is to follow the rules of the signs that the railways put up for everyone's safety. Also, not to destroy property, or try to collect a piece of history which does not belong to them. (Hugh and Liz – USA)

Good manners – work well with others and give and take … share photo spots, do not step in front of photographers while they are photographing. Talking while others are videotaping is extreme bad manners. Trespassing to get pictures on railway property is also bad manners and illegal. Climbing telephone poles or up into areas where pedestrians are not allowed is also frowned upon. Disobeying traffic rules while following a train to get photos is also bad manners. Jeopardizing other peoples' lives passing and speeding along the highway is also bad manners. There are in-car rules as well. If the photo trip is a long trip, then rules as to when someone pays for gas, dinner and rest stops are done in advance. (Miles – USA)

Amongst rail fans there is something of an 'in-house' view of the poor skills of others. This leads to concern that the behaviour of others will bring the activity into disrepute:

Many railfans are not socially evolved enough to realize the main issues. (Nick – USA)

Railfans in New Zealand don't have a very good reputation among the public at large, the main complaint being a complete lack of consideration to other railfans and the public at large when they are chasing trains, or when they are travelling as passengers on trains. I believe they should stand back and have a good look at their behaviour and say to themselves – 'what would I think of someone who behaved like I do when I am in railfan mode?' (Owen – New Zealand)

Some respondents, however, suggest that inappropriate behaviour is largely the result of lack of experience, and that naïve fans represent a danger to themselves:

It's nearly always the inexperienced fan that falls foul of these protocols, and natural selection tends then to prevail – these people are the most likely ones to get taken out by accidents, thus purifying the railfan breed. (Steve – New Zealand)

Given the perceived common-sense nature of appropriate behaviour when train-watching, this group are clearly 'risk-takers' (e.g. Lupton 1999). Yet experience is not the only way in which some rail fans distance themselves from inappropriate behaviour. There is also some blaming of the 'stranger', the 'other':

Some railfans are foolish. We Canadians tend to presume that they are American tourists. (Damien – Canada)

As Norbert Elias and John Scotson (1994: xvi) argue, in any community the 'established' group (in terms of a given territory, or over a longer period of time) will tend to 'close ranks' and stigmatize a group of 'outsiders': they 'look upon themselves as the "better" people, as endowed with a kind of group charisma, with a special virtue shared by all its members and lacked by the others'.

Train Fans Breaking the Law

For some rail enthusiasts (including some of those represented above), disrespect for the feelings of others, even breaking the law, is worth it on occasion. When we asked if they had ever been stopped by the police, the following accounts were typical of others:

> Yes. But I was young and foolish. I shouldn't have been lying down between tracks (not between rails) to take a photo of a passing freight train – this was in Canada – it was in a yard, there was a lot of room between tracks, no live wires and a very low speed limit. I was nineteen and showing off to my girl-friend – it was a stupid thing to do, as freight trains can occasionally drag debris that would have smacked me in the head. After the train passed, I got up to discover a CN track test car beside me with four angry employees on it shouting at me in French. I apologised profusely and quickly ran for my life! I have been stopped by railway police many times over the years. It was usually a case of trespassing on property that was off limits without a pass. I must confess that my usual response when confronted by the officer was to act innocent and say something like, 'Oh really? I was unaware of that.' The only consequences were to be evicted from the property. (Damien – Canada)

> Yes, once I was photographing a tunnel from the subway platform in Edmonton Alberta. The PA announcer said I should move away from the end of the platform. I ignored him till I got my pics. By that time he said that police had been dispatched, so I ran out of the station and five blocks away in a zigzag pattern. I didn't hear any sirens or see any police. I've photographed from platform ends many times and never had a problem. It's not like anyone rides the Edmonton system anyway. Also I've been warned not to photograph in the London Tube. I still took a few pics afterwards, but slyly. Generally though, I try very hard to stay within the law and observe property rights. (George – Canada)

In the grand scheme of things, though, railway trespass has historically not been considered to be that serious a crime and authorities have behaved accordingly:

Yes, I have been asked by a railway policeman to remove myself from their property because, after all, I was trespassing. However, in general, officials of the railway locally get to know who we are and that, in fact, we are not a threat to them or our ourselves and tend to turn a blind eye to the issue of trespassing. However, having said that, I will not go on railway property unless I'm on business or invited on by a local official – I believe the railway has the right to ask us to stay off their property just as we have the right to withhold access to our property for whatever reason. I will then find another way to accomplish what I wanted to do in most cases. In the case that the police stopped me, I was asked to leave and did so without an argument. (Archie – Canada)

The worst I've seen is two railway constables (a kid and an older one) in civilian clothes running to us with their guns drawn. Then a heated exchange about us not having any business taking pictures of the trains. Meanwhile, the train we wanted to see (a first run of a new route) shows up, and we take the pictures anyway right in the face of the constables. Obviously, the guns didn't intimidate us very much … Then, suddenly the constables simply put back their guns and left muttering 'it's not the guys we're looking for', but not without telling us not to cross any tracks. (Alex – Canada)

This could lead us to suggest that the social control of the rail enthusiast largely takes place within the group, with, yet again, there being a necessary period of socialization before one is accepted as a full member of the group. On the other hand, there is a time-specific dimension to this issue; since nine-eleven and the increased threat of terrorist attack worldwide, the social control authorities may not be so lenient to the rail enthusiast.

Emotion

As Simon Williams and Gillian Bendelow (1998: xvi/xvii) argue:

the 'deep sociality' of emotions – offers us a way of moving beyond micro-analytic, subjective, individualistic levels of analysis, towards more 'open-ended' forms of social inquiry in which embodied agency can be understood not merely as 'meaning-making', but also as 'institution making' … In short, the emphasis here is on the active, emotionally expressive body, as the basis of self, sociality, meaning and order, located within the broader sociocultural realms of everyday life and the ritualized forms of interaction and exchange they involve.

In other words, an analysis of emotions is necessary to fully understand the social world.

Anxiety, Embarrassment, Sadness and Joy

Our respondents recounted a mixture of emotions surrounding rail travel. Henry, for example, expresses some personal anxiety:

> The only other things I've got on my list are journey anxiety – if you have a heart monitor, you find the beginning of the journey and the end are stressful times for the heart. You are alert for things going wrong – station emotions, heart rate gets up. Get to your seat on the train and heart rate drops. Train emotions – on the train, made it, heart rate drops. Fellow passengers annoying, tension goes up, phone annoyance, possibility of missing connection, heart rate goes up. Those are the things that try.

For others, there is the stress of managing the emotions and behaviour of others:

> Well, it's a bit more fraught if I am with my mum because she is very anxious about travelling ... I have to do everything I can to make the experience more pleasurable ... In a sense this puts greater stress on me because if I miss a train it's a nuisance to me, I might get a bit irritated with myself, but it feels a disaster if it happens with my mum ... it's funny 'cos it's sort of like role reversal, I'm sure she must have had to keep me occupied as a child when we were travelling because we used to travel quite a bit. It feels like I am doing a little bit of the same back. (Rhian – UK)

> Some of the worst experiences I've had on trains is when sharing the carriage with young children and their parents. Often it's not the kids that disturb you but their parents with their anxiety. One particular occasion I remember is a woman literally screaming at her three children to be quiet, sit still, not to drop food. It was sad really she was obviously so anxious in case the children disturbed anyone and she really went overboard in trying to control their behaviour. But the kids were fine, just being kids, playing and talking but not in a way that would disturb most people. (Gayle)

> I noticed when the children were little and they were playing up. You do get scowling looks. (Julie – UK)

A comparison of travel in different parts of Britain and across countries and cultures seems to highlight different emotional norms. Henry and Gillian observe cultural differences between and within countries:

> well I went to South Africa on a train trip and people with nothing would wave at the train and you feel embarrassed. I wasn't on a smart train, I was on a very antique train but even so we probably had a standard of living

hundreds of times above the people and they would come and wave with no context, totally spontaneously, then you come back to Paddington ... and everybody is miserable – and you've got everything there! There is so much, and everybody's like this [expression of misery]. I think it is sad, if you travel on the North London trains, that is very sad ... But it varies – I think trains outside London are much more cheerful ... In Paddington the train was overcrowded and when it's overcrowded people don't move down the centre of the train, they tend to be at the door ends. More people wanted to get on and people were saying 'I'm not moving, I'm not moving' and you know it wouldn't have taken anything for them to fill up that centre aisle, to move from the two ends of the carriage so that more people could get on. In the end, some New Zealand people on holiday came on and they got everyone to move, but what I did notice on that train journey was that as people got out they were replaced by people who were that much nicer, more relaxed. The further we got from London, the nicer the people became, the more amenable they became. When we got to Reading it got a bit better, when we got to Swindon it got better, people became more relaxed and more human the further down that line we got and the more the commuters got out. It was fascinating. (Henry – UK)

certainly the last few miles into Nairobi through the shanty towns – hundreds and hundreds of kids lined up both sides of the railway track, begging for money and it gets under your skin when you experience that kind of inequality and you are on the winning side as it were, it fundamentally alters the way that you live among other people. But the year before last, a couple of our Kenyan friends came over to visit us, and he was telling the story that he got in the train at Euston and came across this empty seat that had a woman sitting one side. So he plonked himself down and started chatting away to her, and she looked completely spaced out and said 'you don't know me do you?' And he said 'no no, but we are going to be spending the next few hours together, so we might just as well get to know each other. And who knows, if the train crashes we may be spending eternity together, so let's get to know each other now' ... But it's that complete clash of cultures, of this 'you're in my space, go away' compared with this Kenyan 'we're in this space together, this is our space, not your space'. (Gillian)

Clearly, the prevailing cultural perception of the traveller as polite and aloof is not the norm across the globe and even varies within Britain. Once more, it is possible to argue that the British owe some of their reserve to the codes set down in Victorian England. As Tim Newton (1998: 71) notes, within English drawing-rooms at that time, 'careful control and display were the order of the day'. In courtly society, too, it was equally important to curb one's emotions and to 'maintain an appropriate appearance and gentility'.

Lust and Love

Sometimes, when the emotions are 'running high', it is not so easy to keep them under control. This, in turn, can cause embarrassment for others:

> I interrupted a couple once making love … again, this was a late night train, one of the old style trains. I had got on and I was moving down the train, came into this carriage, and you know how you do a double-take? You think 'no, this isn't happening' but it was clear that they were being very 'friendly'. They weren't fully, but they were well on the way! So I just walked straight past – what can you say? I just carried on. Is that a weird experience? It is the only time in all the years that I've been commuting that I've come across anything like that. (Derek – UK)

This resonates with the experience of Jon Horne (undated and unpaginated), who, whilst sketching at New Street Station in Birmingham, observes:

> There is a stampede through the gates. The City Boys are as I remember them, radiating confidence. Each of them is picked out and hugged. A fair-haired specimen is being pawed and gently bitten by the girl in green, who rubs herself against his hip. He head rocks back and her lips snarl. The boy accepts the proffered orgasm with easy grace, and strokes the girl down her spine from neck to coccyx. Hand on buttock, they trot outside to the taxi rank.
> The rest of them are at it too: fervent kissing and body-rubbing. Sex is everywhere.

Holmes and Reeves (2003: 106) outline a story that apparently 'hit' the headlines concerning a couple who were engaging in sexual intercourse on a packed train:

> Not one person raised an objection. Most either diverted their eyes, busied themselves with their work … or did anything they could to ignore the succession of grunts and pants as the couple went at it like a steam engine. Only when they had completed their act and lit up cigarettes did the tirade of abuse follow. Not about their lovemaking, you understand, but about them smoking in a non-smoking carriage … If there was a 'no sex' sign they would have been up in arms, but without it they did not have the permission to protest.

None of our respondents admitted to having sexual intercourse – or anything near it – on or near a train, but some did tell us about their experience of romance at the railway station or on the train:

I met Rosie on the train and I always remember how I was on there with my mum and dad going to Blackpool, then I suddenly got talking to Rosie, and that's how we met. (Joe – UK)

And I saw this pretty girl, I was attracted by this coat she used to have actually – and the first time I made approaches, she got into a carriage so I followed her in and I just spoke to her, would she mind if I travelled with her. That was alright with her so that was it. Then all of a sudden out of the blue another bloke got in and sat alongside her and started chatting with her while I was still breaking ice. So I couldn't stand that and without a word I just got my bag off the rack and went off up the train. And that was it until the following week. (Theo – UK)

This particular day it was absolutely bunged up with people going on holiday and soldiers ... And I was thinking 'there aren't going to be any seats' and I'm dashing down this train looking for seats, and all at once this window comes down – you know the old windows – and he said 'here you are' and he opened the door and he'd saved me a seat in the corner. (Jessica – UK)

To top it all, a lovely day out to London with [name of partner] where we bought an engagement ring at a jeweller's in Piccadilly Circus. I refused to have it put on my finger in a very crowded posh restaurant so finally we became engaged at Kings Cross Station, waiting for the train to take us back home. (Sue – UK)

None of these appear to have been the illegitimized 'brief encounter' that Celia Johnson and Trevor Howard shared, but all led to long-term relationships. Ian Marchant's experience, on the other hand, resonated precisely with the 'best-loved train film of Britain' (see Chapter 3):

We were both married. She lived with her husband in a terraced house by the Harbour; we walked to the station together after rehearsal, and she would wait with me on the platform for the last train before crossing the tracks to go home. We had our first kiss on that platform, said a hundred desperate good-byes on that platform, waiting for the last train ... She was Celia Johnson to my Trevor Howard. (Marchant 2003: 34)

As Lynn Jamieson (1998: 19) notes, sex is no longer 'harnessed to marriage-like arrangements and couples negotiate their own rules of sexual conduct on a we-will-do-what-we-enjoy basis'. Furthermore, the public display of intimate affection (for heterosexuals at least) is more acceptable than it once was. Even so, and despite the early association of the railway with sexual intercourse – even sexual abuse (see Chapter 3) –

the car is the vehicle now most likely to be associated with actual sex acts and sexual aggression (Davison 2004). The train, on the other hand, is perceived as the vehicle that connects lovers to each other rather than providing a copulative space.

Irritation, Anger and Rail Rage

Negotiating time spent with strangers in a confined public space can lead either to potential relationships, or to feelings of irritation, as Georg Simmel noted in his various discussions of the modern metropolis (Frisby 1992). Feelings of irritation arise simply because there is always the risk and its associated 'existential anxiety' (Giddens 1991: 39) that a stranger brings different (and therefore unpredictable) expectations of both the space and other people. Distinctions between irritation and anger are very blurred and both were experienced by our respondents. Noise was a major source of tension on a train journey: loud noise, or noise of children's electronic toys, or raucous laughter, loud enough to be intrusive. There is clearly a contested acceptable level of 'everyday' noises. But the limit for irritation is not solely about volume. Henry, for example, experienced irritation when someone sat opposite him on a train, wearing a headset and playing music:

> I could hear the tick-tick-tickety-tick and after a while I started to do the hand-jive to the rhythm, just to make a point. He got cross with me!

For a significant number of respondents, mobile phones are, without doubt, a source of irritation on a train journey. Again, the historical time in which we are researching and writing – the early twenty-first century – is relevant here in terms of consumerism and popular technology. Although we have discussed mobile phones in the context of working on the train (see Chapter 5), there are clearly other uses for such 'gadgets'. Henry, for example, sees people using them as 'toys' to alleviate boredom:

> I'm not bored on a train, but I see a lot of people who are bored. They are on their mobiles 'I'm on the train, I'm really bored, it's another two hours.' (Henry – UK)

Respondents, perhaps predictably, varied in the degree of annoyance experienced from mobile phones. Kenneth, for example, experiences only slight irritation:

I do find the tones on them, the rings on them, a little bit irritating, but I just look at it with wry amusement. Really, the person who is using the mobile phone is behaving in an interesting way, in a way that suggests they simply aren't aware of how loud their voice is, or that other people can hear the banal things they're saying to the person at the other end ... [but] I can't say that I find myself being deeply disturbed, I am a profoundly nosy person and ... I believe that people who hold conversations at the top of their voice on railway trains are fair game to be listened to.

Rhian and Grace, on the other hand, feel more affected:

I don't understand mobile phones, I've never had one, but it seems that you have to fiddle with them a lot and there's all the jingling going on ... There was a mother and her daughter, and they both had their own mobile phones. As a joke the daughter rang her mother who was sitting right opposite her and they had a conversation via their mobile phones ... I couldn't believe it! (Rhian – UK)

I do actually find mobile phones very intrusive on a train journey because people talk much more loudly on their mobile phones than they do to their companions. So you become a kind of integral part of the conversation, even when you're not. (Grace – UK)

The tension created by being 'drawn into' the listening side of a conversation, whilst at the same time being excluded from it, can rapidly turn irritation into anger.

Anger directed towards other travellers is often distinctively different from anger directed towards railway workers, which is more often a consequence of a breakdown on the provision of a service (e.g. cancelled trains, missed connections, perceived rudeness). Anger, of course, can escalate into rage, sometimes experienced or labelled as uncontrolled anger. Arguably, the promotion of the railway of consumerism and quality, including the production of customer charters and punctuality tables, can act as a catalyst for rage. Customers are encouraged to develop expectations in order to drive up the standards of a public service and this can legitimate the anger or rage that many people feel. As far as trains are concerned, this often occurs when you are unable to get a seat, when the train is late or perhaps – worst of all – when the train is at the station and so are you, but you cannot get on because the automatic doors have already been locked in preparation for departure (see Fig. 14). There is something of a tension here between consumer expectations and perceived risks that are managed by the service provider. Given some of the current problems on the British railways, there is often sympathy for the 'perpetrators' of rage:

Figure 14 Rail rage and locked doors. Copyright: line drawing by David Bill (Billy). By permission.

It was Christmas and the train was packed. I stood up from Coventry to Wolverhampton. To make it worse someone was arrested on the train at Coventry and we had to wait about half-an-hour for the police to arrive and for him to be removed. There had been a mix-up over the seats and two guys were arguing about who a particular seat belonged to. One guy started to push the other and the first one made a complaint and decided to press charges. I felt really sorry for the guy that was arrested, he was just frustrated.

Another time I travelled on a coach from Stafford to Stoke with a travel cop. He told us that he had just had to arrest someone for punching someone else. He said 'I had to arrest him of course, but I didn't blame him, I feel like punching someone myself.' (Gayle)

It is thus not only other passengers who bear the brunt of the rage of others but railway workers too. In her influential 1983 book – *The Managed Heart: Commercialisation of Human Feeling* – Arlie Hochschild details, amongst other things, the relationship between the (predominantly) female flight attendant and her passengers:

of all workers in an airline, the flight attendant has the most contact with passengers, and she sells the company the most. When passengers think of service they are unlikely to think of the baggage check-in agent ... the cabin clean-up crew, the lost and found personnel, or the man down in commissary pouring gravy on a long line of chicken entrees. They think of the flight attendant. (Hochschild 1983: 92)

The flight attendant, Hochschild argues, is expected not only to manage her own emotions – and always to appear calm, cheerful and pretty – but to also manage the negative behaviour and emotions of others: for example drunkenness, anger and rage. Because of this, Hochschild (1983: 98 suggests that the airline recruiters:

look for someone who is smart but can also cope with being considered dumb, someone who is capable of giving emergency safety commands but can also handle people who can't take orders from a woman, and someone who is naturally empathetic but can also resist the numbing effect of having that empathy engineered and continuously used by a company for its own purposes.

Hochschild adds that this type of emotional labour is gendered in that it is more likely to be an aspect of a female-dominated occupation rather than a male one (other examples include nursing and secretarial work). Yet, as Jean Duncombe and Dennis Marsden (1998) argue, it is important to consider differences between individual women and men and not to automatically assume that emotion work is women's work. Hochschild herself notes, however, that the job of flight attendant 'is not the *same job* for a woman as it is for a man':

Male flight attendants tended to react to passengers *as if they had more authority* than they really did. This made them less tolerant of abuse and firmer in handling it. They conveyed the message that *as authorities* they expected compliance without loud complaint. Passengers sensing this message were discouraged from pursuing complaints and stopped sooner. Female flight attendants, on the other hand, assuming that passengers would honor their authority less, used more tactful and deferential means of handling abuse. (Hochschild 1983: 178, original emphasis)

There are occupations undertaken by as many (if not more) men as women that involve the emotional management of both the employees' and the clients'/customers' emotions. The position of train manager is one such occupation. Furthermore, the display of rage as an emotion is much more likely than it was over twenty years ago when Hochschild was researching for and writing her book. Fuelled by the increasing number of 'reality' TV shows where individuals are put in positions designed to test their tempers, 'road rage' has already become fully integrated into everyday language – there are even interactive internet games which enable us to 'play out' our rage – and 'air rage' and 'rail rage' are not far behind.

Despite the proliferation of anxiety-inducing headlines such as 'Violence against rail staff reaches 30-year high' (Clement 2001) and '"Shocking and unacceptable" rise in rail rage attacks on staff' (O'Neill 2001), we suggest that much of the 'rail rage' that passengers feel is, in reality, not directed at those they are really angry with. Equally, it can be argued that the anger is to some extent socially manufactured by modern consumerist cultures. As Henry (UK) says:

> I do think that people get angry because it's a safe area in which to get angry, and it's partly the media saying that nothing the trains do is right ... Now if you take away some of the anger against the transport then it's got to be something else, it can't be the home, the domestic situation, or disappointment about themselves and their lives, or lack of self-esteem, it will have to go somewhere else, so maybe it's safe to have it there.

Fellow passengers and railway workers bear the brunt of the individual's dissatisfaction with the railway of consumerism and quality and/or their disappointment at the loss of the romantic railway of their dreams. Although arguably more blameworthy, it is unsurprising that the train companies' solution to this problem – of the threat to their customers and staff – is to install surveillance cameras on trains and station platforms. The fact that there is often (unlike the flight attendants' experience on the aeroplane) only one train manager on duty on each train further necessitates the need for another form of 'protection' for railway workers and users. The following notice can be seen on all South West Trains and stations; similar signs are produced by most train operating companies in Britain:

> Violence is unacceptable. Our staff have the right to work without fear or threat of violence – whatever the form and whatever the reason. We will seek to prosecute anyone who assaults or intimidates any South West Trains Employee. Recorded CCTV is used throughout our network and will be used in evidence if necessary.

Closed-circuit TV was perceived by a small number of our respondents as a useful way of helping individuals to assess some of the risks associated with travelling in public spaces:

There were people smoking all the time and this was a non-smoking carriage. People were not only smoking but they were drinking cans of lager ... [and] it occurred to me: what if all this bubbling tension does turn into acts of violence, what do you do? And again it struck me that what they want in these carriages is closed circuit TV. (Kenneth – UK)

An advantage of such technology is the impact it might have on incidences of crime on the railways. As Wolfgang Schivelbusch (1986) argues, the traditional British railway carriage with its enclosed carriages notoriously became a crime scene with no witnesses. Although most modern trains do not expose passengers (or train managers) to the same risk, they can still be unsafe at times:

I witnessed a fight on a late night train; I was in the same carriage ... I moved to another carriage. I had no wish to get involved with drunken teenagers. Because at night there's not many people on trains ... I suppose you're very conscious on late night trains that if something blows off there isn't really anywhere for you to go, you can only go to the next carriage and if you are on a two-carriage train, it's not very funny ... that was a bit scary, yes. (Derek – UK)

There have been other times, perhaps travelling back from Manchester late at night on a local train where there are only a few people on the train, where I have felt much less secure. Perhaps the lads in the next carriage have obviously been drinking and they are messing around. I have had that sort of experience. (Stuart – UK)

However, as David Lyon (2001: 21) notes, surveillance is always something of a double-edged sword. In this instance cameras may serve to offer the railway worker and rail passenger some protection but they also monitor her or his working life or travel time, respectively. The presence of surveillance cameras also removes pretensions to privacy and renders entirely public the space and place of the train (through the medium of video recording), long after the traveller has alighted. We need to ask the question, as Lyon does: is privacy ever possible within 'surveillance society'?

Status and Identity

As we have noted in previous chapters, some of our respondents, despite the encouragement mentioned earlier to maintain 'reserve', enjoy the camaraderie that the train space provides. Here, we acknowledge some general differences between rail enthusiasts and rail travellers, and also differences between British cultures and others (especially in Canada and North America) (see Chapter 3). In Britain, for example, camaraderie tends to increase when there is a delay or another particular problem with the train, or as a consequence of the 'vestibule blues':

> The only time I think I enter into conversations with people on trains is when we are all standing, and often that is in those bits between the carriages ... that's kind of nobody's 'territory'. (Gillian)

At these times the 'well-we're-all-in-this-together' spirit appears to kick in. However, it is important not to overemphasize the 'levelling' aspect of shared experience on the railways, as difference is also relevant to our analysis. Although 'difference' can be defined in different ways, for the purposes of this chapter we refer to difference as diversity of experience (e.g. between different social classes, between women and men, between not-disabled and disabled people) (see Letherby 2003 for a further analysis of 'difference' within feminist theory). Pierre Bourdieu (1984: 466) argues that: 'one's relationship to the social world and to one's proper place in it is never more clearly expressed than in the space and time one feels entitled to take from others; more precisely, in the space one claims with one's body in physical space, through a bearing and gestures that are self-assured or reserved, expansive or constricted'. Our data here largely support Bourdieu's analysis; however, we would suggest that there is always capacity for resistance, challenge and transgression within the train. This is because the public nature of the space and its changing occupancy mean that it is constantly being de-constructed and re-constructed as a 'new' social place. Such sites are thus of value in exploring the personal politics of status and identity.

Class

'Class' as a status distinction is difficult to define and is a contested concept (e.g. Adam et al. 2000), but the train is a place where the distinctions are, superficially at least, very clear. The railway worker is subservient to the railway customer and the customers themselves are easily classified by where they sit. In some countries – including Britain and Canada – railway carriages are still graded by class (see Chapter 1). People have very different attitudes towards the concept of first class: 'Robson frequently travels First Class – and is unapologetic about it "I don't associate my political beliefs with poverty. I feel I've earned the right to travel comfortably. Yes I earn well but then I pay higher taxes, some of which goes into public transport"' (Barber 2004: 20). Our respondents were typically diverse in their views:

> I'm usually in First Class, *so all I can drink*, snack, dine, sleep, read, look out the window, talk with the other passengers about how the service could be improved, and other such stuff. (Robbie – Canada, original emphasis)

> Basically, they could take away all these stupid First Class carriages that nobody uses, and kit them out as carriages that are actually useful to people, as well as being affordable … like family carriages. (Julie – UK)

> I think that it [concept of first class] is disgusting, I think it is particularly disgusting when there is overcrowding in the rest of the train and you have to pay more to go into First Class or they won't let you in … You know often you are dealing with people who have got young kids or they are old or, you know, have found the journey wearisome, and they are not allowed to move to basically sit down, which if you had paid on a coach you pay for your seat and your seat is guaranteed. I find it really offensive that people can be standing … I think it's disgusting that people can't get a seat. I think the concept, as a whole is awful, I think that I would rather see a determination to accrue the standard of facilities across the board; I think it would be abolished then. I think everybody's experience of train travel should be good enough, get enough leg room, enough ventilation, a good enough seat. Sometimes the old ones I'm travelling on, the seats actually stink, you know. Accumulation of certain travellers, the seats are falling off. (Rhian – UK)

Having a seat in first class, however, does not necessarily mean that you have worked harder (as Robson Green suggests – note here the comparison with achieving I-SPY Train-Traveller First Class; see Chapter 4) or paid more (as Rhian says). Indeed, when we asked Rhian if she would sit in first class if there were no available seats elsewhere, she told us this story:

> the whole station was full of these people and then the train pulled in and there wasn't very many carriages and there was one guy who said 'I've paid my money to go back to Stoke so I am going to go into First Class and the rest of you can follow me if you like' and everyone did and I followed as well and I have never seen anything like it and it was like power to the people stuff – everyone shoved into the First Class carriage which was completely empty, there was nobody in there and the guard was very good. He anticipated that there was going to be trouble if he charged us anyway but also I think he was quite sympathetic and we all travelled quite happily in First Class.

Other respondents told us similar stories, but some were more reticent about adopting this type of protest. Joseph, for example, said:

> What, do you mean and not pay? [pause] I'd have to wait and see what the situation was. I'm not averse to protest, I have been on protests [but] I'm not a very confrontational person really, I don't like confrontation, and I also feel to some extent that it would be hard enough for the particular individual [train manager] who is only doing his job.

And Henry said:

> I wouldn't go into First Class. It's funny, isn't it? ... well I'm breaking a bye-law basically aren't I? I'd have the ignominy of being turfed out at some stage. I think it's more deference really, old-fashioned deference. We were on a [name of train operator] train that stopped because a track had buckled or something and they stopped another train that wasn't a [name of train operator]. And when we got on, we got into First Class, a great load of us – I think we were indicated in there, yes, which annoyed the people who had paid for it enormously but that was fine ... I'd do Weekend First, yes, when I get to sixty I will probably do it because my fares will drop, and there are various schemes for travelling First Class at that sort of time.

As well as reflecting an attitude of deference instilled in British society, not least by the division of people into first, second and third class on the railways of Victorian Britain, Henry's account above serves to highlight one perceived challenge to the concept of first class in contemporary society:

> I bought an up-grade to a Weekend-First ticket and settled myself in a nice comfortable seat. A man who was already in there suddenly looked up at me, saw the 'Weekend First' sign on the window, and promptly said to the woman with him, 'Oh, this isn't *really* First Class, it's Weekend-First. Let's move', and off they went to the next First Class coach – not a Weekend-First! (Gillian)

Gender

As two women academics whose work is informed by feminist thought, this book is permeated with a gendered sensitivity. This is true of everything that we do. With this in mind this section allows us not only to raise new issues but also to recap on the specific relationship between men, women and trains because of course – and contrary to some opinion – taking a gendered perspective necessitates a consideration of male as well as female status and experience (Letherby 2003).

Traditionally, the train, like the rest of the public sphere, was a masculine space. Women who entered the public sphere in nineteenth-century Britain, including the space of the train, were considered to have committed an act of 'deviance' but some women of that time felt that the travel afforded them both independence and dignity (Muellner 2002). This sense of freedom came, though, with great risk. As Kim Stevenson (2002: 1) notes, Victorian society expected that women protect themselves against any unwarranted advances which 'in practice meant that women, in order to preserve their reputation and morality, were often faced with no choice but to extricate themselves from such situations, if necessary by death defying escapes out of open carriage windows'. Women's physical safety – and their reputations – are still at risk:

It was in 1968 and I was travelling from Exeter to Redruth on one of the old-fashioned trains with a corridor down the side and compartments for six to eight people. It was summer and very hot – I was sitting nearest to the corridor, so I left the sliding door open for a breeze. The only other occupants of the compartment were a middle-aged, rather sour-looking couple who didn't speak either to each other or to me. I noted that the lights in the carriage weren't working, but didn't think anything of it. My small son was asleep on my lap and I was quite pregnant then with my first daughter, and wearing a fashionable 'mini' maternity dress. We were actually moving into our new house in Helston. At some point – I can't remember where – there is a long tunnel. Of course, when we went into it, the carriage was in total darkness. I felt a movement up my leg and, thinking it was my son's hand, started to remove it gently. Then I realized it was an adult's hand! I screamed and rammed the sliding door shut on it, intending to trap it till we came out of the tunnel. But it was too strong and wriggled away. By the time we came to the end of the tunnel, I was in a bit of a state, and tried to explain to the couple what had happened. But the only response was 'Well, what do you expect when you're wearing a skirt as short as that?' I was shocked and numbed into total silence for the rest of the journey! (Gillian)

So on the train that was going up to the North East [of India] I slept in the corridor, which was really not very good at all, because I spent most of the night fending off Indian men who were sitting on the bunk. It was horrid really. It wasn't nice at all. Fortunately there was a family in the little compartment opposite me and the father of the family a couple of times came to my rescue and sent them packing, but it was really unnerving. I dealt with it in the end by just blanking it all out. People still sat on my bunk and they would just sit and stare, because – I mean I don't know what was going on really but I'm sure part of it was that a woman on her own, a white woman on her own, travelling, is very unusual, and not something that would happen in Indian culture. You don't see women generally travelling on their own, they

are usually going as part of a family or there will be group of women travelling together but there's usually a man with them. So to have a woman on
their own, and a white woman on their own, I think was just so unusual. But
it was just unnerving because they would stare, they would just sit and stare.
(Sandie – UK)

Perhaps not surprisingly, virtually every source of data about women
and transport in Britain mentions the desire to have more staff on stations
(Hamilton et al. 2002). If asked, we feel sure that many women (and men)
would feel safer if there were more staff on trains. Thus, we were particularly disturbed, when undertaking research for this chapter, by the very
many articles about sexual assault and rape of women on or near trains,
in which we came across a comment assuring the reader and possible
passenger that the attack had been an 'isolated event'. We know that
women are more at risk of attack in the private rather than the public
sphere, but we also know that violence against women is often supported,
even promoted, by the media and not given serious attention by the criminal justice system (e.g. Stanko 1985; Lees 1996; Gillespie 2000).

In addition – as our own experience, and that of our respondents, highlights – in both reality and public perception, the world of the railway
remains a space which is appropriated more comfortably and 'naturally'
by men. However, just as the advent of the railways enabled women to
challenge to some extent their 'natural' place in the home (Stevenson
2002), women's relationship with the contemporary railway – as workers,
as passengers and as enthusiasts – challenges the assumption that trains
are the concern of men and boys. This book is one example of that challenge.

Other Others

In addition to issues of class and gender, other 'differences' are relevant
to any social analysis of trains and train travel. As we have previously
noted, the train space is not always a comfortable place for children.
Similarly, older people and people with disabilities often experience the
train as an unfriendly space:

> [I like to] look out the window at the scenery, take photographs, read at night,
> talk to other passengers when possible [but] disabled accommodations in
> long-distance trains often separate you from other passengers. (Dan – USA)

But space for luggage, we found that quite difficult because managing heavy
luggage if you are getting on, is not easy, and neither is getting in and out of

the train. People are very helpful most times but it – but the doors that come out then along, not something that you just open with a handle and a nice strap on the front of it. (Joseph – UK)

This is not to say that no attention is paid to the needs of older passengers and/or passengers with disabilities, especially as a consequence of the Disability Discrimination Act (1995):

It looks from an outsider's point of view that they have made travelling better for people with disabilities ... I think there's recognition of the fact that some people use wheelchairs. That's good. People are still a bit marginalized with special places [marked out in the carriage] but it is possible to travel now. (Rhian – UK)

The fact remains, however, that with only a limited number of railway staff aboard each train, a personal service – even when needed and however much it is promoted – is often impossible in practice:

You get lots and lots of public information announcements that are clear and polite sometimes to the point of hilarity as they are so obviously reading from a script. But, for instance, I recently asked a station to assist a disabled passenger. They were great at the station, they phoned up the next station where the transfer was going to be. We had a seat number, carriage number, everything. [But] the person on the journey was never even approached. The train was late which made the transfer even more difficult, for anybody, but especially for someone with a disability. (Janet – UK)

Although not something that respondents referred to in detail, racial discrimination is also an aspect of the contemporary railway. We have each witnessed, for example, the sniggering that takes place when a train manager whose first language is not English, but who probably speaks English much better than the majority of people on the train speak any language other than English, makes announcements. Arguably, marginalization and ridicule of the 'other' in this way is just one way in which individuals can claim space for themselves (Bourdieu 1984). Once again, though, we acknowledge a deficiency in our data collection. We have demonstrated in this book that gender and class are integral to any understanding of trains and train travel. What is lacking – both here and elsewhere – is a systematic consideration of the significance of other differences, both the discrete variations in experience and interconnections between differences (Letherby 2003).

As Philip Mellor and Chris Shilling (1997: 164) point out: 'In the absence of an overarching social contract that can be agreed upon by people of different classes, ethnic backgrounds and genders, individuals make their way on the basis of transient, individualized contracts. Made in writing, orally, or even in the mind, these contracts link ... [individuals] through a reciprocity which is easily agreed and easily broken.' Without a thorough grounding in the narratives of difference regarding experiences on or near the train, there can be no firm or lasting understanding of a common etiquette for travellers.

Reflections

The focus of this chapter on the personal politics of trains and train travel brings us to the end of our substantive analysis. Our grounded exploration of behaviour, emotion and identity has enabled us to challenge once more the widely held perception that trains are merely vehicles which transport us from A to B; on the contrary, we have argued that 'all of life' can be found on the train. Affected as it is by the legacy of historical norms and values, our behaviour on and around the train reveals as much about wider society as it does about work, play and politics on the railways. The fact that within and outside the train we experience emotion that is connected to and a part of the railways again indicates the significance of trains and train travel to an understanding of social life in the twenty-first century. That identity and difference are as significant on the railways as elsewhere enables us to consider individual and group life course issues.

What we have found from our data is that, in at least two areas, there is a mismatch between different discourses of train travel and railway interest. On the one hand, whereas the discourse of consumerism encourages – even coerces – a sense of individual rights and responsibilities, the discourse of safety and accountability takes control of the issues of risk away from the individual. The resulting ultimate tendency towards rail rage as a means of expressing frustration is largely a consequence of the tension between these different discourses. On the other hand, there is a similar discrepancy between the discourse of individualism, which seeks out the 'punctual' and 'reliable' train of consumerism and quality, and the discourse of romanticism and nostalgia, which seeks out the 'train of our dreams'.

Final Reflections
Light at the End of the Tunnel?

In this our final space for reflection, we consider what we have and have not achieved in the writing of this book and the research that preceded it. We look to the future for our own work and for others whose work might also explore the complex issue of trains and train travel.

On the Right Lines? What we Have and Have Not Done

We have deliberately chosen to refer to this part of our book as 'reflections' rather than 'conclusions' and to end with a question mark, because of the inconclusive and incomplete aspects of some of our analyses and because we do not believe that the journey (both for ourselves and for others working in this area) is over. However, we must also re-emphasize the conclusive points which we do make in this book, namely:

- that the railways and rail travel are part of the corporate, almost generic, identity of 'Britishness';
- that from the perspective of British railway workers, and British, Canadian, American and New Zealand (at least) rail fans and rail users, trains and train travel have personal, public and political significance;
- that the train is not merely a box on wheels – a vehicle that gets one from point A to point B; and
- that (almost) all social life can be identified on the train.

With reference to our final point above, although we have few data referring to birth and death, we know that they do occur on and around the train. There may well be some other significant life course events that do not occur on the train (for example, we do not know of any marriage ceremonies that have taken place on trains but we are happy to be corrected) but we have clearly demonstrated the many personal, as well as public, activities that take place on or around the train.

With all of this in mind, many of the major current debates in the social sciences are relevant to our discussion. Thus, we have made contributions to debates surrounding issues such as time, space and place, identity, power and risk (see Fig. 15). The railways, of course, have structured time itself, but in addition our contributions have furthered understandings of multiple time: e.g. historical time, clock time, biological time, work and leisure time, reflexive time. Our analysis of place and space demonstrates a consideration of 'macro' politics and policy surrounding the railways and rail travel and the train as a material and iconic place and space for individual people. With reference to identity, power and risk, our analysis of the gendered and classed experience of the railways and train travel has led us to challenge some of the previous work in this area. In relation to all of these themes and issues, we suggest that a sophisticated awareness of the public and private significance of the train and train travel is necessary.

Overall, we feel that our book contributes to a more complex understanding of the place of the train and train travel in people's lives. By grounding our analyses in the 'insider' perspectives of people who engage with the train and train travel, we have been able to highlight some of the deficiencies of previous literature and challenge those who poke

Figure 15 Risk society: light at the end of the tunnel, or an oncoming train? Copyright: line drawing by David Bill (Billy). By permission.

fun at the train-spotter; underestimate the complex identity of the railway worker; ignore the agency of the rail traveller.

There is incompleteness, however, in what we have done. For us, each of our chapters has huge gaps – literature and respondent accounts that we have had to exclude due to lack of space. Although some of these may not be evident to the reader, we feel sure that other limitations will. For example, as we have already mentioned, we have not considered the experience of those who commute but who are unable to undertake work on the train, and we have not fully explored all aspects of identity difference. Neither have we included the experience of those who travel for 'work' legitimately without paying – for example, the soldier or, indeed, the railway worker travelling to work; or the experience of those who travel for leisure illegitimately without paying – for example, the 'rail rider' or 'hobo'. Also missing are the discourses of those who feel less affection for the railways and train travel; who travel less, including people forced to travel, such as those taken to their death on the train (e.g. in the Second World War), illegal immigrants and asylum seekers.

The Long Haul? What Future for the Railways?

Thus, having begun to consider issues of work, play and politics on the railways, we feel we still have lots left to do. We look forward to undertaking further research and writing and to engaging in debate with those who have influenced us and others whom we may influence.

Throughout this book we insist that the train and its surrounding space are real: a place in its own right. However, our consideration of the competing discourses surrounding the train, including the nostalgic railway of our dreams discourse and the discourse of the railway of consumerism and quality, would seem to contradict this. Not so; both are real. Compare the accounts of Damien and Elaine, both people who love trains:

> I always feel disappointed when my train journey is ended and I 'return to the real world'. It occurs to me that the feeling is similar to that experienced upon disembarking from a ride in an amusement park such as a roller coaster. For a few minutes you are part of that special group aboard the ride. Then you get off again, return to normal and glancing back see others taking your place. I think I feel a sense of being special or even being catered to when I am aboard a train. I only get to travel by intercity train about once or twice a year. Boarding with my ticket in hand I feel important perhaps. I have a right to be there. When I disembark I have only the stub and am ordinary again. (Damien – Canada)

What would I like to see on trains, it is very much a personal wish list and is fraught with all kinds of commercial implications (in terms of increased cost and service provision) and probably ethical connotations too, but what the heck and in no particular order:

- The Quiet Zone to really mean the 'Quiet Zone' and therefore extended to exclude adult group travel and family group and noise abatement to be suitably enforced by a member of staff.
- More luggage space via mid carriage luggage stacks, between seats and overhead racks.
- Introduction of a security system for luggage and belongings to counter-act theft.
- Priority seating pitches throughout carriages.
- A way of displaying that a seat is 'taken' even though it might not be occupied (for example if you are travelling on your own and you make a trip to the buffet or toilet … and you want the same seat to be available on your return …).
- A wider range of healthy 'snacks' with the ingredients printed on the packaging.
- A vegan breakfast option, at seat service.
- Pressure pad activated automatic doors that also close more gently when a passenger finds themselves caught between the doors closing.
- Zero tolerance to litter – clean trains for the entire journey not just at turn-around.
- More conspicuous litter bins, sometimes passengers want to dispose of their litter but do not know where the bins are located and so leave litter either on the table, on the seat back tables, on the floor or in the pockets designed for in-house train-operator magazine. (Elaine – UK)

Both historically and to date – pre- and post-Beeching, before and after privatization – those who control the railways have been concerned to make money, and those who work and travel on the railways have wanted to contribute to, and experience, a comfortable and speedy service. At the same time, though, the railway has held – and does hold – a special charm for many people. We could argue, as do some writers, that nostalgia is a dangerous thing that distracts us from wider social and political concerns. Conscious as we are of the significance of safety and risk, environmental awareness, efficiency and reliability, power and control within space and place, we cautiously propose that there is enough about the train and train travel that is exciting and enriching to suggest the continuing survival of the nostalgic railway of our dreams over the railway of consumerism and quality. The quote with which we started this book represents a humorous challenge concerning everything that people perceive to be 'wrong with the railways'. The account that we end with perhaps suggests all that is right?

> I enjoy the things you can do on a train so much that I don't care if they are late. (Jasper – UK)

Bibliography

Adam, Barbara (1990), *Time and Social Theory*, Cambridge/Oxford: Polity/Blackwell.

—— (1995), *Timewatch: the Social Analysis of Time*, London: Polity/Blackwell.

—— Beck, Ulrich and Van Loon, Joost (eds) (2000), *The Risk Society and Beyond: Critical Issues for Social Theory*, London: Sage.

Aitchison, Cara (1999), 'New Cultural Geographies: the Spatiality of Leisure, Gender and Sexuality', *Leisure Studies*, 18(1): 19–40.

Aitken, Ian (ed.) (1998), *The Documentary Film Movement: An Anthology*, Edinburgh: Edinburgh University Press.

Alfasi, Nurit and Portugali, Juval (2004), 'Planning Just-in-time versus Planning Just-in-case', *Cities*, 21(1), February: 29–39.

Allcroft, Britt (2000), *Thomas the Tank Engine and Friends: 25 of the Best Stories from The Railway Series by the Rev. W. Awdry OBE*, London: Egmont Children's Books.

Anderson, Janice and Swinglehurst, Edmund (1981), *Ephemera of Travel and Transport*, London: New Cavendish Books.

Bagwell, Philip (1996), *The Transport Crisis in Britain*, Nottingham: Spokesman.

Bakhtin, Mikhail (1981), *The Dialogic Imagination*, transl. Caryl Emerson and Michael Holquist, Austin: University of Texas Press.

Barber, Richard (2004), 'Ever Green' [interview with Robson Green], *e-motion*, South West Trains' Customer Magazine and Interactive Website Issue 4: 18–20.

Barrett, Michèle (1991), *Politics of Truth: from Marx to Foucault*, Cambridge: Polity.

Barthes, Rolland (1972), *Mythologies*, transl. by A. Lavers, London: Jonathan Cape, in D. Tallack (ed.) (1995), *Critical Theory: a Reader*, Hemel Hempstead, Hertfordshire: Harvester Wheatsheaf.

Barton, Susan (2002), 'Learning how to Behave on Nineteenth Century Railways', paper presented to *Off the Rails – Behaving Badly on the Railways Conference*, York Railway Museum, 20 April.

Bauman, Zygmunt (1992), *Intimations of Postmodernity*, London: Routledge.

—— (1997), *Postmodernity and its Discontents*, Cambridge/Oxford: Polity/Blackwell.

—— (1998), *Work, Consumerism and the New Poor*, Buckingham: Open University Press.

BBC (2004), 'DNA Kits Help Stop Train Spitting', *BBC News*, 28 April. http: //news.bbc.co.uk/1/hi/scotland/3667145. Accessed 6.5.04.

Beck, Ulrich (1992), *Risk Society: Towards a New Modernity*, London: Sage.

Bell, Kathleen (1998), 'Poop, Poop! – An Early Case of Joy-Riding by an Upper Class Amphibian', in D. Thoms, L. Holden and T. Claydon (eds), *The Motor Car and Popular Culture in the 20th Century*, Aldershot: Ashgate.

Bender, Barbara (1993), *Landscape: Politics and Perspectives*, Oxford: Berg.

Bertilsson, Margareta (1991), 'Love's Labour Lost? A Sociological View' in M. Featherstone, M. Hepworth and B.S. Turner (eds), *The Body: Social Processes and Cultural Theory,* London: Sage.

Bhatti, Mark and Church, Andrew (2001), 'Cultivating Natures: Homes and Gardens in Late Modernity', *Sociology*, 35(2): 365–83.

Billington, Michael (2003), 'Up the Junction', *Guardian Archives*, 17 November. Accessed 4.12.03.

Bourdieu, Pierre (1984), *Distinction: a Social Critique of the Judgement of Taste*, London: Routledge.

Carr-Brown, Jonathon (2002), 'All Aboard for the Bad Old Days', *The Sunday Times*, 13 January: 12–13.

Carter, Ian (2000), 'The Lost Idea of a Train: Looking for Britain's Railway Novel', *The Journal of Transport History*, 21(2), September: 117–39.

—— (2002), 'The Lady in the Trunk: Railways, Gender and Crime Fiction', *The Journal of Transport History* 23(1), March: 46–59.

Clement, Barrie (2001), 'Violence against Rail Staff Reaches 30–year High', *The Independent*, 7 September.

Cole, Beverley and Durack, Richard (1992), *Railway Posters 1923–1947*, National Railway Museum, York, London: Laurence King Publishing.

Concise Oxford Dictionary (1982), Oxford: Oxford University Press

Cook, William (2001), 'Goodbye to All That', *New Statesman*, 26 March. http: //home.clara.net/gw0hqd/media/. Accessed 7.01.04.

Cooke, Brian (1990), *The Grand Crimean Central Railway*, Knutsford, Cheshire: Cavalier House Publishing.

Cotterill, Pam and Letherby, Gayle (1993), 'Weaving Stories: Personal

Auto/biographies in Feminist Research', *Sociology*, 27(1): 67–79.

Craik, Jennifer (1997), 'The Culture of Tourism', in C. Rojek and J. Urry (eds), *Touring Cultures: Transformations of Travel and Theory*, London: Routledge.

Crompton, Gerald (2003), 'Money isn't Everything', *New Statesman Special Supplement: On the Right Lines? The State of the Railways*, 24 November: x–xi.

Crouch, David (2000), 'Places Around Us: Embodied Lay Geographies in Leisure and Tourism', *Leisure Studies*, 19(2): 63–76.

David, Miriam E. (2003), *Personal and Political: Feminisms, Sociology and Family Lives*, Stoke-on-Trent: Trentham Books.

Davison, Graeme (2004), *Car Wars: How the Car Won our Hearts and Conquered our Cities*, Crows Nest, Australia: Allen and Unwin.

de Boer, Edward (1986), *Transport Sociology: Social Aspects of Transport Planning*, Oxford: Pergamon.

Delgado, Alan (1977), *The Annual Outing and Other Excursions*, London: George Allen and Unwin.

Derby Evening Telegraph (2003), 'Train Company Profits Up by 11 Per Cent', 12 September http: //www.businessderbyshire.co.uk/company. Accessed 11.01.04.

Dey, Ian (1989), 'Flexible "Parts" and Rigid "Fulls": the Limited Revolution in Work and Time Pattern', *Work, Employment and Society*, 3(4): 465–90.

Dickens, Charles (1966), *Dombey and Son*, Oxford: Oxford University Press.

Divall, Colin (2003), 'Transport Museums: Another Kind of Historiography', *The Journal of Transport History*, 24(2): 259– 65.

Duncombe, Jean and Marsden, Dennis (1998) '"Stepford Wives" and "Hollow Men": Doing Emotion Work, Doing Gender and "Authenticity" in Intimate Heterosexual Relationships', in G. Bendelow and S.J. Williams (eds), *Emotions in Social Life: Critical Themes and Contemporary Issues*, London: Routledge.

Edwards, Rosalind (1993), *Mature Women Students: Separating or Connecting Family and Education*, London: Taylor and Francis.

Elias, Norbert (1978), *The Civilizing Process, Volume 1: The History of Manners*, New York: Urizen and Oxford: Basil Blackwell.

—— and Scotson, John (1994), *The Established and the Outsiders*, London: Sage.

Featherstone, Mike (1995), *Undoing Culture: Globalization, Postmodernism and Identity*, London: Sage.

Filmer, Paul (1998), 'Image/Text', in C. Jenks (ed.), *Core Sociological Dichotomies*, London: Sage.

Foucault, Michel (1972), *Archaeology of Knowledge*, transl. by A.M. Sheridan Smith, London: Routledge.

——(1980), 'Two Lectures', in C. Gordon (ed.), *Michel Foucault: Power/Knowledge*, London: Harvester Wheatsheaf.

——(1984), *The History of Sexuality Volume 1: An Introduction*, London: Penguin.

Francis, John (1967) (first published 1851), *A History of the English Railway: its Social Relations and Revelations*, London: David and Charles.

Freeman, Michael (1999a), *Railways and the Victorian Imagination*, New Haven and London: Yale University Press.

——(1999b), 'The Railway as Cultural Metaphor: "What Kind of Railway History?" Revisited', *The Journal of Transport History*, 20(2), September: 160–7.

Frisby, David (1992), *Simmel and Since: Essays on Georg Simmel's Social Theory*, London: Routledge.

Giddens, Anthony (1991), *Modernity and Self-Identity: Self and Society in the Late Modern Age*, Cambridge: Polity.

Gilbert, Nigel (1993), *Researching Social Life*, London: Sage.

Gillespie, Terry (2000), 'Virtual Violence? Pornography and Violence against Women on the Internet', in J. Radford, M. Friedberg and L. Harne (eds), *Women, Violence and Strategies for Action*, Buckingham: Open University Press.

Glaister, Stephen and Travers, Tony (1993), *New Directions for British Railways? The Political Economy of Privatisation and Regulation*, London: Institute for Economic Affairs.

Glucksmann, Miriam (2000), *Cotton and Casuals: the Gendered Organisation of Labour in Time and Space*, Durham: Sociology Press.

Goffman, Erving (1963), *Behaviour in Public Places*, Harmondsworth: Penguin.

——(1969), *The Presentation of Self in Everyday Life*, London: Allen Lane.

Golding, Harry (ed.) (1918), *The Wonder Book of Railways for Boys and Girls*, London: Ward Lock.

Gooch, Rebecca (2004), 'Green Goddess' [interview with Charlie Dimmock], *e-motion*, South West Trains' Customer Magazine/ Interactive Website. Issue 3: 18–20.

Goodman, Edward (ed.) (2001), *Writing the Rails: Train Adventures by the World's Best-loved Writers*, New York: Black Dog and Leventhal.

Gourvish, Terry (1980), *Railways and the British Economy 1830–1914*, Basingstoke: Macmillan.

Green, Nicholas (1990), *The Spectacle of Nature: Landscape and*

Bourgeois Culture in 19th Century France, Manchester: Manchester University Press.

Grint, Keith (1991), *The Sociology of Work*, Cambridge: Polity.

Hadfield, John (1973), *Love on a Branch Line*, London: Pan Books.

Halford, Susan (2004), 'Towards a Sociology of Organizational Space', *Sociological Research Online*, 9(1). www.socresonline.org.uk/9/1/halford.html.

Hall, Colin and Page, Stephen (1999), *The Geography of Tourism and Recreation: Environment, Place and Space*, London: Routledge.

Hall, Stanley (1999), *Hidden Dangers: Railway Safety in the Era of Privatisation*, Shepperton, Surrey: Ian Allan.

Hall, Stuart (1997), Introduction, in S. Hall (ed.), *Representation: Cultural Representations and Signifying Practices*, London: Sage.

Hamilton, Kerry and Potter, Stephen (1985), *Losing Track*, London: Routledge Kegan Paul.

—— Ryley, Susan and Jenkins, Linda (2002) *Women and Transport: the Research Report*, University of East London, Transport Studies Unit. www.uel.ac.uk/womenandtransport. Accessed 30.4.04.

Harrington, Ralph (1994), 'The Neuroses of the Railway', *History Today*, 44(7), July: 15–21.

—— (1999a), 'The Railway Accident: Trains, Trauma and Technological Crisis in Nineteenth-century Britain', University of York, Institute of Railway Studies, http: //www.york.ac.uk/inst/irs/irshome. Accessed 4.4.03.

—— (1999b), 'Perceptions of the Locomotive Driver: Image and Identity on British Railways, *c*.1840–*c*.1950', Paper given to the *Occupational Identity and Railway Work Conference*, National Railway Museum, York, 15–16 September. http: //www.york.ac.uk/inst/irs/irshome. Accessed 4.4.03.

Harvey, David (1993) 'From Space to Place and Back Again: Reflections on the Condition of Postmodernity', in J. Bird, B. Curtis, T. Putman, G. Robertson and L. Tickner (eds), *Mapping the Futures: Local Cultures and Global Change*, London: Routledge.

Harvey, Michael, G. (2004), *Forget the Anorak: What Trainspotting was Really Like*, Stroud: Sutton Publishing.

Henley Centre (2003), 'Beyond Commuterland', *Financial Times*, 24 May. http://www.henleycentre.com. Accessed 4.4.03.

Hochschild, Arlie (1983), *The Managed Heart: Commercialisation of Human Feeling*, Berkeley, Los Angeles, London: University of California Press.

Hogarth, T. and Daniel, W. (1987), 'The Long-distance Commuters', *New Society*, 29 April: 11.

Holmes, Andrew and Reeves, Matthew (2003), *Pains on Trains: a Commuter's Guide to the 50 Most Irritating Travel Companions*, Chichester: Capstone Publishing.

Horne, Jon (undated), *Sex in a Railway Station*. http: //www.horne. demon.co.uk/bsides-station.

Huntley, John (1993), *Railways on the Screen*, Shepperton: Ian Allen.

Jack, Ian (2003), 'Picture of Perfection', *New Statesman Special Supplement: On the Right Lines? The State of the Railways*, 24 November: 19–20.

Jameson, Fredric (1984), 'Postmodernism: the Cultural Logic of Late Capitalism', *New Left Review*, 146: 53–93.

Jamieson, Lynn (1998), *Intimacy: Personal Relationships in Modern Societies*, London: Polity Press.

Jordan, Arthur and Jordan, Elisabeth (1991), *Away for the Day: the railway excursion in Britain 1830 to the Present Day*, Kettering, Northants: Silver Link Publishing.

Kampfner, John (2003), 'The Boss of the Rail Network Urges us All to be "More Understanding" of its Problems, but Insists that Motoring is Too Cheap', *New Statesman*, 10 February. http: //www.findarticles. com. Accessed 7.1.04.

Kent, Ian (1999), 'TV Gives its Time to Carnforth', *The Visitor*, 13 January. http: //home.clara.net/gw0hqd/media/tvtime. Accessed 30.7.04.

Kirby, Lynne (1997), *Parallel Tracks: the Railroad and Silent Cinema*, Exeter: University of Exeter Press.

Kraus, Nancy, Malmfors, Torbjörn and Slovic, Paul (2000), 'Intuitive Toxicology: Expert and Lay Judgments of Chemical Risk', in P. Slovic (ed.), *The Perception of Risk*, London: Earthscan.

Kroto, Harry (2003), 'Our Country must be the Only One in which Passengers do not Know from which Platform their Trains will Leave – if they Leave at All', *Times Higher Educational Supplement*, 16 May: 15.

Layton, Lyndsey (2002), 'Public Primping Raises Eyebrows, Metro Riders Clip, Curl and Annoy', *Washington Post*, 3 March. UrbanTransitAficionados@yahoogroups.com.

Leake, Christopher (2003) 'Tilting Trains "Make us Sick"', *Mail on Sunday*, 16 November: 42.

Lechner, Frank (1991), 'Simmel on Social Space', *Theory, Culture and Society*, 8(3): 195–201.

Lees, Sue (1996), *Carnal Knowledge: Rape on Trial*, London: Hamish Hamilton.

Lefebvre, Henri (1981), *The Production of Space*, Oxford: Basil Blackwell.

Leicestershire County Council (2003), 'A Slice of Life: The Railway Station Past and Present: An Exhibition by Susan Yeates'. http: //www.leics.gov.uk/community. Accessed 26.5.04.

Leiss, William, Kline, Stephen and Jhally, Sut (eds) (1986), *Social Communication in Advertising: Persons, Products and Images of Well-being,* London: Methuen.

Letherby, Gayle (2003), *Feminist Research in Theory and Practice,* Buckingham: Open University Press.

—— and Reynolds, Gillian (2003), 'Making Connections: the Relationship between Train Travel and the Processes of Work and Leisure', *Sociological Research Online,* 8(3). http: //www.socresonline.org.uk/8/3/letherby.

Levine, David (1991), 'Simmel as Educator: on Individuality and Culture', *Theory, Culture and Society,* 8, No. 3: 99–117.

Levitas, Ruth (2000), 'Discourses of Risk and Utopia', in B. Adam, U. Beck and J. Van Loon (eds), *The Risk Society and Beyond: Critical Issues for Social Theory,* London: Sage.

Locke, Tom (2004), 'Ghost Town', *hotline,* Virgin Trains' Guide to Onboard Audio, Shopping and Safety, Summer: 38–41.

Low, Sui Pheng and Chan, Yue Meng (1997), *Managing Productivity in Construction: JIT Operations and Measurements,* Aldershot: Ashgate.

Lubben, Richard (1988), *Just-in-time Manufacturing,* New York: McGraw-Hill.

Lupton, Deborah (1999), *Risk,* London: Routledge.

Lyon, David (1994), *Postmodernity,* Buckingham: Open University Press.

—— (2001), *Surveillance Society: Monitoring Everyday Life,* Buckingham: Open University Press.

Manning, Maria (1989), 'On the Tebbit Express', *New Statesman and Society,* 8 December: 10–11.

McDowell, Linda (1999), *Gender, Identity and Place: Understanding Feminist Geographies,* London: Polity.

McHoul, Alec and Grace, Wendy (1995), *A Foucault Primer: Discourse, Power and the Subject,* London: University College London Press.

McNab and Pryce (1987), 'Lineside Landscape', *Landscape Design,* December: 14–15.

Marchant, Ian (2003), *Parallel Lines: or Journeys on the Railway of Dreams,* London: Bloomsbury.

Marshall, P. David (1997), Celebrity and Power: Fame in Contemporary Culture, Minneapolis: University of Minnesota Press.

Martin, Andrew (2003), 'Romance and Reality', *New Statesman Special Supplement: On the Right Lines? The State of the Railways,* 24 November: xxi.

Masberg, Barbara (1998), 'Defining the Tourist: is it Possible? A View from the Convention and Visitors' Bureau', *Journal of Travel Research*, 37(1): 67–70.

Massey, Doreen (1993), 'Politics and Space/Time', in M. Keith and S. Pile (eds), *Place and the Politics of Identity*, London: Routledge.

Mellor, Philip and Shilling, Chris (1997), *Re-forming the Body: Religion, Community and Modernity*, London: Sage.

Melucci, Alberto (1996), *The Playing Self*, Cambridge: Cambridge University Press.

Mills, C. Wright (1970), *The Sociological Imagination*, Harmondsworth: Penguin.

Moscowitz, Howard (1994), *Food Concepts and Products: Just-in-time Development*, Trumbull, USA: Food and Nutrition Press.

Muellner, Beth (2002), 'The Deviance of Respectability: Nineteenth-century Transport from a Woman's Perspective', *The Journal of Transport History*, 23(1): 37–45.

Murray, Andrew (2002), *Off the Rails: the Crisis on Britain's Railways*, London: Verso.

Murray Schafer, Raymond (1977), *The Tuning of the World: A Pioneering Exploration into the Past History and Present State of the Most Neglected Aspect of our Environment: The Soundscape*, New York: Knopf.

Mykhalovskiy, Eric (1996), 'Reconsidering Table Talk: Critical Thoughts on the Relationship between Sociology, Autobiography and Self-indulgence', *Qualitative Sociology*, 19(1): 131–51.

Nesbit, Edith (1995), *The Railway Children*, Harmondsworth: Penguin.

Newton, Tim (1998), 'The Sociogenesis of Emotion: a Historical Sociology?' in G. Bendelow and S.J. Williams (eds), *Emotions in Social Life: Critical Themes and Contemporary Issues*, London: Routledge.

Nowotny, Helga (1994), *Time: the Modern and Postmodern Experience*, Cambridge/Oxford: Polity/Blackwell.

Okely, Judith (1992), 'Anthropology and Autobiography: Participatory Experience and Embodied Knowledge', in J. Okely and H. Callaway (eds), *Anthropology and Autobiography*, London: Routledge.

—— and Callaway, Helen (1992) 'Introduction', in J. Okely and H. Callaway (eds), *Anthropology and Autobiography*, London: Routledge.

O'Neill, Rory (ed.) (2001), '"Shocking and Unacceptable" Rise in Rail Rage Attacks on Staff', *Risks*, 18, 8 September, in *Hazards* magazine, September.

O'Sullivan, Tim (1998), 'Transports of Difference and Delight: Advertising and the Motor Car in Twentieth-Century Britain', in D.

Thoms, L. Holden and T. Claydon (eds), *The Motor Car and Popular Culture in the 20th Century*, Aldershot: Ashgate.

Pacey, Philip (2003), *Music and Railways.* http: //www.uclan.ac.uk/ library/musrail.htm. Accessed 8.8.03.

Page, Stephen, J. (1999), *Transport and Tourism,* Harlow, Essex: Addison Wesley Longman.

Parker, Peter (1991), *For Starters: The Business of Life*, London: Pan.

Parsons, Talcott and Bales, Robert (1955), *Family Socialisation and Interaction Process*, London: Routledge.

Payton, Philip (1997), 'An English Cross-country Railway: Rural England and the Cultural Reconstruction of the Somerset and Dorset Railway', in *Railway, Place and Identity: Working Papers in Railway Studies No. 2*, compiled by Colin Divall, York: University of York, Institute of Railway Studies.

Pike, Richard (ed.) (1884), *Railway Adventures and Anecdotes*, London: Hamilton, Adams.

Pilling, Alison, Murray, Stuart and Turner, Jeff (1998), *Catching them Young Project: a community-based Project to Increase Transport Awareness and Influence Travel Behaviour amongst Young People*, University of Manchester.

Pitts, Victoria (1998), 'Reclaiming the Female Body: Embodied Identity Work, Resistance and the Grotesque', *Body and Society*, 4(3): 67–84.

Povey, R.O.T. (1974), *The Bedside Book of Railway History*, Yorkshire: Dalesman Books.

Purvis, June (1994), 'Doing Feminist Women's History: Researching the Lives of Women in the Suffragette Movement in Edwardian England', in M. Maynard and J. Purvis (eds), *Researching Women's Lives from a Feminist Perspective*, London: Taylor and Francis.

Quinion, M. (1996), *World Wide Words.* http: //www.quinion.com.

Rallis, Tom (1977), *Intercity Transport: Engineering and Planning*, London and Basingstoke: Macmillan.

Ransom, Judith (1993), 'Feminism, Difference and Discourse: the Limits of Discursive Analysis for Feminism', in C. Ramazanoglu (ed.), *Up Against Foucault: Explorations of some Tensions between Foucault and Feminism*, London: Routledge.

Ransom, P.J.G. (2001), *Snow, Flood and Tempest: Railways and Natural Disasters*, Hersham, Surrey: Ian Allan Publishing.

Reinharz, Shulamit (1992), *Feminist Methods in Social Research*, Oxford: Oxford University Press.

Ribbens, Jane (1993), 'Facts or Fiction? Aspects of the Use of Autobiographical Writing in Undergraduate Sociology', *Sociology*, 27(1): 323–42.

—— and Edwards, Rosalind (1998), 'Living on the Edges: Public Knowledge, Private Lives, Personal Experiences', in J. Ribbens and R. Edwards (eds), *Feminist Dilemmas in Qualitative Research: Public Knowledge and Private Lives*, London: Sage.

Richards, Jeffrey and MacKenzie, John M. (1986), *The Railway Station: a Social History*, Oxford: Oxford University Press.

Richardson, Miles (1989), 'Place and Culture: Two Disciplines, Two Concepts, Two Images of Christ, and a Single Goal', in J. Agnew and J. Duncan (eds), *The Power of Place: Bringing Together Geographical and Sociological Imaginations*, Boston, USA: Unwin Hyman.

Ritzer, George (1993), *The McDonaldization of Society: an Investigation into the Changing Character of Contemporary Social Life*, Newbury Park, California: Pine Forge.

Rix, Mick (2003), 'It Doesn't Have to be Like This', *Guardian Archives*, 4 July.

Robinson, Ronald (1991), 'Conclusion: Railways and Informal Empire', in C. Davis and K. Wilburn (eds), *Railway Imperialism*, Westport, USA: Greenwood Press.

Rodaway, Paul (1994), *Sensuous Geographies: Body, Space and Place*, London: Routledge.

Rojek, Chris and Urry, John (eds) (1997), *Touring Cultures: Transformations of Travel and Theory*, London: Routledge.

Rowling, J.K. (1997), *Harry Potter and the Philosopher's Stone*, London: Bloomsbury.

Sargent, Caroline (1984), *Britain's Railway Vegetation*, Huntingdon: Institute of Terrestial Ecology.

Schivelbusch, Wolfgang (1986), *The Railway Journey: the Industrialization of Time and Space in the 19th Century*, Leamington: Berg.

Shaw, Chris (2004), 'Picture This', *The Big Issue in the North*, 506: 46.

Shields, Rob (1997), 'Spatial Stress and Resistance: Social Meanings of Spatialization', in G. Benko and U. Strohmayer (eds), *Space and Social Theory: Interpreting Modernity and Postmodernity*, Oxford: Blackwell.

Shilling, Chris (1993), *The Body and Social Theory*, London: Sage.

Shurmer-Smith, Pamela and Hannam, Kevin (1994), *Worlds of Desire, Realms of Power: a Cultural Geography*, London: Arnold.

Simmons, Jack (compiler) (1991a), *Railways: an Anthology*, London: Collins.

—— (1991b), *The Victorian Railway*, London: Thames and Hudson.

Slovic, Paul, Fischhoff, Baruch and Lichtenstein, Sarah (2000), 'Facts and Fears: Understanding Perceived Risk', in P. Slovic (ed.), *The Perception of Risk*, London: Earthscan.

Smith, Dorothy (1974), 'Women, the Family and Corporate Capitalism', in M.L. Stephenson (ed.), *Women in Canada*, Toronto: New Press.

Smith, W.H. (19th century, undated), *The Illustrated Railway Anecdote Book: a Collection of the Best and Newest Anecdotes and Tales to the Present Day, Selected for the Reading of Railway Passengers*, London: W.H. Smith.

SRA (2003), 'Some Facts about the Railway', in *New Statesman Special Supplement: On the Right Lines? The State of the Railways*, 24 November.

Stacey, Meg (1981), 'The Division of Labour Revisited or Overcoming the Two Adams', in P. Abrams, R. Deem, J. Finch and P. Rock (eds), *Practice and Progress: British Sociology 1950–1980*, London: Allen and Unwin.

Stanko, Elizabeth, A. (1985), *Intimate Intrusions: Women's Experience of Male Violence*, London: Virago.

Stanley, Liz (1993), 'On Auto/biography in Sociology', *Sociology*, 27(1): 41–52.

—— and Wise, Sue (1990), 'Method, Methodology and Epistemology in Feminist Research Processes', in L. Stanley (wd.), *Feminist Praxis: Research, Theory and Epistemology in Feminist Sociology*, London: Routledge.

—— and Wise, Sue (1993), *Breaking Out Again: Feminist Ontology and Feminist Epistemology*, London: Routledge.

Stevenson, Kim (2002), 'Damsels in Distress or Female Monsters', Paper presented to *Off the Rails – Behaving Badly on the Railways Conference*, National Railway Museum, York, 20 April.

Stoneham, Jane and Jones, Ray (1997), 'Residential Landscapes: their Contribution to the Quality of Older People's Lives', in S. Wells (ed.), *Horticultural Therapy and the Older Population*, New York: Haworth Press.

Strangleman, Tim (1999), 'The Nostalgia of Organisations and the Organisation of Nostalgia: Past and Present in the Contemporary Railway Industry', *Sociology*, 33(4), November: 725–46.

—— (2002a), 'Constructing the Past: Railway History from Below or a Study in Nostalgia?', *The Journal of Transport History*, 23(2): 147–58.

—— (2002b), 'Nostalgia for Nationalisation – the Politics of Privatisation', *Sociological Research Online*, 7(1). http://www.socresonline.org.uk/7/1/strangleman.

—— (2004), *Work Identity at the End of the Line? Privatisation and Culture Change in the UK Rail Industry*, London: Palgrave Macmillan.

Swinglehurst, Edmund (1974), *The Romantic Journey: the Story of Thomas Cook and Victorian Travel*, London: Pica Editions.

Tate Gallery Online (2003), http: //www.tate.org.uk/. Accessed 26.5.04.

Taylor, B. (1993), 'Unconsciousness and Society: the Sociology of Sleep', *International Journal of Politics, Culture and Society*, 6(3): 463–71.

TEST (1991), *Wrong Side of the Tracks? Impacts of Road and Rail Transport on the Environment: a Basis for Discussion*, London: TEST.

Thomas, Helen and Walsh, David (1998), 'Modernity/Postmodernity'. in C. Jenks (ed.), *Core Sociological Dichotomies*, London: Sage.

Thrift, Nigel (1996), *Spatial Formations*, London: Sage.

Tulloch, John and Lupton, Deborah (2003), *Risk and Everyday Life*, London: Sage.

Urry, John (1990), *The Tourist Gaze: Leisure and Travel in Contemporary Societies*, London: Sage.

Walsh, Margaret (2002), 'Gendering Transport History: Retrospect and Prospect', *The Journal of Transport History Special Issue: Gender and Transport History*, 23(1): 1–8.

Walters, Joanna (2000), 'A Year of Pain and Rising Anger. Special Report: Paddington Train Crash', *The Observer*, 1 October. http: //www.guardian.co.uk/traincrash/. Accessed 4.4.03.

Walvin, James (1978), *Beside the Seaside*, London: Allen Lane/Penguin.

Weber, Max (1930), *The Protestant Ethic and the Spirit of Capitalism*, London: Unwin University Books.

—— (1947), *The Theory of Social and Economic Organisations*, New York: Free Press.

Wernick, Andrew (1991), *Promotional Culture: Advertising, Ideology and Symbolic Expression*, London: Sage.

White, Peter (1995), *Public Transport: its Planning, Management and Operation* (3rd edition), London: UCL Press.

Whitelegg, Drew (2002), 'Cabin Pressure: the Dialectics of Emotional Labour in the Airline Industry', *The Journal of Transport History*, 23(2) 73–86.

Whittaker, Nicholas (1995), *Platform Souls: the Trainspotter as 20th Century Hero*, London: Indigo.

Willan, Philip (2002), 'Revisiting Mussolini's Railways', *Guardian*, 16 January. http: //www.guardian.co.uk/elsewhere/journalist/. Accessed 21.9.03.

Williams, Simon J. (2003), *Medicine and the Body*, London: Sage.

—— and Bendelow, Gillian (1998), 'Introduction: Emotions in Social Life: Mapping the Sociological Terrain', in G. Bendelow and S. J. Williams (eds), *Emotions in Social Life: Critical Themes and Contemporary Issues*, London: Routledge.

Williams, Stephen (1998), *Tourism Geography*, London: Routledge.

Witz, Anne (1993), 'Women at Work', in D. Richardson and V. Robinson (eds), *Introducing Women's Studies*, Basingstoke: Macmillan.

—— (2000), 'Whose Body Matters? Feminist Sociology and the Corporeal Turn in Sociology and Feminism', *Body and Society*, 6(2): 1–24.

Wolff, Jonathan (2002), 'Policy and Risk: Railway Safety and the Ethics of the Tolerability of Risk', in *Railway Safety Research Programme*, London: WCA Consulting and University College.

Wolmar, Christian (2001), *Broken Rails: How Privatisation Wrecked Britain's Railways*, London: Aurum Press.

Young, Iris (1990), 'The Ideal of Community and the Politics of Difference', in L. Nicholson (ed.), *Feminism and Postmodernism*, London: Routledge.

Leaflets and Magazines

CHURNET VALLEY RAILWAY Proudly Presents SANTA & STEAM (2003) A Victorian Christmas: Timetable and Booking Form.

e-motion South West Trains' Customer Magazine and Interactive Website Issue 3.

e-motion South West Trains' Customer Magazine and Interactive Website Issue 4.

Hotline (2003) Virgin Trains' Customer Magazine.

I-SPY with David Bellamy ON A TRAIN JOURNEY (1984), Horsham, West Sussex: Ravette.

Just Press Play (undated), www.rentadvdplayer.co.uk.

Panorama (2003), 'Promises, Promises', BBC1, screened 16th February.

Pennington, Nigel (2003), *Leaf Fall Train Times*, London: Central Trains Information Leaflet.

Risks: issue no. 18–8 September 2001.

That's Life (2004), Edition 28.

'Transetiquette' (2002) *Ottawa Transit Riders Association Newsletter*, March.

Windowgazer Guide Edinburgh/Glasgow–Penzance, Virgin Trains.

Index